Making the most of Chicken, Poultry & Game

ROBERT CARRIER'S KITCHEN

Making the most of
Chicken, Poultry
& Game

Marshall Cavendish   London Sydney & New York

Contents

Chicken & Turkey

Duck, Goose & Guinea Fowl

Editor	Grizelda Wiles
Editorial Staff	Carey Denton
	Felicity Jackson
	Carol Steiger
Designer	Ross George
Series Editor	Pepita Aris
Production Executive	Robert Paulley
Production Controller	Steve Roberts

Photographers
Bryce Attwell: 61, 62, 107
Tom Belshaw: 89
Paul Bussell: 13, 22, 24, 30, 37, 38, 40, 57, 58, 59, 64, 67, 70, 74, 106, 108
Laurie Evans: 73, 92, 93, 94, 110
John Hall: 10
James Jackson: 25, 97, 99
Chris Knaggs: 15, 20, 33, 34, 36, 72
Peter Myers: 2, 7, 9, 17, 26, 27, 31, 32, 44, 68, 85, 87, 88, 90, 105
Ian O'Leary: 18
Paul Webster: 14
Paul Williams: 11, 12, 16, 21, 28, 39, 66
Cover picture: **Theo Bergstrom**

Weights and measures
Both metric and imperial measurements are given. As these are not exact equivalents, please work from one set of figures or the other. Use graded measuring spoons levelled across.

Time symbols
The time needed to prepare the dish is given on each recipe. The symbols are as follows:

simple to prepare and cook

straightforward but requires more skill or attention

time-consuming to prepare or requires extra skill

must be started 1 day or more ahead

On the cover: Coq au vin rouge, page 32

This Edition Published 1984
© Marshall Cavendish Limited 1984

Printed in Spain by
Artes Graficas Toledo, S.A.
D.L.TO:- 912-1984

Typeset by Performance Typesetting, Milton Keynes.

Published by Marshall Cavendish House
58 Old Compton Street
London W1V 5PA
ISBN 0 86307 264 X (SERIES)
ISBN 0 86307 266 6 (THIS VOLUME)

Here is the second in my super series of cookery books. *Making the most of Chicken, Poultry & Game* is a volume full of ideas for all occasions, from a simple snack to a dish impressive enough for the grandest dinner.

Chicken is one of the least expensive of meats, and because of this we tend to cook it often – usually in the same few ways – and as a result we get bored with it. But with the 50 or so chicken recipes in this volume you – and your family – need never be bored again. I show you how simple it is to dress up chicken for a special occasion – try roasting it with tarragon butter, then adding a brandy or cream sauce. Or casserole it in red wine with button onions, bacon and mushrooms for the classic *Coq au vin rouge*. I also provide you with lots of quick and easy family recipes. Try crunchy, Spicy stir-fried chicken or grilled chicken joints, moist and aromatic with oregano.

Turkey tends to be thought of as a special-occasion dish, particularly associated with festivals. Follow my instructions for that all-important Christmas turkey and it's bound to delight all the family, with the skin crisp and golden brown, and the meat tender and juicy. Then the leftovers will practically take care of themselves – my recipes range from a curry served in a ring of rice to a creamy double-crust pie. I'll bet you never thought of grilling or deep frying turkey, but now that ready-cut portions are so easily available, why don't you try grilled Turkey tournedos with almonds or Deep-fried turkey packets deliciously stuffed with dried apricots and walnuts?

Duck, goose and guinea fowl are birds that many of us never think of cooking. But any of them make superb dinner-party dishes, while roast goose has long been considered a traditional Christmas dish in Eastern Europe. So why not ring the changes once in a while, and stuff a goose with sausage-meat, prunes and apples, casserole guinea fowl with pears, white wine and port, or try your hand at *nouvelle cuisine* with *Magrets de canard au cassis* – pan-fried duck breasts with a blackcurrant glaze.

Game used to be regarded as a luxury reserved for the favoured few, but now that frozen game is available all year round from butchers and supermarkets, we can all enjoy the distinctive flavour of such birds and animals as pheasant, pigeon, grouse, venison, hare and rabbit. A simple roast is superb, if your game is young and tender; if not, make a casserole or pie – you'll find a tempting selection of recipes here, from the classic Jugged hare to the exotic and spicy Moroccan grouse.

Besides the many recipes packed into this volume, there's all sorts of useful information: how to choose the very best, how to store it and how to prepare it. I take all the worry out of jointing, boning, trussing and carving with my step-by-step instructions, and provide lots of informative charts for roasting times, and storage and thawing times for frozen poultry and game – in fact, all you need to know about chicken, poultry and game.

Happy cooking and bon appetit!

Robert Carrier

Chicken & Turkey

ROASTING CHICKEN & TURKEY

Chicken and turkey were once prized delicacies, but now they are widely available. Roasted until crisp and golden-skinned with juicy and flavoursome flesh, they make a memorable meal for any occasion.

When we see the plentiful poultry sections of our supermarkets today, it is difficult to believe that chickens and turkeys were once rare and very expensive birds, treats reserved for Christmas and other festive occasions. Modern production techniques mean that they are now readily available in all sizes all year round.

Choosing chicken for roasting

There are several types of chicken sold, and out of these the boiling fowl is the only one unsuitable for roasting.
Poussins are baby chickens, 4–6 weeks old. They are best spit-roasted or oven-roasted whole or halved. Larger poussins, weighing about 500 g / 1 lb, will serve one, or two if they are stuffed. Smaller poussins are sufficient for only one. Chickens of 8–10 weeks, 800–900 g /1¾–2 lb in weight – known as double poussins – serve two or three.
Spring chickens are slightly larger than poussins and better value. They weigh up to 1.1 kg /2½ lb and serve two or three.
Large roasting chickens are tender chickens of 1.4–1.8 kg /3–4 lb or more. The best ones have well-rounded bodies and full breasts. A 1.4 kg /3 lb chicken will feed four people; a 1.8 kg /4 lb chicken will feed five to six.
Capons are de-sexed male chickens. Large (over 2 kg /4½ lb) and delicately flavoured, they are excellent roasted.

When you buy a chicken from the butcher it will be 'dressed' – that is plucked, drawn and cleaned. The 'dressed weight' of the bird is the weight after plucking and drawing, but includes the cleaned giblets (neck, heart, liver and gizzard). A cleaned, trussed chicken is often sold as 'oven ready'.

Storing chicken

Remove any wrappings from a fresh chicken, remove the giblets, if there are any, and any wrappings round them. Loosely cover the chicken with greaseproof paper or foil. It can then be stored near the bottom of the refrigerator for 2–3 days. Remove from the refrigerator 1–2 hours before cooking. The giblets can be used to make gravy, but must be cooked on the day of purchase.

If you are intending to use a chicken that is frozen, keep it in the freezer until 24 hours before cooking it (see *page 104* for thawing times).

Preparing chicken for roasting

Rinse the chicken and pat dry, inside and out, then season it with salt and pepper.

You can smear the skin with a little butter which has been blended with some herbs, spices, garlic or lemon juice, or put some in the body cavity. Stuffing can be carefully eased between the skin and flesh of the breast, or put inside the neck cavity and held in place by the neck skin.

Roasting chicken

Although you can prepare a poultry stuffing the day before and refrigerate it, never stuff the chicken until just before roasting, as the stuffing may go sour. Make sure the stuffing is cold before you stuff the bird, and never pack the stuffing in tightly.

When the chicken is stuffed and trussed (*page 10*), place it on a rack in a roasting tin and either bard it with strips of streaky bacon or cover it with buttered muslin or aluminium foil. Remove this 20 minutes before the end of cooking to brown the skin. For roasting times for plainly cooked chicken see the chart on *page 105*.

To test that the chicken is cooked, push a skewer through the thickest part of the inside leg; the juices should run quite clear.

Transfer the chicken to a warmed serving dish and carve it at the table (see *page 15*).

Choosing turkey for roasting

Turkeys are available either fresh, chilled or frozen. Whichever you buy, the breasts should be plump and white, the drumsticks firm and rounded. Allow 350–450 g /12 oz–1 lb per person for a bird weighing up to 7.5 kg /16 lb; 450–550 g /1–1¼ lb per person for a bird weighing between 7.5–10.5 kg / 16–23 lb. A really big bird, between 10.5–11.5 kg /23–25 lb, will give 16–20 servings. If you buy a fresh turkey, allow 1.4 kg /3 lb for the weight of the head, feet and innards. Remember about 5 per cent of the weight of a frozen bird is water.
New York dressed turkeys: on a fresh or New York dressed turkey, which is the one seen hanging in the butcher's window at Christmas – plucked but with head and feet still attached – look for smooth black legs; these indicate a young, tender bird.

Hens are usually reckoned to be more tender than cocks, though modern breeders say there is little difference. Both are hung for 5-7 days after they have been killed to tenderize them.
Chilled turkeys have had their innards removed; they are then dressed for the oven on the farm before they are air-chilled. This process involves no intake of water (unlike deep freezing), so there is no weight loss later on. They are usually available from butchers and supermarkets, prewrapped and with the giblets wrapped separately inside them. Chilled turkeys range in weight from 2.5–11.5 kg /5½–25 lb.
Frozen turkeys are sold oven ready in the same sizes as chilled turkey. This is the cheapest way to buy turkey, though the weight includes extra water. Lengthy, slow thawing is a necessity to make the bird tender and safe to eat (see chart on *page 105*).

There is a variety of frozen turkey called the self-basting turkey. This has had butter or vegetable oil injected under its skin before

freezing and thus it will need no basting while it is roasting.

Storing turkey

A fresh turkey, loosely covered on a plate, will keep for up to 2 days in the coldest part of the refrigerator. Giblets should be kept separately and cooked on the day of purchase. They can be used to make stock for gravy. Follow the manufacturer's instructions for storing chilled turkeys. Frozen turkey should be thawed in the bottom of the refrigerator (see *page 105*).

Preparing turkey for roasting

A fresh bird may have a few quills left on – a sharp tug will quickly remove these.

Rinse the bird in cold water and pat dry inside and out. Season inside and out with salt and pepper before stuffing. If you are not stuffing the bird, put a lemon, cut in half, 2–3 sprigs of fresh herbs and some garlic, if you like inside the cavity to add flavour to the meat.

Traditionally two stuffings are used, one in the body cavity and one at the neck end.

Never fill the body cavity more than half full to ensure the inside of the bird cooks fully. If you are using one stuffing only, stuff the neck. Pull the neck skin over the back of the bird, then secure it with a skewer. The turkey can then be trussed, if wished.

Roasting turkey

Always bring the bird to room temperature first; allow at least 2 hours.

When the turkey is stuffed and trussed, place it on a rack in a roasting tin and either bard it with strips of streaky bacon or cover it with buttered muslin. Alternatively, the turkey can be spread all over with a paste of softened butter and salt and covered with a dome of aluminium foil. Remove this 20 minutes before the end of cooking to brown the skin. Unless you have bought a self-basting turkey, regular basting will be necessary to prevent the meat becoming dry.

If the breast appears to be getting overcooked, cover it with foil until the leg meat is done. A skewer inserted in the thickest part of the leg should produce clear juices when cooked and the leg should wiggle easily in its socket. For roasting times see the chart on *page 105*.

A turkey is carved in basically the same way as a chicken (see *page 15*) though the drumsticks can be sliced.

Roast chicken with herbs

bringing to room temperature, then 1½ hours

Serves 4
1.4–1.6 kg /3–3½ lb roasting chicken,
  dressed weight
75 g /3 oz softened butter
1.5 ml /¼ tsp dried rosemary
1.5 ml /¼ tsp dried marjoram
5 ml /1 tsp lemon juice
salt and freshly ground black pepper
a little flour
45–60 ml /3–4 tbls boiling water
90 ml / 6 tbls dry white wine
5 ml /1 tsp butter
fresh herbs, to garnish
buttered asparagus spears, to serve
sauté potatoes, to serve

1   Bring the chicken to room temperature. Heat the oven to 220C /425F /gas 7. Place the butter in a bowl and blend in the dried rosemary, marjoram and lemon juice. Season with salt and pepper. Put half the seasoned butter in the cavity of the chicken.
2   Truss the chicken (see *page 10*) and

spread the remaining seasoned butter over the breast. Sprinkle with salt and pepper.
3   Lay the chicken on its side in a roasting tin and roast in the oven for 20 minutes, until it is lightly browned. Turn the chicken onto its other side and roast for a further 15–20 minutes. Remove the chicken from the oven and reduce the temperature to 180C /350F /gas 4.
4   Turn the chicken onto its back in the tin and sprinkle a little flour over the breast. Spoon over 45–60 ml /3–4 tbls boiling water, return the chicken to the oven and roast for 35 minutes, basting frequently.
5   When the chicken is cooked, remove the trussing string and transfer the chicken to a heated serving dish.
6   Pour off most of the fat from the roasting tin. Add the dry white wine, place it over a high heat and bring to the boil, stirring and scraping the base and sides of the tin.
7   Boil the gravy for 3–5 minutes, until it is reduced by about half. Season with salt and freshly ground black pepper and add the butter. Pour into a heated sauce-boat.
8   Garnish the chicken with herbs and arrange the asparagus spears and sauté potatoes around it. Serve at once with the gravy handed round separately.

Roast chicken with herbs

Trussing a chicken

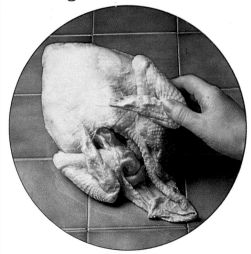

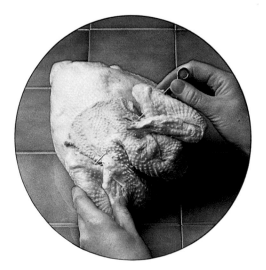

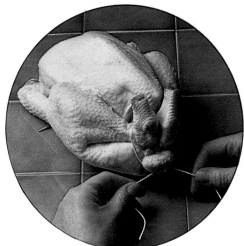

Lay the chicken on its breast, with the neck end facing you. Bring round the wings and lay them flat across the back.

Draw the neck skin over the body. Pass a skewer through one wing, through the neck skin and through the other wing.

Turn the chicken onto its back. Tie the legs together with string, draw the string under the 'parson's nose' and tie it tightly.

Roast turkey with sausage-meat stuffing and whole chestnuts

🔪🔪🔪 making stock, 2 hours,
3½–4 hours roasting, then 10 minutes

Serves 8–10
*4.5 kg /10 lb turkey, dressed weight, giblets
    reserved*
salt and freshly ground black pepper
100 g /4 oz butter, melted
For the turkey giblet stock
1 Spanish onion, coarsely chopped
1 bay leaf
*4 sprigs each celery leaves and
    parsley*
salt and freshly ground black pepper
150 ml /5 fl oz dry white wine
For the sausage-meat stuffing
75 g /3 oz fat bacon slices
25 g /1 oz butter
*100 g /4 oz crustless stale white bread, cut
    into 10 mm /⅓ in cubes*
500 g /1 lb pork sausage-meat
*225 g /8 oz boned pork sparerib or veal,
    minced*
1 small onion, finely chopped
*30 ml /2 tbls finely chopped fresh
    parsley*
1.5 ml /¼ tsp dried thyme
1.5 ml /¼ tsp dried marjoram
a pinch of dried sage
1 egg, beaten
salt and freshly ground black pepper
For the chestnut stuffing
1 kg /2 lb chestnuts
45 ml /3 tbls oil
15–25 g /½–1 oz butter
salt and freshly ground black pepper
For the gravy
15 ml /1 tbls cornflour
salt and freshly ground black pepper

1 Remove the turkey from the refrigerator. Make the turkey giblet stock: cut the wing tips from the turkey at the first joint. Wash the neck, heart, gizzard and wing tips and place them in a pan with the coarsely chopped onion, bay leaf, celery leaves and parsley and a little salt and freshly ground black pepper. Add the dry white wine and enough water to cover the giblets. Bring to the boil, skim the surface, cover the pan and simmer over a gentle heat for 1½ hours, topping up with water, when necessary, to keep the giblets covered. Wash the turkey liver, add it to the pan and simmer for a further 30 minutes. Strain the stock into a measuring jug. You should have at least 425 ml /15 fl oz of turkey stock; make it up to this amount with water, if necessary.
2 Make the sausage-meat stuffing: cook the bacon slices in a large frying-pan over a low heat until the fat runs and the bacon slices are crisp and dark golden. Remove them from the pan with a slotted spoon and crumble them into a large bowl (or snip them with kitchen scissors).
3 Add the butter to the bacon fat in the frying-pan and heat until foaming. Add the bread cubes and toss over a moderate heat until they are crisp on the outside but still soft and spongy inside. Add to the crumbled bacon. Add the remaining sausage-meat stuffing ingredients and 60 ml /4 tbls of the turkey giblet stock to the bowl, and mix by hand until all the stuffing ingredients are thoroughly blended. Let cool.
4 Make the chestnut stuffing. First shell and skin the chestnuts: with the tip of a small knife, cut a small slit in the shell on the rounded side of each chestnut. Heat the oil in a wide, heavy saucepan. Add enough of the chestnuts to make a single layer in the pan, and sauté them over a high heat for 5 minutes, shaking the pan to keep the chestnuts moving and to prevent them from charring. Using a slotted spoon, transfer the chestnuts to a colander. Rinse them briefly with cold water until they are cool enough to

handle, then remove the shells and peel away the thin inner skins, being careful not to break the nuts. Repeat the shelling and skinning process with the remaining chestnuts.
5 Cook the shelled and skinned chestnuts in boiling salted water for 35–40 minutes or until they are quite tender. Drain the chestnuts thoroughly, reserving a little of the liquor, then return the empty pan to the heat, add the chestnuts, butter and 15–30 ml /1–2 tbls of the reserved liquor and swirl the pan until the chestnuts are coated with the buttery liquid. Season the chestnuts to taste with salt and freshly ground black pepper and let cool.
6 Heat the oven to 220C /425F /gas 7. Using a damp cloth or absorbent paper, wipe the turkey clean both inside and out, then pat it dry. Using a pair of tweezers, or the point of a knife and your thumb, pluck out any bits of feather or quill. Weigh the turkey and calculate the cooking time, allowing 44 minutes per kg /20 minutes per lb for well-cooked meat.
7 Loosen the skin all over the breast of the turkey by carefully easing your hand down between the skin and the flesh. Take great care that you do not tear the skin. If the skin refuses to come away from the flesh at any point, release it with a pair of scissors or the point of a sharp knife.
8 Push the sausage-meat stuffing between the breast skin and flesh of the turkey, making sure that you push it right to the end and down the sides of the breast. Do not pack it too tightly though, as it tends to swell during cooking. Draw the neck skin loosely over the back. Stitch with strong thread, or use skewers or cocktail sticks, to hold the neck skin in position and the wings folded under.
9 Stuff the chestnuts loosely into the body cavity. If you have any chestnuts left over, they can be added to the roasting tin for the last 30 minutes of the turkey's cooking time, then removed from the tin with a slotted spoon just before serving. Sew the vent shut

with strong thread and tie the legs together with string.

10 Put the turkey, breast side up, in a large roasting tin. Season generously with salt and freshly ground black pepper. Using a sharp skewer or cocktail stick, prick the breast skin all over. This helps to prevent it bursting should the stuffing swell during the cooking time.

11 Cut a piece of double-thick muslin, large enough to drape over and cover the tukey completely. Rinse the muslin in cold water and wring it out as dry as possible. Soak the muslin in the melted butter and gently squeeze out the excess. Drape the buttered muslin over the turkey.

12 Roast the turkey on the lowest shelf of the oven for 15 minutes of the calculated cooking time. Then reduce the oven temperature to 180C /350F /gas 4, turn the turkey onto its breast and roast for a further 15 minutes of the cooking time to allow the back to take on some colour. Turn the turkey back to its original position, breast side up, and roast for the rest of the calculated cooking time.

13 Meanwhile combine the remaining melted butter with 150 ml /5 fl oz of the turkey giblet stock. Baste the turkey with this buttery liquid after the first 30 minutes of cooking time, then baste every 15 minutes with the buttery liquid and the juices in the roasting tin, making sure that the muslin is completely remoistened with each basting. About 45 minutes before the end of the cooking time, remove the muslin to allow the turkey to brown. To test that the turkey is cooked, insert a skewer into the thickest part of the inside leg close to the body; the juices should run clear and if you cut the string and move the leg, the leg joint should wiggle loosely in its socket.

14 Remove the trussing threads, string and skewers from the cooked turkey and transfer the turkey to a heated serving platter. Turn off the oven, then slide the turkey back into the oven to keep warm while you make the gravy.

15 Skim the excess fat from the juices in the roasting tin. Bring the skimmed juices to the boil, add 275 ml /10 fl oz of the turkey giblet stock and return to the boil, stirring and scraping the base and sides of the pan with a wooden spoon to dislodge any bits that are stuck to the pan.

16 Taste and season the gravy if necessary. Blend the cornflour to a smooth paste with a little cold water, add to the pan and stir thoroughly. Bring to the boil and simmer for 2–3 minutes, stirring constantly. Strain the gravy into a heated sauce-boat and serve with the roast turkey.

Roast turkey with oyster stuffing

🍴 bringing to room temperature, then 2½–3 hours

Serves 6-8
3.6 kg /8 lb turkey, dressed weight
1 lemon, cut in half
salt and freshly ground black pepper
8 thin slices of streaky bacon
125–175 g /4–6 oz butter
15 ml /1 tbls whisky
For the stuffing
75 g /3 oz butter
2 medium-sized onions, finely chopped
4 sticks celery, chopped
1 small green pepper, finely chopped
125 g /4 oz button mushrooms, thinly sliced
30 ml /2 tbls finely chopped fresh parsley
125 g /4 oz fresh white breadcrumbs
2.5 ml /½ tsp dried marjoram
2.5 ml /½ tsp dried thyme
2.5 ml /½ tsp freshly grated nutmeg
salt and freshly ground black pepper
125 g /4 oz canned smoked oysters, chopped
15 ml /1 tbls whisky
For the garnish
sprigs of watercress
thin slices of lemon

1 Remove the turkey from the refrigerator and bring to room temperature. Meanwhile, make the stuffing: melt the butter in a large frying-pan and cook the onions, celery, green pepper, mushrooms and the parsley until soft, about 15 minutes.

2 Place the mixture in a large bowl and stir in the breadcrumbs. Add the marjoram, thyme, nutmeg and salt and pepper. Add the oysters, together with any liquid from the can, and the whisky. Stir well and let cool.

3 Heat the oven to 220C /425F /gas 7.

4 Wipe the turkey inside and out with a damp cloth, dry, then pack the stuffing into the cavity. Truss the bird neatly, then rub the skin all over with the lemon and season with salt and pepper. Lay the bacon slices over the breast and place in a roasting tin.

5 Melt 125 g /4 oz butter in a small saucepan. When it is bubbling, pour over the turkey. Cover the turkey loosely with foil and place in the oven. After 15 minutes turn the heat down to 170C /325F /gas 3 and cook for a further 2–2½ hours, basting every 15 minutes with the melted butter. Melt more butter for basting if necessary. Remove the bacon slices when the bird is almost cooked, to allow the breast to brown. When the juices run clear if the thickest part is pierced with skewer, the turkey is done.

6 Place the turkey on a warmed serving platter, remove any strings, garnish with watercress and lemon and keep warm in the turned-off oven while you make the gravy.

7 Skim the fat from the cooking juices and add 30–45 ml /2–3 tbls water to the roasting tin. Bring to the boil, add the whisky and boil for 2 minutes. Pour into a warmed sauce-boat and serve with the turkey.

Roast turkey with sausage-meat stuffing and whole chestnuts

Poulet à l'estragon

bringing to room temperature,
then 1½ hours

Serves 4–6

1.8 kg /4 lb chicken
50 g /2 oz butter
30 ml /2 tbls freshly chopped tarragon
leaves or 30 ml /1 tbls dried tarragon
1 garlic clove, crushed
salt and freshly ground black pepper
15 ml /1 tbls oil
50 ml /2 fl oz brandy
75 ml /3 fl oz thick cream

1 Bring the chicken to room temperature. Heat the oven to 190C /375F /gas 5. Mash together the butter, tarragon, garlic, salt and pepper. Divide the mixture into 3.
2 Gently push your fingers between the skin and the breast of the chicken and insert one third of the butter mixture on each side of the breast, under the skin. Flatten slightly by patting the skin. Put remaining butter into the cavity of bird.

Poulet à l'estragon

3 Rub a little oil on the outside of the bird. Arrange the chicken so it rests on one breast on a rack in a roasting tin and roast for 35 minutes. Turn it onto the other side and roast for a further 35 minutes.
4 Remove the tin from the oven, lift out the bird, take out the rack and return the bird to the tin.
5 Put the brandy into a soup ladle and warm it gently. Light it with a taper and pour it over the chicken. When the flames subside, remove the chicken, tipping the juices from the cavity into the tin. Place the bird on a serving dish and keep warm.
6 Add the cream to the pan and warm it through gently, stirring well. Pour the sauce over the chicken and serve immediately.

Roast chicken with saffron and lemon

Typically French in feeling, this tender roast chicken is flavoured with lemon juice and saffron.

bringing to room temperature,
then 1¾ hours

Serves 4

1.4–1.6 kg /3–3½ lb roasting chicken,
dressed weight
salt and freshly ground black pepper
75 g /3 oz butter
a good pinch of powdered saffron or crushed
saffron strands
1 small garlic clove, finely chopped
juice of ½ lemon
a little flour
45–60 ml /3–4 tbls boiling water
sprigs of watercress, to garnish
For the sauce
50 g /2 oz butter
100 g /4 oz button mushrooms, sliced
zest of ½ lemon, finely shredded
2 medium-sized egg yolks
150 ml /5 fl oz thick cream
juice of ½ lemon
20 ml /4 tsp sugar
90 ml /6 tbls dry white wine
salt and freshly ground black pepper

1 Bring the chicken to room temperature before cooking. Heat the oven to 220C /425F /gas 7.
2 Wipe the chicken clean both inside and out, then pat it dry. Season inside the cavity with salt and freshly ground black pepper.

12

3 Put the butter in a bowl and, using a wooden spoon, work in the saffron, finely chopped garlic and lemon juice. Season generously with salt and freshly ground black pepper. Place half of this seasoned butter in the cavity of the chicken.

4 Truss the chicken as shown in the step-by-step pictures on *page 10*.

5 Spread the remaining seasoned butter over the breast and thighs of the chicken. Sprinkle with more salt and freshly ground black pepper.

6 Lay the chicken on its side in the roasting tin and roast in the oven for about 20 minutes, until it is lightly browned. Turn the chicken onto its other side and roast for a further 15–20 minutes. Remove the chicken from the oven and reduce the oven temperature to 180C /350F /gas 4.

7 Turn the chicken onto its back in the tin and sift a dusting of flour over the breast. Spoon over 45–60 ml /3–4 tbls boiling water and roast for a further 30–35 minutes, or longer if necessary, basting frequently, until the chicken is cooked. To test that the chicken is cooked, push a skewer through the thickest part of the inside leg; the juices should run quite clear and golden. Similarly, when you tip up the chicken the juices from the cavity should be clear.

8 While the chicken is roasting, prepare the sauce. Melt the butter in a pan and lightly sauté the sliced mushrooms. Remove them from the pan with a slotted spoon. Blanch the shredded lemon zest by cooking it in boiling water for about 2 minutes. Drain thoroughly.

9 Place the egg yolks in a bowl with the cream, sautéed mushroom slices, lemon juice and blanched shredded lemon zest. Mix together lightly.

10 Place the sugar in a small, heavy pan and melt over a gentle heat. When the sugar has melted completely, bring it to the boil and boil to a rich brown caramel. Hold the pan at arm's length and add 30 ml /2 tbls water, then stir over a gentle heat until the caramel has dissolved and continue to cook until the mixture is syrupy. Stir the caramel into the egg yolk, cream and mushroom mixture.

11 Remove the trussing string and skewer from the roast chicken. Drain the juices from the chicken into the roasting tin and transfer the chicken to a heated serving dish.

12 Pour off most of the fat from the roasting tin. Add the dry white wine to the tin, place the tin over a high heat and bring to the boil, stirring, and scraping the base and sides of the tin with a wooden spoon to dislodge any stuck bits. Boil the contents of the tin for 3–5 minutes, until reduced to about half the original quantity.

13 To finish the sauce, place the cream mixture in the top of a double boiler, over boiling water. Strain the contents of the roasting tin into the cream and whisk the mixture over the boiling water for about 5 minutes, until it has lightly thickened. Do not allow the sauce to boil or it will curdle. Season the sauce to taste with salt and freshly ground black pepper, then pour it into a heated sauce-boat. Garnish the chicken with watercress and serve at once, with the sauce handed round separately.

Roast poussins with dill stuffing

🔪🔪 bringing to room temperature, then 1½ hours

Serves 4
2 × 500 g /1 lb poussins, dressed weight, with giblets
50 g /2 oz butter
sprigs of dill, to garnish
For the dill stuffing
25 g /1 oz softened butter
2 medium-sized eggs, separated
50 g /2 oz dry white breadcrumbs
15–20 ml /3–4 tsp finely chopped fresh dill
salt and freshly ground black pepper

1 Make sure that the poussins are at room temperature. Heat the oven to 180C /350F / gas 4.

2 Using a damp cloth or absorbent paper, wipe the poussins clean both inside and out, then pat them dry. Clean the livers, chop them finely and reserve them for the stuffing. (Use the remaining giblets to make stock to use in another recipe.)

3 Make the stuffing: place the softened butter in a mixing bowl with the egg yolks and, using a wooden spoon, beat until well blended. Blend in the breadcrumbs and the reserved chopped livers. Mix in the finely chopped fresh dill and season to taste with salt and pepper. Whisk the egg whites until stiff but not dry. Fold them, gently but thoroughly, into breadcrumb mixture.

Roast poussins with dill stuffing

4 Loosen the skin all over the breast of each poussin by carefully easing your fingers down between the skin and the flesh. Take great care that you do not tear the skin. If the skin refuses to come easily away from the breast at any point, do not force it, but use the point of a sharp knife, or a pair of small scissors, to cut it from the breast.

5 Push enough of the stuffing between the skin and breast of each poussin to cover the entire breast with a thin, even layer. Divide the remaining stuffing between the poussin cavities. Skewer or sew up the cavities, and make sure that the stuffing cannot slip out from under the breast skin.

6 Truss the poussins as shown in the step-by-step pictures on *page 10*.

7 Choose a roasting tin large enough to take the poussins side by side. Place the tin over a medium heat, add the 50 g /2 oz butter and heat until foaming. Turn the poussins over in the butter so that they are coated evenly. Turn them on their backs in the tin and roast in the oven for 45 minutes, basting frequently with the juices in the tin. To test that they are cooked, push a skewer in the thickest part of the inside leg, close to the body. The juices should run clear.

8 Remove the roast poussins from the roasting tin and, using a very sharp knife, slice each one in half right down the middle. Put the 2 halves back together and arrange the 2 reassembled poussins on a heated serving dish. Garnish with sprigs of dill. Strain the pan juices into a heated sauce-boat and serve with the poussins.

Boning out a chicken

1 Cut off the ends of the legs at the first joint and the wings at the second joint. Cut cleanly along the backbone, through the skin and flesh, down to the bone.

2 Holding the knife flat against the carcass, cut the flesh away from the rib cage, working close to the ribs. Work down to the thigh joints. Do not puncture the skin.

3 Cut through each thigh joint, to separate the thigh bone from the carcass. Working down the thigh bone, scrape away the flesh until you reach the drumstick joint.

4 To remove each drumstick (optional), continue working the flesh away from the drumstick bone, pushing the bone in from the outside. Draw out the complete leg bone.

5 Scrape the flesh away from each wing bone; sever the bone from carcass and draw out. Finish working the flesh away from the ribs and then the breastbone.

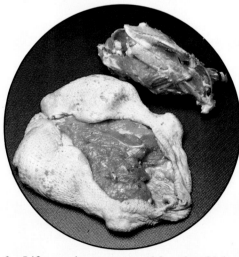

6 Lift out the carcass and lay the chicken out flat. Push the legs and wings into the body so there is no skin hanging out. Lay the stuffing along the centre and sew up.

Stuffed chicken

boning chicken, then 3 hours plus overnight chilling

Serves 6–8

1.6 kg /3½ lb roasting chicken, boned out
  except for the drumsticks
15 g /½ oz sultanas
15 ml /1 tbls brandy
75 g /3 oz long-grain rice
salt and freshly ground black pepper
50 g /2 oz butter
150 g /5 oz onion, finely chopped
350 g /12 oz minced pork
50 g /2 oz button mushrooms
25 g /1 oz toasted almonds, finely chopped
15 g /½ oz pine kernels, chopped
grated zest of ½ medium-sized orange
a good pinch each of dried sage and thyme,
  or fresh sage and thyme, finely chopped
a generous pinch of grated nutmeg
2 medium-sized eggs, beaten separately
watercress and orange slices, to garnish

1 Soak the sultanas in the brandy. Boil the rice in plenty of lightly salted water for about 15 minutes until just done. Rinse in a sieve under cold running water. Drain.
2 In a medium-sized frying-pan, melt 15 g /½ oz butter and cook the onion until soft and translucent. Turn into a mixing bowl. Add another 15 g /½ oz butter to the pan, turn up heat to medium and cook the pork, stirring and turning to break up any lumps, until light brown. Add to the mixing bowl.
3 Add another 15 g /½ oz butter to the pan and cook the mushrooms until golden brown, then turn into the mixing bowl along with the pan juices.
4 Add the almonds, pine kernels, sultanas and any unabsorbed brandy, grated orange zest, the herbs, salt and black pepper and nutmeg. Then add the rice and 1 egg.
5 Mix the stuffing with your hands, squeezing and kneading, until it holds together. If the first egg has not bound the mixture sufficiently, add part or all of the second egg until the stuffing binds. Let the stuffing cool completely.
6 Heat the oven to 200C /400F /gas 6. Spread the stuffing evenly down the centre of the boned-out chicken. Pull the skin together on top. Sew it up neatly with strong thread, making sure the neck and tail ends do not gape. Gently pat into shape.
7 With a string, make a series of ties around the chicken, but not so tightly as to squash it. Tie it once from neck to tail.
8 Melt the remaining butter and brush over the chicken. Sprinkle lightly with salt and pepper and place in a roasting pan in the middle of the oven. After 15 minutes, lower the heat to 190C /375F /gas 5. Shake the pan gently to ensure that the chicken is not sticking and baste with the juices in the pan. Continue roasting for another 1¼ hours, basting at half-hourly intervals.
9 Remove from the oven and cool completely. Refrigerate overnight, wrapped in foil. Bring it to room temperature 1 hour before serving. Carefully remove the strings and stitching. Garnish with watercress and orange slices and carve in slices to serve.

Carving a large chicken, capon or turkey

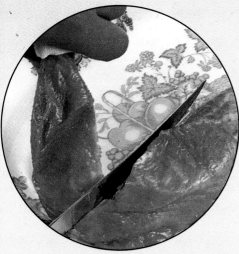  

Carve one side completely first. Place the bird, breast side up, with the neck facing you. Insert the fork in the breast. Cut the skin between the thigh and breast; bend the thigh outwards to find the ball and socket joint. Slice through the joint (see below); remove the whole leg. Place the leg, skin side up, on the dish. Holding the drumstick, cut firmly through the joint between thigh and drumstick (see above). Carve slices off the thigh bone and drumstick.

With the neck still facing you, and the fork firmly inserted in one breast, cut through the other breast just above the wing and ease the wing away from the body to expose the ball and socket joint. Cut firmly through the joint and carve off the wing with the slice of breast attached.

Still with the neck facing you, cut down vertically through the breast to carve a complete slice. Continue to carve slices in this way until you reach the carcass. Lift each slice away between the back of the fork and the knife. Carve the other side of the bird in the same way.

GRILLING CHICKEN & TURKEY

Grilling chicken and turkey is quite an art, but it is a good method for creating a simple but succulent dish. Marinades and herbs help to keep the meat moist and add subtle but delicious flavours.

Half a tender young spring chicken, grilled until its skin crackles crisply, served with a tossed green salad, is a dish fit for a king. Joints from a larger chicken – though a little less impressive to look at – are equally tasty and very good value. Buy only young, tender chickens for grilling – poussins, spring chickens and small roasting chickens.

Turkey was once a bird reserved for roasting, but now that turkey portions are so readily available turkey becomes yet another lean, tender meat ideal for grilling. Choose boneless meat that can be cut into portions of even thickness. Both light and dark turkey meat can be cut into steaks or escalopes, or into smaller pieces for threading on skewers to make kebabs.

Both chicken and turkey are delicious cooked over charcoal – the smoky flavour complements them particularly well.

Preparing to grill
It is not possible to grill a whole chicken successfully; it will cook too unevenly. A small chicken of not more than 1 kg /2 lb dressed weight can be spatchcocked: split down the middle and secured with skewers, then grilled to serve two people.

To spatchcock a chicken cut down each side of, and remove, the backbone. Remove the breastbone carefully, keeping the skin intact and therefore not separating the two halves of the bird (but leave in the rib bones), and open the bird out like a book. A single skewer through the legs and across the body will hold a small bird flat during grilling; for a larger bird also thread a skewer through the wings. Remove the skewers and rib bones before serving.

A chicken any larger than 1 kg /2 lb should be cut into four or even eight portions (see below). To make sure the breast portions will lie flat on the grill grid, remove the rib bones by simply running a knife underneath them. Trim off the wing tips and foot joints if the butcher has left them on, as these will burn very easily.

Remember to remove the bird from the refrigerator well before you intend to cook it, to allow it to come to room temperature. Wipe it dry with absorbent paper and season it with freshly ground black pepper. Just before cooking, season the joints with salt and perhaps some more pepper and brush with oil and melted butter, or another moist dressing. Alternatively, give the meat a little extra flavour by marinating it for at least 4 hours. Don't marinate in the refrigerator unless the marinating period is longer than 12 hours or it is a particularly hot day and, even then, try to remove the meat from the refrigerator in time to bring it to room temperature.

Preparing the grill: heat the grill to maximum before you start to cook. How long this takes will depend on the individual cooker, but remove the grid from the grill pan so that the grid itself doesn't get hot. When you are ready to cook, brush the grid lightly with olive oil to prevent the meat from sticking to it.

How to grill
Arrange the bird on the grid with the side that will be served uppermost on top, which usually means skin side upward. This is because the side grilled first always has the better appearance.

Times for grilling poultry depend on thickness rather than weight. For this reason chicken leg joints need longer cooking than breast and wing joints. Start the legs cooking first, turning them twice during cooking so that the skin doesn't burn before the meat is cooked through. The breasts and wings can be added to the grid 5–10 minutes after the legs have started cooking, and need to be turned only once. To test that chicken is cooked, insert a skewer or knife in the thickest part of the meat, nearest to the bone. The juices should run clear. Boneless turkey escalopes or steaks are cooked through when the meat is just beige and opaque all the way through, but still juicy.

Spatchcocking a chicken

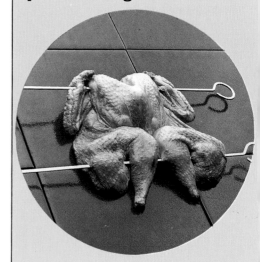

Thread two skewers through the legs and wings, across the body, to hold the bird flat.

Jointing a chicken

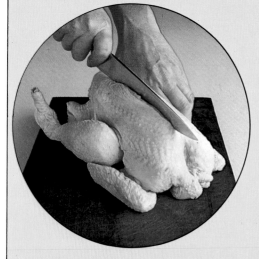

Cut along and through the length of the breastbone. Open out and cut through and remove the backbone.

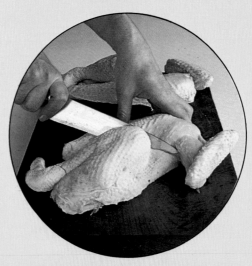

Skin side up, cut diagonally behind the thigh, through the ball and socket joint, to separate the leg from the wing and breast.

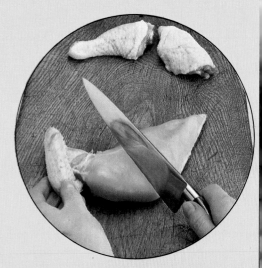

For 8 portions cut the drumstick from the thigh. Cut the wing diagonally through the breast, sliding the knife along the rib cage.

Grilled spring chicken

⏱ bringing to room temperature, then 25 minutes

Serves 2
1.1 kg /2½ lb spring chicken, dressed weight
salt and freshly ground black pepper
30 ml /2 tbls paprika
15 ml /1 tbls lemon juice
60 ml /4 tbls melted butter
60 ml /4 tbls fresh white breadcrumbs
olive oil
sprigs of watercress, to garnish
lemon wedges, to garnish

1 Joint the bird into 4 pieces, removing the rib bones from the breasts. Wipe the pieces with absorbent paper, season with freshly ground black pepper and sprinkle with paprika. Leave the chicken to come to room temperature before grilling.
2 Heat the grill without the grid to high.
3 Sprinkle the chicken pieces with lemon juice, brush with melted butter, sprinkle with breadcrumbs and season with salt.

4 Brush the grill grid with olive oil and place the chicken legs on the grid, meaty side upwards. Grill, with the grid 12.5 cm /5 in from the heat, for 5–10 minutes. Place the chicken breast portions on the grid, skin side upwards, turn the legs and grill for a further 10 minutes, or until cooked, turning all the portions once during this time and brushing frequently with melted butter.
5 Serve immediately, garnished with sprigs of watercress and lemon wedges.

Grilled chicken oregano

⏱ 20 minutes, 4 hours marinating, then 30 minutes

Serves 4
1.6 kg /3½ lb chicken
60 ml /4 tbls lemon juice
90 ml /6 tbls olive oil
10 ml /2 tsp dried oregano
1–1½ garlic cloves, finely chopped
30 ml /2 tbls finely chopped fresh parsley
salt and freshly ground black pepper
olive oil for greasing

Grilled spring chicken

1 Wipe the chicken and joint into 4 pieces, removing the rib bones from the breasts.
2 Combine the lemon juice, olive oil, dried oregano, garlic and parsley in a small bowl and season with salt and pepper to taste. Mix with a fork to blend the marinade.
3 Place the chicken pieces in a large flat gratin dish. Pour the oregano marinade over the chicken and leave it to marinate for at least 4 hours, turning the chicken pieces once or twice during this time.
4 Heat the grill without the grid to high. When ready to cook, brush the grid with oil, place the chicken legs on the grid, fleshy side up, and brush with marinade. Grill the legs, 10–15 cm /4–6 in from the heat, for 5–10 minutes, spooning the marinade over the chicken from time to time.
5 Turn the chicken legs over. Place the chicken breasts, skin side up, on the grid, brush with marinade mixture and continue to grill for 15–20 minutes, turning all portions once and spooning over the marinade from time to time. Cook until the chicken is crisp and golden brown and the juices run clear when the meat is pierced with a skewer or knife. Serve with the pan juices.

17

American devilled chicken

⏱ 20 minutes, 4 hours marinating, then 40 minutes

Serves 4
1.4 kg /3 lb chicken, dressed weight
60 ml /4 tbls olive oil
1.5 ml /¼ tsp cayenne pepper
2.5 ml /½ tsp ground ginger
salt and freshly ground black pepper
60 ml /4 tbls flour
1 egg, beaten
75 g /3 oz fresh white breadcrumbs
olive oil for greasing
75 g /3 oz butter
4 slices back bacon, rinds removed
2 tomatoes, halved
200 g /7 oz canned sweetcorn kernels
extra cayenne pepper for seasoning
parsley sprigs, to garnish

1 Joint the chicken into 4 pieces, removing the rib bones from the breasts. Combine the oil, cayenne pepper and ginger in a shallow dish. Wipe the chicken pieces with absorbent paper, season with freshly ground black pepper and place in the cayenne and ginger marinade. Turn to coat well, then leave to marinate for 4 hours, turning the pieces from time to time so that they remain coated with the marinade.
2 Place the flour, beaten egg and fresh breadcrumbs on 3 separate plates. Remove the chicken legs from the marinade and blot well with absorbent paper. Coat the legs with flour, shaking off the excess. Dip the legs in beaten egg and then in the breadcrumbs, making sure they are evenly coated. Season with salt. Melt 50 g /2 oz of the butter in a small saucepan.
3 Heat the grill without the grid to high.
4 Brush the grill grid with olive oil, place the chicken legs on the grid and brush them with melted butter. Grill, fleshy side upwards, with the grid 12.5 cm /5 in from the heat, for 10 minutes. Meanwhile, blot the breast portions, then coat them evenly in the flour, egg and crumbs in the same way. Season with salt and brush with butter.
5 Place the chicken breasts, skin side upwards, on the grid and turn the legs. Grill for 10 minutes, brushing frequently with melted butter.
6 Turn all the chicken portions and brush again with melted butter. Place the bacon and the tomato halves, cut side up, on the grid. Season the tomatoes with salt and freshly ground black pepper. Grill for a further 5 minutes, or until the chicken is cooked through, turning the bacon once.
7 Meanwhile, heat the canned sweetcorn in the liquid from the can.
8 To serve, drain the corn, add the remaining butter and toss until the butter has melted. Season to taste with salt, freshly ground black pepper and cayenne pepper. Pile the sweetcorn in the centre of a heated serving dish, arrange the devilled chicken pieces around it and garnish the chicken with the tomatoes, bacon and parsley sprigs. Serve immediately.

Turkey tournedos with almonds

⏱ 15 minutes, bringing to room temperature, then 20 minutes

Serves 4
700 g /1½ lb rolled turkey breast
4 slices streaky bacon, rind removed
freshly ground black pepper
salt
olive oil
75 g /3 oz ground almonds
For the garnish
250 g /8 oz mange-tout
salt
25 g /1 oz butter
freshly ground black pepper

1 Untie the string from the rolled turkey breast and cut the breast into 4 even steaks. (Each one should be 4 cm /1½ in thick and 5–7.5 cm /2–3 in in diameter.) Wrap a bacon slice around the sides of each one and tie with string. Season the steaks on both sides with freshly ground black pepper and allow to come to room temperature.
2 Prepare the garnish: wash the mange-tout and cut off the stems. Blanch them in a saucepan of boiling salted water for 1 minute. Drain, refresh under cold running water and drain again.
3 Heat the grill without the grid to high. Season the steaks on both sides with salt and freshly ground black pepper, dip them in olive oil and coat them with the ground almonds. Brush the grill grid with olive oil and grill the steaks, with the grid 7.5 cm /3 in from the heat, for 12 minutes or until cooked through, turning once and brushing frequently with olive oil.
4 Meanwhile, melt the butter in a frying-pan and sauté the mange-tout for 2–3 minutes, until cooked through but still crisp to the bite. Season with salt and freshly ground black pepper.
5 Arrange the turkey tournedos on a heated serving platter and remove the strings. Garnish with the mange-tout and serve immediately.

Grilled chicken with mustard crumbs

⏱ 25 minutes, 4 hours marinating, then 35 minutes

Serves 4
1.4 kg /3 lb chicken, dressed weight
olive oil
60 ml /4 tbls flour
1 egg, beaten
75 g /3 oz fresh white breadcrumbs
salt and freshly ground black pepper
30 ml /2 tbls melted butter
For the marinade
60 ml /4 tbls olive oil
60 ml /4 tbls lemon juice
½ Spanish onion, finely chopped
freshly ground black pepper
a pinch of cayenne pepper

For the mustard sauce
40 g /1½ oz butter
45 ml /3 tbls flour
150 ml /5 fl oz dry white wine
300 ml /10 fl oz milk
1 chicken stock cube, crumbled
15 ml /1 tbls Dijon mustard
salt and freshly ground black pepper

1 Joint the chicken into 4 pieces, removing the rib bones from the breasts. Remove the skin from all the pieces. Wipe the pieces with absorbent paper.
2 In a shallow dish combine the marinade ingredients. Add the chicken pieces, turn to coat them well, cover and leave to marinate for 4 hours, turning from time to time.
3 Meanwhile, make the mustard sauce: melt the butter in a saucepan, add the flour and stir over a low heat for 4–5 minutes, to form a pale roux. Gradually add the white wine and milk, stirring vigorously with a whisk to prevent lumps from forming. Add the crumbled chicken stock cube, then bring to the boil, stirring. Reduce the heat and

For the marinade
45 ml /3 tbls clear honey
15 ml /1 tbls Dijon mustard
15 ml /1 tbls olive oil
100 ml /4 fl oz pineapple juice
juice of 1 orange
90 ml /6 tbls tomato ketchup
freshly ground black pepper
1.5 ml /¼ tsp ground ginger
a good pinch of cayenne pepper

1 Joint the chicken into 4 pieces, removing the rib bones from the breasts. Wipe the pieces with absorbent paper.
2 Make the marinade: in a small saucepan mix together well the honey, mustard, olive oil, fruit juices and tomato ketchup. Bring to the boil, reduce the heat and simmer for 20 minutes. Season with pepper to taste, the ginger and cayenne pepper. Allow to cool.
3 Place the chicken pieces in a shallow dish, pour the marinade over and coat the chicken well. Cover and marinate for 4 hours, turning occasionally.
4 Heat the grill without the grid to high.
5 Season the chicken pieces with salt. Brush the grill grid with olive oil and lay the chicken legs on the grid, fleshy side up. Grill, with the grid 12.5 cm /5 in from the heat, for 5–10 minutes. Place the breast portions on the grid, fleshy side up, turn the legs and brush all the pieces with the marinade. Grill for 15 minutes more, or until the chicken is cooked through, turning and brushing all the pieces once more. Serve immediately.

Grilled herbed poussins

15 minutes, bringing to room temperature, then 25 minutes

Serves 4
4 × 450 g /1 lb poussins
4 garlic cloves, finely chopped
10 ml /2 tsp dried thyme
freshly ground black pepper
olive oil
salt
40 g /1½ oz softened butter
sprigs of thyme, to garnish

1 Cut the poussins in half lengthways. Lay the halved poussins flat. Ease the skin away from the breast with a small, sharp knife, and push the finely chopped garlic and dried thyme underneath. Season the skin with freshly ground black pepper and leave to come to room temperature.
2 Heat the grill without the grid to high.
3 Brush the grill grid with olive oil and place the halved poussins on the grid, skin side up. Season generously with salt and freshly ground black pepper and spread a little softened butter on each halved poussin.
4 Grill 7.5 cm /3 in from the heat for 8 minutes. Turn over, season generously with salt and pepper and spread the remaining softened butter on the halved birds. Cook for 8 more minutes, or until cooked through.
5 Arrange the poussins on a heated serving dish. Garnish with sprigs of thyme and serve.

American devilled chicken

simmer for 20 minutes, or until the sauce has reduced to 300 ml /10 fl oz. Stir in the Dijon mustard and season to taste with salt and freshly ground black pepper. Cool the sauce, cover with damp greaseproof paper and chill in the refrigerator until cold, and solid enough to spread thickly.
4 Heat the grill without the grid to high.
5 Remove the chicken pieces from the marinade and dry each piece with absorbent paper. Brush the grill grid with olive oil and place the chicken legs, fleshy side down, on the grid. Grill, with the grid 12.5 cm /5 in from the heat, for 10 minutes.
6 Place the breast portions on the grid, fleshy side down, and grill all the portions for a further 5 minutes. Meanwhile, place the flour, beaten egg and breadcrumbs on 3 separate plates.
7 Remove the chicken pieces from the grill and coat the uncooked surface of each piece with flour, shaking off the excess. Spread the mustard sauce over the floured chicken and lay the surface of the sauce in the breadcrumbs. Dip the surface in beaten egg, then lay in the breadcrumbs again. Season the crumbed pieces with salt and freshly ground black pepper.
8 Return the chicken pieces to the grill grid, coated side up. Grill for a further 10 minutes, or until cooked through, brushing with melted butter from time to time.

Chicken with honey fruit marinade

This marinade is perfect for adding flavour when the poultry is bland.

25 minutes plus cooling, 4 hours marinating, then 25 minutes

Serves 4
1.4 kg /3 lb chicken, dressed weight
salt
olive oil

PAN FRYING CHICKEN & TURKEY

Pan frying is a foolproof formula that can transform plain chicken or turkey into an Oriental delight, an American family classic or a glamorous dinner-party dish.

Pan frying is an ideal way to cook chicken and turkey. They can be fried very simply with a crispy coating. Or you can treat them more elaborately and serve with a rich sherry and cream sauce made, in a few minutes, from the pan juices.

Choosing the right bird
For the best results when pan frying poultry choose young and tender birds. Older birds, with tougher flesh, are better cooked in recipes calling for slower, moister cooking.

Poussins weighing 350–500 g /12 oz–1 lb are ideal, they are usually halved for pan frying. One bird will serve one or two people.

Spring chickens are slightly larger than poussins, and better value. They can be halved or quartered for pan frying. A spring chicken amply serves two.

Roasting or frying chickens are most commonly available. These are young birds weighing between 1.1 kg /2½ lb and 1.6 kg / 3½ lb. They are usually jointed into four portions for pan frying, and will serve four people. Birds larger than this are best cooked by other methods.

Turkeys, which traditionally were roasted, are now increasingly used for frying. You can buy ready-cut turkey breasts for escalopes, but far better to my mind is to buy a small turkey, joint it and cut your own succulent escalopes. The bird is so economical that you can make several family dishes for the freezer from the remainder of the meat.

Jointing a chicken
To pan fry chicken successfully the bird needs to be jointed into equal-sized portions so they will cook evenly. Joint it into four or, if it is large, into six. Keep the backbone to add to the pan when the chicken is cooking, as it will add extra flavour.
Breasts and suprêmes: for more elegant chicken dishes use boned and skinned chicken breasts or suprêmes. First remove the legs and wings from the chicken. With a sharp knife, cut through the flesh along the breastbone and work each breast in turn away from the carcass, scraping the rib cage clean. Each breast consists of two pieces – one large piece (the suprême) and one small (the fillet). Carefully remove the skin. Use the breasts whole, or separate the fillets from the suprêmes and use the suprêmes alone.

Turkey escalopes can be made in the same way, cutting several from large breasts.

Fats to use for pan frying
Butter is the best fat to use for pan frying because of the richness and flavour it gives the finished dish. However, it burns at a surprisingly low heat, so to avoid the danger it must be combined with a little oil. Alternatively, use clarified butter.

Olive oil, used on its own, is preferable in dishes with a tomato or garlic-flavoured sauce, while peanut or a light vegetable oil is the most suitable for Chinese stir-frys.

Chicken fat, made by rendering the lumps of fat from inside the birds, adds to the flavour, and can be heated to a high temperature without danger of burning. Use it in pan frying recipes in place of the butter, without adding any oil.

Starting to pan fry
You will need a large, heavy-bottomed frying-pan, so that heat is conducted evenly and there is less chance of burning. When the poultry pieces are in the pan they should not overlap, and should touch the base of the pan as much as possible. On the other hand it should not be too big or the fat will be too thinly spread and will burn. You may well have to use two small pans.

To prepare the poultry, blot the pieces dry with absorbent paper and season them generously with salt and pepper.

Open frying chicken and turkey
Heat the chicken fat, oil or butter and oil over medium-high heat until thoroughly hot. If you are using butter it will foam up and then subside. At this point put in the pieces of poultry, fleshy side down, and cook until lightly browned on the underside.

Use a fish slice or tongs to turn the pieces over – never use a fork because if you pierce the meat the juices will escape and the flesh toughen. Quickly brown the other side, then reduce the heat and cook, turning once, until the meat is tender and the juices run clear when you pierce the thickest part with a skewer. If you are pan frying chicken drumsticks, turn them over as they cook until they are evenly browned all over.

Steam frying chicken
Meat that is to be open fried must not be too thick. It is normally fried well spread out in a shallow, open pan, because high sides or overcrowding will lead to steam being trapped in the pan. This has the effect of reducing the surface crispness of the meat.

If you want to fry thicker pieces of meat like joints of chicken, a period of frying in their own steam is a bonus. Choose a pan for which you have a tight-fitting lid. If you initially fried in two pans, transfer all the meat to a single pan at this point. After searing the meat on all sides, turn down the heat. Add any flavouring ingredients and cover the pan tightly. Sometimes a little liquid is added, but this is not necessary.

Allow the chicken to cook through gently for 15 minutes. Then remove the wings and breasts as these are more delicate and cook more quickly. Keep them warm. Re-cover the pan and cook the legs for a further 5 minutes. Remove the legs from the pan and keep them warm with the breasts. Use the juices in the pan to make a sauce.

Stir-frying chicken and turkey
Stir-frying is a method of pan frying that is easy and quick, and ideal for small strips of chicken or turkey breast. The secret is to have all the ingredients prepared before you start cooking, as you won't have time, once you've started, to chop anything. Use a wok if you have one, but a heavy frying-pan will do very well too.

Chicken Maryland

Preparing chicken suprêmes

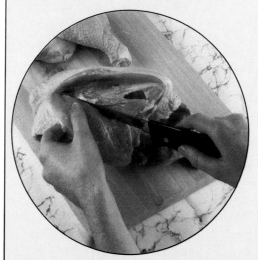 

Remove the legs and wings from the chicken. Cut through the flesh along the breastbone and work each breast away from the carcass, scraping the rib cage clean.

Each breast consists of two pieces – the large suprême and the small fillet. Remove the skin, then separate the fillets from the suprêmes. Trim the suprêmes neatly.

Chicken Maryland

 1 hour

Serves 4
1.4 kg /3 lb chicken, jointed into 4 pieces
30—45 ml /2—3 tbls flour, seasoned with salt,
freshly ground black pepper, 1.5 ml /¼ tsp
cayenne and 2.5 ml /½ tsp dry mustard
2 medium-sized eggs, beaten
60—90 ml /4—6 tbls fine dried breadcrumbs
75 g /3 oz butter
30 ml /2 tbls oil
4 medium-sized bananas
lettuce leaves, to garnish
For the sweetcorn fritters
225 g /8 oz frozen corn kernels, thawed, or
350 g /12 oz canned sweetcorn, drained
100 g /4 oz flour
5 ml /1 tsp salt
1 medium-sized egg
100 ml /3½ fl oz milk combined with 25 ml /
1 fl oz water

1 Remove the skin from the chicken pieces. Dip each piece first into the seasoned flour, then into the beaten egg and finally in the breadcrumbs to coat. (It is necessary to press hard to make the breadcrumbs stick.) Refrigerate the coated chicken pieces.
2 Prepare the sweetcorn fritter batter. Sift the flour and salt into a bowl. Make a well in the centre and add the egg and half the milk mixture. Stir until smooth and thick, then beat in the remaining milk. Stir in the sweetcorn. Set aside.
3 Heat 50 g /2 oz butter and the oil in a large frying-pan over a high heat until sizzling, and fry the chicken for about 2½ minutes on each side. Reduce the heat and gently fry the chicken for a further 10 minutes each side, until done. Keep warm.
4 Halve the bananas lengthways, then cut each half in 2 crossways. Heat the remaining butter in the pan and fry the bananas until lightly browned. Remove from the pan with a slotted spoon and keep warm.
5 Drop 15 ml /1 tbls sweetcorn batter at a time into the hot butter in the pan and fry until firm and golden, turning once.
6 Serve the chicken surrounded by the fried bananas and sweetcorn fritters, garnished with lettuce leaves.

Little chicken rolls, Chinese-style

 1 hour

Serves 4
4 chicken breasts, boned and skinned
salt and freshly ground black pepper
1 large cucumber
6 spring onions
225 g /8 oz mange-tout
30 ml /2 tbls white wine vinegar
20 ml /4 tsp sugar
90 ml /6 tbls soy sauce
90 ml /6 tbls sake or dry sherry
90 ml /6 tbls peanut or light vegetable oil

1 Place each chicken breast between 2 sheets of cling film and beat with a wooden rolling pin to a 10 × 18 cm /4 × 7 in rectangle. Season with salt and pepper.
2 Cut the cucumber into 4 sections lengthways, then cut each section into 3 strips. Place them in a saucepan and cover with cold water. Bring to the boil, drain immediately and refresh the strips under cold running water. Drain them again on absorbent paper.
3 Cut the green leaves from the spring onion tops so that the leaves are the same length as the cucumber strips. (Discard the whites or use them in another recipe.) Place 3 strips of cucumber and 4 green strips of spring onion on each rectangle of chicken. Wrap the chicken round the vegetables to form a roll and tie each roll in 2 places with fine string.
4 Wash and trim the mange-tout and string them if necessary. Bring a saucepan of water to the boil and blanch them for 1 minute, then drain and refresh under cold running water. Pat dry with absorbent paper.
5 Place the mange-tout in a small bowl. Add the white wine vinegar, 10 ml /2 tsp sugar and salt to taste; stir well and marinate until needed.
6 In another small bowl combine the soy sauce, sake or sherry and remaining sugar.
7 Heat the oil in a heavy-based frying-pan. Fry the chicken rolls, turning to brown them evenly, for 5 minutes.
8 When the chicken is golden, drain the excess oil from the pan and pour in the soy mixture. Simmer gently for 6—7 minutes, turning the chicken frequently in the sauce. Remove the rolls from the pan with a slotted spoon. Remove the strings and cut each roll into 3 segments. Keep warm.
9 Bring the remaining sauce to the boil and simmer for 3—5 minutes, or until it is reduced to a thick glaze.
10 Stand the rolls upright on warmed individual, flat serving dishes. Pour a little glaze over each roll and garnish with the marinated mange-tout.

Turkey escalopes chasseur

 30 minutes

Serves 4
4 × 125 g /4 oz fillets of turkey breast
40 g /1½ oz butter
15 ml /1 tbls olive oil
3 shallots or 1 medium-sized onion, chopped
350 g /12 oz tomatoes, blanched and
skinned, seeds and juice removed
½ garlic clove, finely chopped
salt and freshly ground black pepper
10 ml /2 tsp arrowroot
50 ml /2 fl oz juice from roast beef or good
beef consommé
125 ml /4 fl oz dry white vermouth
2.5 ml /½ tsp freshly chopped basil or
tarragon (optional)
350 g /12 oz button mushrooms, sliced
basil leaves and chopped parsley, to garnish

Turkey escalopes chasseur

1 Flatten the turkey breasts slightly with a rolling pin to make escalopes. Pat dry with absorbent paper. Heat 15 g /½ oz butter with the oil in a frying-pan over moderate heat until the butter foams. Put in the escalopes. Fry for 4—5 minutes on each side to seal and brown. Remove from the pan and keep warm.
2 Fry the shallots or onion in the pan for 1 minute, scraping up the sediment from the bottom of the pan. Slice the tomato flesh and stir into the pan with the garlic and seasoning. Cover and simmer for 5 minutes.
3 Mix the arrowroot with a little of the beef juice or consommé. Add the vermouth, arrowroot mixture and remaining beef juice or consommé to the pan and boil rapidly until it is reduced by half.
4 Season the escalopes and return them to the pan. Sprinkle with the herbs, if available. Reduce the heat and simmer very gently for for 4—5 minutes.
5 Meanwhile, melt 25 g /1 oz butter in a separate pan and sauté the mushrooms for 4 minutes over moderate heat, tossing them until they are brown. Season with salt and freshly ground black pepper.
6 Transfer the escalopes and sauce to a heated serving dish. Spoon over the sautéed mushrooms and serve, garnished with basil leaves and chopped parsley.

Stir-fried chicken and vegetables

🍴 2 hours marinating,
then 30 minutes

Serves 4–6
3 boned chicken breasts
30 ml /2 tbls soy sauce
30 ml /2 tbls oyster sauce
30 ml /2 tbls dry white wine
105 ml /7 tbls peanut or light vegetable oil
a dash of Tabasco sauce
30 ml /2 tbls chopped onion
1 green pepper, in 25 mm /1 in squares
1 red pepper, in 25 mm /1 in squares
16 button mushrooms, trimmed
4 spring onions, in 25 mm /1 in segments

1 Slice each chicken breast in 2 lengthways. Cut each section into 25 mm /1 in squares.
2 In a bowl, combine the soy sauce, oyster sauce, dry white wine and 30 ml /2 tbls oil. Season with a dash of Tabasco. Add the chicken pieces and the chopped onion. Toss well to coat, then leave to marinate for at least 2 hours.
3 When you are ready to cook, drain the chicken, reserving the marinade. Pat dry with absorbent paper.

4 In a large frying-pan or wok, heat 45 ml /3 tbls oil over a high heat. Add half the marinated chicken pieces and quickly stir-fry them in the hot oil, tossing continuously with a spatula for 1½ minutes, or until they are brown on all sides.
5 Remove the browned chicken pieces with a slotted spoon and keep warm. Repeat with the remaining chicken.
6 Add the remaining oil to the pan or wok. Add the peppers and toss for 2 minutes or until they begin to lose their hard edges. Add the mushrooms and cook for a further minute.
7 Return the chicken pieces to the pan or wok with the spring onion segments and the reserved marinade. Bring to boiling point.
8 Adjust the seasoning and serve immediately in a heated serving dish.

Turkey escalopes marinated in sherry

🕐🍴 24 hours marinating,
then 30 minutes

Serves 4
4 × 150–175 g /5–6 oz turkey escalopes
30 ml /2 tbls olive oil
15 ml /1 tbls thick cream
freshly chopped coriander leaves, to garnish

For the marinade
65 ml /2½ fl oz dry sherry
50 ml /2 fl oz olive oil
4 ml /¾ tsp fresh lime juice
2.5 ml /½ tsp cumin seeds, crushed
2.5 ml /½ tsp fenugreek seeds, crushed
1.5 ml /¼ tsp coriander seeds, crushed
2.5 ml /½ tsp clear honey
1 garlic clove, crushed
salt and freshly ground black pepper

1 Combine the marinade ingredients in a large bowl and add the escalopes. Leave in a cool place for 24 hours, turning several times.
2 Heat the olive oil in a large frying-pan over a low heat. When it is nearly smoking, remove the escalopes from the marinade with tongs (do not dry) and place in the pan in 1 layer.
3 Raise the heat to seal the escalopes on both sides. Then lower the heat to low and sauté gently for 10–12 minutes each side, until crisp on the outside and tender inside. Remove with a slotted spoon to a warmed serving platter and keep warm.
4 Add the remaining marinade to the pan and bring to the boil. Let it bubble for 1–2 minutes, stirring constantly, then lower the heat and add the cream. Stir well but do not allow the sauce to boil. Pour over the escalopes, garnish with coriander leaves and serve at once.

DEEP FRYING CHICKEN & TURKEY

Chicken and turkey are perfect for deep frying – the fine meat responds well to quick, high temperature cooking, giving you a crispy, crunchy outside and tender, juicy meat inside.

One of the advantages of deep frying chicken and turkey is the variety of ways to present it. Try whole joints in breadcrumbs, boneless portions wrapped around a stuffing, or leftovers made into pancakes – the results will be equally delicious.

A whole chicken is too large and cumbersome to deep fry, but a chicken up to about 1.6 kg /3½ lb in weight is excellent if quartered first. Turkey portions are better boneless; both dark and white meats can be deep fried.

Preparing the meat

Be sure to allow the chicken or turkey to come to room temperature first and dry it thoroughly with absorbent paper. Remove all skin and any bones that stick out awkwardly, for example the wing tips on a chicken breast. If you are serving breast portions only you may prefer to remove all the bone to make a neater portion. This is an ideal way to serve chicken for a dinner party or another elegant occasion.

If you are making escalopes, put the portion between cling film or two sheets of greaseproof paper and beat to an even thickness with a meat bat or rolling pin. Spoon any stuffing onto the meat and roll it up, carefully enclosing the stuffing on all sides. You can secure the roll with a wooden cocktail stick if you wish, though this is not normally necessary.

Frying

I prefer olive oil for frying most poultry dishes; however, Oriental-style dishes such as my Twice-fried chicken are better fried in a lighter oil such as peanut. For economy, though, you may use an ordinary vegetable oil or corn oil for everything.

Half fill the pan with oil; there must be sufficient oil to cover the food completely, but never fill the pan too full, as the hot oil will foam up when the cold food is added and may spill over the sides.

Heat the oil slowly to the required temperature and then keep it steadily at that temperature: if the temperature rises too high the outside of the meat will burn before the centre is cooked through. If you do not have a thermostatically controlled deep-fat frier, use a thermometer. If you don't have a thermometer you can make an approximate check with a crustless 15 mm /½ in cube of day-old white bread. At 160C /320F the cube will turn a crisp, golden brown in 2½ minutes; at 170C /340F it will take 75 seconds, and at 180C /350F it will take 60 seconds.

Add the food to the hot oil in small portions: overcrowding the pan results in a lowering of the temperature which will spoil the finished dish. Each piece of food should have room to roll and turn in the bubbling oil. For large portions like whole chicken legs, and also for large quantities of small pieces, use the frying basket. For small portions and individual pieces a spoon may be

Deep-fried turkey packets

easier. I like to use an open-meshed wire spoon of the sort they sell in Chinese stores, as they do the job of draining much better than a slotted spoon or fish slice. Heat the basket or the spoon in the oil before putting the food in.

Keeping fried food hot
When your first batch of food is cooked, remove it from the oil and drain on absorbent paper. Keep it hot in a low oven on a plate or baking tray lined with absorbent paper. Never cover fried food while it is being kept hot or the coating will go soft.

Check the temperature of the oil again before you go on to fry the next batch. Always serve fried food as quickly as possible after cooking and be sure that it is piping hot.

For extra flavour try marinating the poultry before frying. Prepare the marinade and leave the meat to soak in it at room temperature for at least 2 hours for large portions and as little as 15 minutes for tiny pieces. When you are ready to deep fry, remove the meat from the marinade with a slotted spoon, drain off the excess liquid on absorbent paper and coat lightly with seasoned flour or cornflour, then fry as usual.

Coating
All poultry needs coating before it is deep fried. The coating protects the surface of the meat from the fierce heat of the oil and prevents it from drying out and hardening. The simplest coating is a light dusting of flour or cornflour. This is sufficient to protect pieces of chicken or turkey which are so small that they cook through in a matter of seconds and do not need a heavy coating.

An egg and breadcrumb coating is more common, especially with larger portions of poultry that need a stronger coating. This is necessary to prevent the surface burning in the more prolonged cooking – up to 15 minutes in some cases.

Use seasoned flour first to dry the surface and give it immediate protection. Then dip in egg and roll in fresh white breadcrumbs – the breadcrumbs will fry to a crisp, golden crunch while the poultry inside stays moist and succulent. For extra protection, for example when the food inside is rolled and may tend to unroll during cooking, the coating can be repeated – flour, egg and crumbs, then more egg and crumbs to give a firmer surface.

It helps to set the coating firmly if you chill the coated food for 15 minutes before frying. Do not leave it in the refrigerator for too long or the meat will become too cold and this will affect the cooking time, but a light chilling prevents the coating from falling off into the hot oil and makes the poultry easier to handle as you lower it into the oil and remove it.

Battered chicken or turkey is not very successful. The thick batter coating protects the poultry from the heat too thoroughly, making it difficult to cook the meat through without burning the batter. But if you are fond of batter, try poaching chicken first, then dip the joints in batter and fry until just golden and piping hot right through.

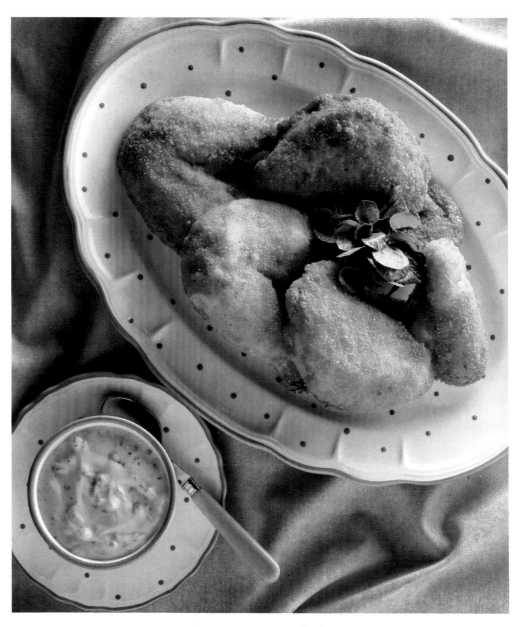

Deep-fried turkey packets

🕐 🍴 soaking apricots, bringing to room temperature, then 1 hour

Serves 4
4 turkey escalopes
50 g /2 oz dried apricots, soaked overnight
50 g /2 oz walnuts, chopped
1 garlic clove, finely chopped
2 egg yolks
salt and freshly ground black pepper
25 g /1 oz flour
1–2 eggs, beaten
fresh white breadcrumbs
oil for deep frying
lemon wedges and parsley, to garnish

1 Bring the turkey to room temperature. Put the apricots with their soaking liquid in a saucepan. Add extra water to cover if necessary. Simmer for 20 minutes, or until tender.
2 Strain the apricots and chop them. In a bowl combine the apricots, walnuts, garlic and egg yolks and season with salt and pepper.

Deep-fried chicken with tarragon mayonnaise

3 Place a turkey escalope between 2 pieces of cling film and flatten it with a meat bat until it is 3 mm /⅛ in thick. Repeat with the remaining escalopes.
4 Cut each escalope in 2 and fill with 15 ml /1 tbls of the stuffing. Fold the edges of the turkey escalope to cover the filling and make a square packet, or shape it into a roll, depending on the shape of the escalope.
5 Put the flour, egg and breadcrumbs in 3 separate shallow dishes and season the flour liberally with salt and freshly ground black pepper. Coat the turkey packets with flour, shaking off the excess. Dip them in egg, drain well, then coat with crumbs; make sure the ends are well coated. Repeat the egg and crumbing, then chill for 15 minutes.
6 Heat the oil in a deep-fat frier to 170C / 340F. Using a wire spoon, deep fry 2 turkey packets for 4 minutes. Remove from the oil, drain on absorbent paper and keep hot. Fry the remaining packets in the same way, drain the packets well on absorbent paper and arrange on a heated serving dish. Garnish with lemon wedges and flat-leaved parsley and serve immediately.

Deep-fried chicken with tarragon mayonnaise

In this recipe a whole chicken is quartered and deep fried, then served with a deliciously piquant mayonnaise.

🔪🔪 2 hours marinating, then 45 minutes

Serves 4

1.6 kg /3½ lb chicken
salt and freshly ground black pepper
cayenne pepper
juice of 1 lemon
30 ml /2 tbls olive oil
25 g /1 oz flour
1–2 eggs, beaten
fresh white breadcrumbs
oil for deep frying
watercress sprigs, to garnish
For the tarragon mayonnaise
150 ml /5 fl oz mayonnaise
22.5 ml /1½ tbls Dijon mustard
15 ml /1 tbls small capers
15 ml /1 tbls finely chopped fresh tarragon
2 gherkins, finely chopped
salt and freshly ground black pepper

1 Joint the chicken into 4 portions, removing the protruding bones from the breast pieces, and all the skin.
2 Put the chicken pieces in a shallow bowl and season generously with salt and freshly ground black pepper and a hint of cayenne pepper. Add the lemon juice and the olive oil, stir the chicken pieces around so they are covered in the marinade and leave to marinate for at least 2 hours.
3 Meanwhile, make the tarragon mayonnaise: combine the mayonnaise and the Dijon mustard with the capers, finely chopped tarragon and gherkins and season with salt and freshly ground black pepper to taste. Stir until well blended, then chill
4 Put the flour, beaten egg and breadcrumbs in 3 separate shallow dishes. Season the flour well with salt and pepper.
5 Remove the chicken pieces from the marinade, drain them on absorbent paper and dip each in the seasoned flour, shaking off the excess. Then dip in the beaten egg, draining well, and then in the breadcrumbs. Pat the breadcrumbs on firmly and chill for 15 minutes.
6 Heat the oil in a deep-fat frier to 170C / 325F.
7 Lower the chicken legs into the hot oil. Fry for 12–15 minutes or until deep golden brown and cooked through. Remove from the oil, drain well on absorbent paper and keep hot while you fry the breasts.
8 Check the temperature of the oil and add the chicken breasts. Fry for 10–12 minutes or until deep golden brown and cooked through. Remove from the oil and drain well on absorbent paper.
9 Arrange the chicken portions on a heated serving dish, garnish with sprigs of watercress and serve, with the tarragon mayonnaise handed round separately.

Deep-fried turkey pancakes

🔪🔪 making and resting batter, then 1¼ hours

Serves 6
2 eggs, beaten
fresh white breadcrumbs
oil for deep frying
For the pancakes
75 g /3 oz flour
2.5 ml /½ tsp salt
2 eggs
30 ml /2 tbls melted butter or oil
150 ml /5 fl oz milk, more if needed
oil for greasing
For the filling
40 g /1½ oz butter
37.5 ml /2½ tbls flour
150 ml /5 fl oz hot milk
1 garlic clove, finely chopped
15 ml /1 tbls tomato purée
15 ml /1 tbls dried oregano
salt and freshly ground black pepper
125 g /4 oz cooked turkey, diced

1 First make the pancakes: sift the flour and salt into a bowl. Beat the eggs and stir them into the flour with the melted butter or oil. Gradually add the milk. Strain the batter through a fine sieve. It should be the consistency of thin cream, so add more milk if necessary. Let the batter stand for 2 hours.
2 Heat a 15 cm /6 in pan and grease it with a wad of absorbent paper dipped in oil. Spoon in about 30 ml /2 tbls batter and tilt the pan so that the batter coats the surface thinly. Cook the pancake over a medium heat for 1 minute or until bubbles start to form underneath.
3 Slip a palette knife round the edges of the pancake and turn it over. Cook 1 minute, then place on a plate under a folded cloth to keep it moist while you fry 11 more pancakes, greasing the pan between each.
4 Make the filling: in a small pan melt the butter and add the flour. Cook, stirring, for 2–3 minutes to make a pale roux. Gradually pour on the hot milk, stirring vigorously with a wire whisk to prevent lumps forming, and simmer until thickened. Add the finely chopped garlic, tomato purée, dried oregano and salt and freshly ground black pepper to

Chicken Kiev

Twice-fried chicken

⏸ 30 minutes, 2 hours marinating, then 35 minutes or longer

Serves 4
1.6 kg /3½ lb chicken
60 ml /4 tbls soy sauce
120 ml /8 tbls sake, or dry sherry diluted with a little water
5 ml /1 tsp sugar
5 ml /1 tsp finely chopped fresh root ginger
oil for deep frying
30–45 ml /2–3 tbls sifted cornflour
To serve
700 g /1½ lb hot cooked rice
100 g /4 oz coarsely grated carrot
5 ml /1 tsp finely grated orange zest
50 g /2 oz butter
salt and freshly ground black pepper

1   Bone and skin the chicken completely and cut the meat into 25 mm /1 in cubes.
2   In a large bowl combine the soy sauce, sake or dry sherry and water, sugar and chopped ginger. Put the chicken pieces in this mixture, turn to coat well and leave to marinate for at least 2 hours.
3   Heat the oil in a deep-fat frier to 160C / 320F. Drain the chicken pieces well, put half of them in a wire basket and deep fry for 1 minute. Remove from the oil and drain on absorbent paper. Repeat with the remaining chicken pieces.
4   Return all the fried chicken pieces to the marinade. Allow to stand in the marinade for at least 15 minutes.
5   Reheat the oil to 180C /350F. Make the orange rice: fold the grated carrot and orange zest into the hot rice. Fold in the butter and season with salt and pepper. Keep hot while you re-fry the chicken pieces.
6   Drain the chicken pieces; dust them lightly with sifted cornflour and re-fry in 2 batches for 30 seconds or until crisp and golden brown. Drain on absorbent paper and serve at once with the orange rice.

Chicken Kiev

Chicken Kiev is the most famous of all deep-fried chicken dishes. Raw chicken breast portions are usually available chilled in good supermarkets, but if you cut the breasts from 2 plump 1.4 kg /3 lb fresh or chilled chickens at home you will have the wing joint attached. Decorate this with a cutlet frill for a truly professional finish that looks very pretty at a party. Warn guests that butter may spurt from inside the chicken when cut.

⏸ making and chilling butter, then 1½ hours

Serves 4
4 chicken breasts, about 200 g /7 oz each, with the wing bone attached
125 g /4 oz butter
30 ml /2 tbls lemon juice
1–2 garlic cloves, finely crushed
15 ml /1 tbl finely chopped parsley or mixed parsley, tarragon and chervil (optional)
salt and freshly ground black pepper
25 g /1 oz well-seasoned flour
2 eggs, beaten
fresh white breadcrumbs for coating
oil for deep frying
lemon slices, to garnish

1   Several hours in advance, cream the butter with half the lemon juice, the garlic and herbs, if using, and season to taste with salt and freshly ground black pepper. Form into a rectangular block roughly 6.5 cm /2½ in long, wrap in greaseproof paper or cling film and chill until very firm. Meanwhile, bring the chicken to room temperature.
2   Cut off the chicken wings below the first joint. Using a sharp knife, remove the rib bones and breast cartilage, but leave the wing bone. Remove the skin and discard.
3   Lay the chicken breasts flat, cut side uppermost. Remove the loose fillet from each one, cut the sinew at the wing end and flatten the breasts with a meat bat to about 15 cm /6 in across. Flatten the fillets as well. Season the breasts and fillets with salt and pepper and rub with the remaining lemon juice.
4   Cut the chilled garlic butter into 4 fingers and place 1 finger on each breast. Place the flattened fillets on the butter fingers, then wrap the breast meat around it, pressing the edges to seal.
5   Spread the flour on a flat plate. Coat the stuffed chicken breasts all over, then shake off any excess flour.
6   Put the beaten eggs in another shallow container and spread the breadcrumbs in a third. Dip the breasts in the beaten egg, drain, then coat them in breadcrumbs. Pat the breadcrumbs on firmly. Repeat the egg and crumbing process, then refrigerate the breasts for 15 minutes to set the coating.
7   Heat the oil in a deep-fat frier to 180C / 350F. Lower the joints carefully, 2 at a time, into the oil and fry for 12-15 minutes or until golden brown. Drain on absorbent paper and keep hot while frying the rest.
8   Slip a cutlet frill on each wing tip, garnish with lemon and serve piping hot.

taste. Cook, stirring occasionally, for 3–4 minutes. Remove the pan from the heat and allow the sauce to cool.
5   Stir the diced cooked turkey into the cooled sauce. Place 15 ml /1 tbls of the turkey mixture at 1 edge of a pancake, roll over once so that the filling is enclosed in the pancake, fold in the sides and roll up completely. Seal with beaten egg and repeat until all the pancakes are filled.
6   Put the remaining beaten egg and the breadcrumbs in 2 separate shallow containers. Coat each pancake roll with beaten egg, allowing the excess to drain off, and roll in breadcrumbs. Chill for 15 minutes.
7   Heat the oil in a deep-fat frier to 180C / 350F.
8   Place 4 pancake rolls in the wire basket and deep fry for 2 minutes or until golden brown. Drain on absorbent paper and keep hot. Repeat with the remaining rolls, arrange on a heated serving dish and serve.

● These crispy stuffed pancakes are just as successful made with leftover chicken instead of turkey.

Preparing Chicken Kiev

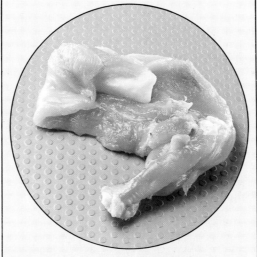

Place the butter on the flattened breast. Lay the fillet over the butter, fold in the end and then the sides to form a neat parcel.

CASSEROLING CHICKEN & TURKEY

Casseroles of chicken or turkey are simple to cook and a pleasure to eat. Economical of both time and money, they are always reliable for dinner parties or family favourites.

Casseroling is ideal for chicken – with its added moistness and extra ingredients, it can put back any flavour that may be lacking in the bird. And the long, slow cooking will always leave the chicken tender as butter at the end.

Turkey is now also an ideal candidate for the casserole pot. The availability of portions has made it much more versatile. You can make tasty family meals or unusual dishes such as Turkey mole (see recipe) if you are entertaining, and the necessity of having a whole army of guests in to eat the giant has now gone.

Casseroling, as a cooking method, has the additional advantage for the cook of needing little or no last-minute attention. All the work for a casserole is done ahead; the most you have to do at the last minute is thicken the sauce and many dishes can go straight to the table without even that much attention being necessary. Braising is a similar method of cooking though it uses slightly less liquid. If chicken is used it is usually left whole as opposed to being jointed. A pot-roast uses much less liquid and, again, a whole bird or portions can be used.

Preparing the poultry

Jointing: joint a chicken into four or eight, depending on its size. You can easily divide a chicken into four (see *page 16*) but for neater serving portions use the following method. Cut the legs from the body, severing the hip joint with the point of your knife; separate the drumstick from the thigh if the chicken is a large one and cut off the end joint if the butcher has left it on.

Cut through the meat on the breast along one side of the breastbone; ease the flesh away from the rib cage with the knife and remove the breast and wing as one single portion. On a large chicken divide this portion in two to give a wing with a small portion of breast attached and a piece of boneless breast. Repeat on the other side, leaving the carcass bare. Always save a chicken carcass and cook it with the giblets for a tasty stock.

Turkey joints can be very large, so for casseroling choose small joints, use boned breast portions or remove the meat from the bone and cut it into cubes.

Preparing the meat: pat the joints dry and, if they have been refrigerated, allow them to come to room temperature before cooking. Season the poultry well with salt and black pepper just before cooking.

Cooking the casserole

Usually the meat is seared in hot fat before cooking in the casserole. This ensures that the juices remain sealed in the meat instead of leaking out into the sauce. It also gives a good golden colour to the poultry. I generally use olive oil and butter for searing,

but you can use chicken fat instead, which adds to the flavour of the finished dish.

Use a flameproof casserole for browning, so that all the flavour is retained for the finished dish. Or you can use a frying-pan and transfer the browned poultry to an ovenproof casserole. Brown or soften the vegetables too, and add stock or wine to moisten. Cover the casserole tightly and simmer very slowly in a moderate oven for the best, most tender results. Check from time to time that the liquid in the casserole is not boiling and adjust the heat if necessary.

One way of ensuring a perfect result is to seal the lid on the casserole with luting paste – this is made from equal quantities of flour and water, mixed to a stiff paste. Put on the lid then spread the paste thickly over the join between the lid and side. Every bit of aromatic moisture is then trapped inside and penetrates the poultry. It means, of course, that you cannot peep halfway through the cooking – but the result is unlikely to be anything but perfect, so don't worry unduly.

Finishing the casserole

To avoid excess fat in the finished dish it is sometimes necessary to skim the sauce at the end, before the final thickening. To skim a greasy sauce you can either use a spoon or, and this is the method I prefer, gently 'wipe' the surface with a thick layer of absorbent paper; the paper soaks up the fat thoroughly and easily.

Thickening: to thicken the sauce, reduction is sometimes enough. Then the concentrated cooking juices make their own sauce without any additions. Or a liaison of egg yolks and

cream may be the answer for a rich, creamy casserole. At a simpler level a starch liaison made with flour, arrowroot or cornflour and a little water can be added to a sauce. This must then be boiled in order to thicken it and remove the taste of flour. Flour can also be added in a *beurre manié*, when it is mashed to a paste with butter and whisked into the sauce piece by piece. This must be cooked until the pieces have melted and been absorbed.

An unusual method of thickening that comes from Mexico is using chocolate. *Mole* sauce, traditionally served with chicken or turkey, is thickened with melted chocolate. Surprisingly enough this does not make the sauce sweet and chocolatey in any recognisable way, but it thickens the sauce admirably and gives it a rich, pinkish-brownish colour.

Turkey mole

 bringing to room temperature, then 1¾ hours

Serves 4–6
900 g /2 lb boned turkey, cut into 25 mm /1 in cubes
salt and freshly ground black pepper
25 g /1 oz butter
30 ml /2 tbls olive oil
50 g /2 oz blanched almonds
50 g /2 oz peanuts
25 g /1 oz fresh green chillies, seeded and coarsely chopped
1 garlic clove, finely chopped
150 ml /5 fl oz chicken stock, home-made or from a cube
1 slice toasted bread
1 green pepper, coarsely chopped
400 g /14 oz canned tomatoes
30 ml /2 tbls sesame seeds
15 ml /1 tbls finely chopped fennel fronds
a pinch of ground cloves
1.5 ml /¼ tsp ground cinnamon
25 g /1 oz dark chocolate, broken up

1 Bring the turkey to room temperature. Heat the oven to 180C /350F /gas 4. Season the turkey with salt and freshly ground black pepper.

2 In a heavy-based flameproof casserole, heat 15 g /½ oz butter and 15 ml /1 tbls olive oil. When the foaming subsides, cook half the meat until golden brown all over. Remove with a slotted spoon. Heat the remaining butter and olive oil and brown the remaining meat. Reserve the cooked meat in the casserole off the heat.

3 Put the almonds and peanuts in a blender and blend until smooth. Add the chopped chillies and garlic and 75 ml /3 fl oz chicken stock. Blend again until smooth.

4 Tear the toast into small pieces and add to the blender with a little more chicken stock. Add the green pepper to the mixture, together with the canned tomatoes, and blend once more.

5 Add half the sesame seeds, the chopped fennel, ground cloves and cinnamon and blend well. Add enough stock to the purée to form a medium thick cream. Season with salt and freshly ground black pepper to taste. Pour into a saucepan and simmer for 5 minutes, stirring occasionally.

6 Add the chocolate to the purée and stir over the heat until completely melted.

7 Add the sauce to the turkey and cook, covered, in the oven for 1 hour or until the meat is tender. Correct the seasoning.

8 Dry fry the remaining sesame seeds and sprinkle over the dish just before serving.

Chicken paprika

 bringing to room temperature, then 1 hour 10 minutes

Serves 4
1.4 kg /3 lb chicken, cut into 4 serving pieces
salt and freshly ground black pepper
125 g /4 oz butter
1 Spanish onion, finely chopped
15 ml /1 tbls paprika
15 ml /1 tbls flour
425 ml /15 fl oz chicken stock, home-made or from a cube
15 ml /1 tbls tomato purée
150 ml /5 fl oz thick cream
juice of ½ lemon
sprigs of watercress, to garnish

1 Bring the chicken to room temperature. Season the pieces with salt and freshly ground black pepper. Melt the butter in a flameproof casserole, add the onion and sauté for 2–3 minutes until transparent.

2 Stir in the paprika and flour. Add the chicken pieces and cook slowly until the pieces are golden all over. Then cover and cook for 10 minutes.

3 Bring the stock to the boil and pour over the chicken pieces. Add the tomato purée and season to taste. Bring to the boil, cover and simmer for 30 minutes.

4 Remove the chicken pieces to a warmed serving dish. Stir the thick cream and lemon juice into the casserole; stir well and simmer for another 5 minutes. Correct the seasoning and pour the sauce over the chicken. Serve the chicken immediately, garnished with a few sprigs of watercress.

Chicken paprika

Moroccan chicken on saffron rice

🕑 2 hours or more soaking,
then 1 hour 10 minutes

Serves 4
1.6 kg /3½ lb chicken
30 ml /2 tbls oil
30 ml /2 tbls lemon juice
2.5 ml /½ tsp ground cardamom
2.5 ml /½ tsp ground turmeric
salt and freshly ground white pepper
sprigs of watercress, to garnish
For the saffron rice
a pinch of saffron strands
60 ml /4 tbls boiling water
225 g /8 oz long-grain rice
5 ml /1 tsp salt
a few drops of yellow food colouring
(optional)

1 Put the saffron strands in a cup, cover with 60 ml /4 tbls of boiling water and leave to soak for at least 2 hours. Bring the chicken to room temperature.
2 In a flameproof casserole large enough to take the chicken, mix together the oil, lemon juice, cardamom, turmeric, salt and pepper. Place over a medium heat, add 125 ml /4 fl oz water and stir well. Bring the liquid to the boil, then put the chicken in, breast side down, and cover the pan tightly. Lower the heat, and simmer for 15 minutes. Turn the bird onto its back and cover the pan again. Simmer for a further 15 minutes. Repeat the turning and cooking process. Cook the bird for a total of 1 hour or until tender.
3 Twenty minutes before the chicken is ready, start the rice. Put the rice and salt in a saucepan and add 500 ml /18 fl oz cold water. Strain in the saffron water, add a few drops of yellow food colouring to strengthen the colour, if wished, and bring to the boil. Stir once, cover the pan tightly and simmer for 15 minutes, or until the rice is tender and has absorbed the liquid. Fluff up with a fork.
4 Transfer the rice to a warm serving dish and place the chicken on top. Stir the pan juices and either spoon them carefully over the chicken or serve separately. Garnish the dish with watercress and serve immediately.

Chicken casserole with mange tout

If mange tout are out of season use fresh green beans instead.

🕑 bringing to room temperature,
then 1 hour

Moroccan chicken on saffron rice

Serves 4
1.6 kg /3½ lb chicken, cut into 4 serving
pieces
25 g /1 oz butter
30 ml /2 tbls olive oil
1 Spanish onion, chopped
425 ml /15 fl oz chicken stock, home-made
or from a cube
salt and freshly ground black pepper
2 celery stalks, chopped
2 leeks, sliced
125 g /4 oz mange tout

1 Bring the chicken to room temperature. Heat the oven to 190C /375F /gas 5.
2 In a large flameproof casserole heat the butter and olive oil. When foaming subsides, sauté the chicken pieces until golden brown. Remove from the pan and add the onion. Cook for 2–3 minutes, stirring occasionally.
3 Pour off any excess fat from the casserole and add the stock. Bring it to the boil and season with salt and freshly ground black pepper. Put the chicken in the pan, cover, and cook for 25 minutes in the oven.
4 Add the chopped celery and the sliced leeks to the stock, and scatter the mange tout over the chicken. Cover again and cook for a further 15 minutes or until the chicken is tender and the mange tout are *al dente*. Correct the seasoning and serve.

Turkey in coconut gravy

⏱ bringing to room temperature,
then 1 hour 40 minutes

Serves 6
6 turkey drumsticks
salt and freshly ground black pepper
60 ml /4 tbls sesame oil
2 large onions, thinly sliced
2 garlic cloves, crushed
2 red chillies, seeded and chopped or sliced
20 ml /4 tsp coriander seeds, crushed
10 ml /2 tsp cumin seeds, crushed
grated zest of 1 lemon
5 ml /1 tsp ground ginger
50 g /2 oz coconut cream
50–275 ml /2–10 fl oz turkey or chicken
stock
15 ml /1 tbls finely chopped fennel fronds
boiled or saffron rice. (page 30), to serve

1   Bring the turkey to room temperature.
Rub the meat with salt and pepper. Heat the
oil in a large saucepan over a moderate heat,
add the onions and sauté until soft.
2   Add the turkey, garlic, chillies, coriander
and cumin seeds, lemon zest and ginger.
Cook for 4–5 minutes, stirring. Make sure
that the meat is coated with the spices.
3   Add 600 ml /1 pt boiling water to the
coconut cream and stir, then add to the
saucepan with 50 ml /2 fl oz stock. Bring to
the boil, then reduce the heat and simmer,
covered, for 40–50 minutes.
4   Uncover the pan and simmer for a
further 20–30 minutes, adding more stock if
needed. Transfer to a warmed serving dish,
garnish with fennel and serve with rice.

Pot-roast chicken with tarragon

⏱⏱ bringing to room temperature,
then 2–2¼ hours

Serves 4
1.6 kg /3½ lb chicken, giblets reserved
salt and freshly ground black pepper
4–6 sprigs of fresh tarragon
salt and freshly ground black pepper
30 ml /2 tbls olive oil
25 g /1 oz butter
60–90 ml /4–6 tbls chicken stock, home-
made or from a cube
150 ml /5 fl oz thick cream
1 egg yolk

1   Bring the chicken to room temperature.
Wipe the chicken inside and out with a
damp cloth. Wash and dry the giblets.
2   Season inside and out and put half the
tarragon sprigs in the cavity of the bird.
Truss the chicken (*page 10*).
3   Strip the leaves from the remaining
tarragon sprigs and reserve both separately.
4   Select a heavy flameproof casserole just
large enough to hold the chicken. Heat the

Turkey in coconut gravy

olive oil and butter and sauté the chicken
until golden all over. Pack the giblets and
tarragon stalks around the chicken.
6   Cover the casserole tightly and simmer
over a low heat for 1¼–1½ hours, or until the
chicken is tender and the juices run clear.
7   Remove the chicken from the casserole,
allowing the juices from the cavity to drain
back into the casserole, and keep it hot.
Remove the trussing strings and discard the
giblets and tarragon stalks.
8   Stir the chicken stock into the juices
remaining in the casserole. Add the reserved
tarragon leaves, bring to the boil and boil
for 2–3 minutes until the liquid is reduced
by half, stirring and scraping the bottom
and sides of the casserole clean.
9   In a small bowl, beat the cream with the
egg yolk until smoothly blended. Blend in a
little of the hot sauce.
10   Turn the heat under the casserole as
low as possible. Pour in the cream mixture,
stirring vigorously to blend it smoothly with
the cooking juices, and continue to stir over
a low heat until the sauce has thickened. Do
not allow it to come to the boil, or the egg
yolk will curdle. Correct the seasoning.
11   To serve, put the chicken on a heated
serving dish and spoon over the sauce.

Chicken with black cherries

⏱ bringing to room temperature,
then 2¼ hours

Serves 4
1.4 kg /3 lb chicken
salt and freshly ground black pepper
10 ml /2 tsp dried rosemary
30 ml /2 tbls olive oil
25 g /1 oz butter
300 ml /10 fl oz chicken stock, home-made
or from a cube
400 g /14 oz canned black cherries, stoned
10 ml /2 tsp cornflour
10 ml /2 tsp lemon juice

1   Bring the chicken to room temperature
and heat the oven to 170C /325F /gas 3.
2   Wipe the chicken inside and out. Rub
the cavity with salt, pepper and the dried
rosemary. Truss the chicken (*page 10*).
3   Heat the oil and butter in a flameproof
casserole and sauté the chicken for 10
minutes or until it is golden brown all over.
4   Bring the chicken stock to the boil in a
saucepan and pour it into the casserole.
Cover and cook the chicken in the oven for 1¼
hours or until the juices run clear.
5   Transfer the chicken to a serving dish,
remove the trussing string and keep warm.
6   Skim off any excess fat from the sauce
and strain in the cherry juice. Bring the
sauce to the boil. In a small bowl blend the
cornflour with 15 ml /1 tbls cold water. Add
a little of the hot sauce, then blend into the
sauce and simmer, stirring, until thickened.
7   Add the cherries and cook for 2 minutes.
Add the lemon juice and correct seasoning.
8   Pour a little of the sauce over the
chicken and serve immediately with the rest
of the sauce in a heated sauce-boat.

Coq au vin rouge

🔪🔪 bringing to room temperature,
then 1 hour 40 minutes

Serves 4
*1.4 kg /3 lb chicken, cut into quarters, with
    backbone and giblets reserved*
1 medium-sized onion, sliced
1 carrot, sliced
2 garlic cloves, cut in half
sprig of thyme
bay leaf
425 ml /15 fl oz red wine
15 ml /1 tbls tomato purée
salt and freshly ground black pepper
40 g /1½ oz butter
30 ml /2 tbls oil
16 button onions, peeled
*100 g /4 oz thick slices unsmoked streaky
    bacon, rind removed and cut into strips*
45–60 ml /3–4 tbls brandy
175 g /6 oz button mushroom caps
For the beurre manié
15 g /½ oz butter, softened
15 g /½ oz flour
For the garnish
fried bread croûtons
sprigs of fresh parsley

1 Bring the chicken to room temperature.
Put the washed giblets, backbone and trimmings from the chicken into a saucepan.
Add the onion, carrot, garlic, thyme, bay
leaf, wine, tomato purée, seasoning and 150
ml /5 fl oz water. Bring to the boil, then
simmer, uncovered, for 20–30 minutes, until
the liquid has reduced to about half. Strain
this stock into a jug.
2 Heat 15 g /½ oz butter with 15 ml /1 tbls
oil in a heavy-based pan and fry the button
onions over moderate heat for about 10
minutes, rolling them around the pan to
brown evenly. Add 150 ml /5 fl oz water,
cover tightly and simmer gently for 20–30
minutes, until tender.
3 Heat the remaining butter and oil in a
flameproof casserole and fry the strips of
bacon for a few minutes.
4 Wipe the chicken portions, pat dry with
absorbent paper; season lightly. Place them
skin side down in the casserole with the
bacon and fry for 5–6 minutes until golden.
Turn the portions, cover the casserole and
fry gently for another 5 minutes.
5 Heat a ladle, pour the brandy into it and
set alight with a taper. Pour it flaming over
the chicken and shake the pan gently.

Coq au vin rouge

6 When the flames die down, pour the
strained giblet stock into the pan containing
the chicken, cover tightly and simmer very
gently for 40 minutes. Add the mushrooms
for the last 5 minutes of cooking.
7 Lift out the chicken portions and
arrange, skin side up, on a heated serving
dish. Remove the mushrooms and bacon
strips and scatter evenly over the chicken.
8 Strain any remaining liquid from the
onions into the casserole, arrange the onions
round the chicken on the dish and keep hot.
9 Measure the liquid remaining in the
casserole; there should be no less than 275
ml /10 fl oz. If there is more, reduce it by
boiling rapidly, uncovered. Season to taste.
10 Blend the butter and flour to form the
beurre manié paste. Bring the liquid in the
casserole to simmering point. Using a wire
whisk, whisk in the *beurre manié*, little by
little, until the sauce is lightly thickened.
11 Spoon the sauce over the chicken and
garnish with croûtons and parsley.

Chicken with Indian spices

🔪 bringing to room temperature,
then 1¼ hours

Serves 4
*2 × 900 g /2 lb roasting chickens, dressed
    weight*
salt and freshly ground black pepper
50 g /2 oz softened butter
45 ml /3 tbls ground coriander
5 ml /1 tsp ground ginger
2 Spanish onions, grated
150 ml /5 fl oz yoghurt
300 ml /10 fl oz thick cream
5 ml /1 tsp ground turmeric
4 cardamom pods, crushed
2 sprigs of watercress, to garnish

1 Bring the chickens to room temperature.
Heat the oven to 180C /350F /gas 4.
2 Wipe the chickens, inside and out, with a
damp cloth or absorbent paper, then pat
them dry. Season generously with salt and
freshly ground black pepper. Prick the skin
all over with a fork.
3 In a small bowl, combine the softened
butter, ground coriander and ground ginger
to a smooth paste. Spread the paste equally
over both chickens. Place them side by side
in a roasting tin.
4 In a bowl, blend the grated onion,
yoghurt, thick cream, ground turmeric and
crushed cardamom pods. Season with a little
salt and freshly ground black pepper to
taste. Pour the mixture over the chickens
and cook, covered, in the oven for 50–60
minutes or until the chickens are tender,
basting frequently. Test that the chickens
are cooked by inserting a skewer in the
thickest part of the inside leg: the juices
should run clear.
5 Cut the chickens in half, cutting beside
the backbone and along the breastbone. Lay
the 4 halves side by side on a large heated
serving platter and coat with the sauce.
Garnish with 2 sprigs of watercress and
serve immediately.

Turkey casseroled in ale

bringing to room temperature, then about 3 hours

Serves 6–8
2.3 kg /5 lb turkey
salt and freshly ground black pepper
150 g /5 oz butter
15 ml /1 tbls flour
30 ml /2 tbls tomato purée
750 ml /27 fl oz pale ale
sprig of thyme or pinch of dried thyme
2 bay leaves
sprigs of thyme, to garnish

1 Bring the turkey to room temperature. Rinse the turkey inside and out and pat dry with absorbent paper. Rub the bird with salt and freshly ground black pepper.
2 Melt 75 g /3 oz of the butter in a large casserole over medium heat. Slowly brown the turkey on all sides, turning it in the

butter. Remove it from pan and keep warm.
3 Add the flour to the butter in the casserole and mix to form a smooth paste, stir in the tomato purée and about 15 ml /1 tbls water. Add the pale ale in a thin stream, stirring constantly.
4 Add the thyme and bay leaves to the sauce and return the turkey to the casserole. Add the rest of the butter, cover and cook over a very low heat for about 2½ hours, or until the turkey is tender and cooked through. When a skewer is inserted into the thickest part of the leg the juices should run clear with with no trace of pink.
5 Transfer the turkey to a warmed serving dish and pour over some of the sauce. Garnish with thyme and serve with the remaining sauce handed round separately.

Turkey in honey and ginger

bringing to room temperature, then 1¼ hours

Turkey in honey and ginger

Serves 4
4 boneless turkey breast portions, skinned
50 g /2 oz butter
125 ml /4 fl oz clear honey
30 ml /2 tbls Dijon mustard
5 ml /1 tsp ground ginger
salt and freshly ground black pepper
watercress, to garnish
boiled rice, to serve

1 Bring the turkey to room temperature. Heat the oven to 180C /350F /gas 4. Melt the butter in a flameproof casserole large enough to take the turkey in a single layer.
2 Stir the honey, mustard and ginger into the butter. Remove from the heat and season to taste with salt and pepper.
3 Arrange the turkey pieces in the mixture in the casserole and turn to coat them well.
4 Cover and cook for 30 minutes, basting occasionally. Turn the turkey portions and continue to cook for 30 minutes, basting.
5 When tender, garnish with watercress and serve with freshly boiled rice.

CHICKEN & TURKEY FOR THE FAMILY

Tender oven-fried chicken drumsticks in a crunchy, cheesy coating, or turkey portions casseroled in a piquant barbecue sauce – chicken and turkey provide easy-to-make dishes which are also easy on the purse.

Chilli chicken

marinating, bringing to room temperature, then 25–40 minutes

Serves 4
1.4 kg /3 lb chicken, divided into 4 serving portions
300 ml /10 fl oz soured cream
10 ml /2 tsp powdered chilli
15 ml /1 tbls paprika
baked potatoes, to serve

1 With a sharp knife, make several deep slits in the flesh of each piece of chicken. Place in a shallow dish.
2 Mix together the remaining ingredients and pour them over the chicken. Turn the pieces so they are well coated and leave to marinate overnight in the refrigerator.
3 Remove the chicken from the refrigerator at least 2 hours before cooking to allow it to come to room temperature. If using a barbecue prepare it in the normal way, or heat the oven to 180C /350F /gas 4.
4 Remove the chicken from the marinade and scrape off any excess, reserving the marinade. Cook the chicken for about 20 minutes on the barbecue or for 30–35 minutes in the oven; the chicken is cooked when the juices run clear when the flesh is pierced with a sharp skewer.
5 Bring the reserved marinade to the boil and simmer gently for 5 minutes, then serve with the chicken and baked potatoes.

Turkey roll with paprika sauce

bringing to room temperature, then 1¼ hours

Serves 4–6
1 rolled turkey breast, about 1 kg /2 lb 3 oz
120 ml /8 tbls olive oil
2 large onions, finely chopped
10 ml /2 tsp sugar
30 ml /2 tbls paprika
10 ml /2 tsp ground allspice
60 ml /4 tbls dry white wine
60–120 ml /4–8 tbls hot chicken stock, home-made or from a cube
300 ml /10 fl oz yoghurt
salt and freshly ground black pepper

1 Bring the rolled turkey breast to room temperature.
2 Heat 60 ml /4 tbls oil in a large saucepan over a low heat and add the onions and sugar. Cook for 10 minutes, or until the onions are soft and golden.
3 Add the paprika and allspice and cook for a further 2–3 minutes. Pour in the wine

and cook until it stops bubbling, about 2 minutes. Push the onions to the sides of the pan, add the remaining oil, then the turkey roll.
4 Turn it to brown on all sides, then add 60 ml /4 tbls stock. Stir well, bring to just under boiling point and then simmer gently, covered, for 30–40 minutes, until the turkey is tender and cooked through. Turn the roll frequently, adding more stock if necessary.
5 Lift the roll onto a warmed serving platter, slice thinly and keep warm. Add the yoghurt to the saucepan over a very low heat, stirring thoroughly to remove any lumps. Heat through gently but do not allow to boil. Check the seasoning, pour the sauce over the turkey and serve at once.

Italian oven-fried chicken drumsticks

30 minutes, 1 hour chilling, then 45 minutes

Serves 4
8 chicken drumsticks
1 egg
30 ml /2 tbls milk
75 g /3 oz fresh white breadcrumbs
40 g /1½ oz freshly grated Parmesan cheese
salt and freshly ground black pepper
flour for coating
60 ml /4 tbls butter
60 ml /4 tbls olive oil
For the garnish
lemon wedges
sprigs of parsley

1 Wipe each chicken drumstick dry with absorbent paper.
2 Beat the egg lightly with the milk in a shallow dish. Combine the breadcrumbs and grated Parmesan cheese in another shallow dish, adding a generous sprinkling of salt and black pepper. Put the flour in a third dish and season with salt and pepper.
3 Dust the drumsticks very lightly with the seasoned flour. Dip each floured piece into the beaten egg and then roll in the Parmesan and breadcrumb mixture, patting the coating on firmly. Chill for about 1 hour to allow the coating to set.
4 Heat the oven to 200C /400F /gas 6. Melt the butter and oil in a roasting tin on top of the stove. When it is sizzling, arrange the drumsticks in the tin, side by side, and spoon the fat over them. Transfer the tin to the oven and bake, turning the pieces once or twice, for 30–35 minutes, or until the drumsticks are tender and a crusty golden brown.
5 Serve very hot on a large serving dish, garnished with the lemon wedges and sprigs of parsley.

Pineapple chicken

1¾ hours

Serves 4–6
1.6 kg /3½ lb chicken, jointed
1 medium-sized onion, sliced
salt and freshly ground black pepper
45 ml /3 tbls oil
100 g /4 oz Chinese or white cabbage, shredded
2 celery stalks, diced
100 g /4 oz Brazil or cashew nuts, chopped
30 ml /2 tbls soy sauce
5 ml /1 tsp sugar
250 g /9 oz fresh or drained canned, unsweetened pineapple chunks
boiled rice or Chinese egg noodles, to serve

1 Put the chicken pieces into a saucepan with 600 ml /1 pt water, the onion and salt and pepper to taste. Bring to the boil, cover and simmer for 1 hour or until the chicken is

tender. Remove the chicken; strain and reserve 300 ml /10 fl oz of the cooking liquid.

2 When it is cool enough to handle, skin and bone the chicken and cut the meat into bite-sized pieces.

3 Heat the oil in a large saucepan or wok. Add the cabbage, celery and chicken. Sauté, stirring constantly, for 5 minutes. Then stir in the nuts, soy sauce, sugar and the reserved chicken cooking liquid. Cook, stirring, until the liquid boils.

4 Add the pineapple, bring back to the boil and cook for 3 minutes. Serve with boiled rice or Chinese egg noodles.

Chicken liver sauce with tagliatelle

Chicken livers are rich in flavour and therefore often used in small quantities. Add one or two to a stuffing for roast chicken, or collect them in the freezer until you have several.

🔪 45 minutes

Serves 4
65 g /2½ oz butter
50 g /2 oz onion, finely chopped
50 g /2 oz smoked streaky bacon, rind removed and finely chopped
250 g /8 oz chicken livers
50 g /2 oz mushrooms, finely chopped
15 ml /1 tbls flour
30 ml /2 tbls medium sherry
225 ml /8 fl oz chicken stock, home-made or from a cube
15 ml /1 tbls tomato purée
salt
freshly ground black pepper
250 g /8 oz green tagliatelle

1 Melt 40 g /1½ oz of the butter in a saucepan, add the onion and bacon and cook them over a low heat for 6–8 minutes, stirring occasionally.

2 Meanwhile, wash the chicken livers, drain well and remove any large veins or discoloured areas. Cut into chunks.

3 Increase the heat under the pan, add the chicken livers and mushrooms and cook, stirring constantly, for 1–2 minutes. Stir in the flour and cook for another minute.

4 Add the sherry and allow to bubble until it is almost evaporated. Then stir in the stock, tomato purée and salt and freshly ground black pepper to taste. Bring to the boil, then simmer gently for 15–20 minutes.

5 About 10 minutes before the sauce is ready, drop the tagliatelle into a large pan of rapidly boiling salted water and cook, uncovered, until *al dente*, tender but still firm to the bite.

6 Drain the tagliatelle thoroughly, return to the pan with the remaining butter and toss lightly.

7 Serve the tagliatelle on very hot plates with the sauce spooned over it.

Rice with turkey and mushrooms

🔪 1¾ hours

Serves 4
½ small turkey breast, boned
425 ml /15 fl oz chicken stock, home-made or from a cube
225 ml /8 fl oz dry white wine
bouquet garni
salt and freshly ground black pepper
50 g /2 oz butter
1 medium-sized onion, sliced
100 g /4 oz mushrooms, sliced
50 g /2 oz cooked ham, cut into thin strips
175 g /6 oz medium-grain rice
100 g /4 oz peas, defrosted if frozen
a pinch of dried marjoram
a pinch of dried thyme
a pinch of dried basil
30 ml /2 tbls freshly grated Parmesan cheese

1 Place the turkey breast in a small saucepan and cover with 150 ml /5 fl oz chicken stock and 150 ml /5 fl oz dry white wine. Add the bouquet garni and salt and pepper to taste, bring to the boil, reduce the heat and simmer gently, covered, for 35 minutes or until tender, turning once. Skin and dice the turkey as soon as it is cool enough to handle.

2 In a flameproof casserole, melt the butter. Add the sliced onion and sauté for 10 minutes or until lightly golden. Add the mushrooms to the pan, together with the strips of ham and the diced turkey. Sauté gently for 2–3 minutes, stirring constantly.

3 Add the remaining wine. Bring to the boil and sprinkle in the rice and peas (if you are using fresh ones) through your fingers. Simmer gently until the wine has been absorbed.

4 Add the remaining chicken stock and the herbs and season with salt and freshly ground black pepper to taste. Simmer gently for 20 minutes or until the rice is tender but not mushy, stirring occasionally to prevent sticking. If using frozen peas, add them when the rise is almost tender.

5 Just before serving, toss in the grated Parmesan cheese. Transfer the rice to a heated serving bowl and serve at once.

● A boned chicken breast can be substituted for the half turkey breast in this recipe.

Chilli chicken

Chicken cacciatore

2   Season the flour liberally with salt and freshly ground black pepper and coat the chicken on both sides with the seasoned flour. In a deep plate, beat the eggs lightly with 30 ml /2 tbls of the finely grated Parmesan or Cheddar cheese.
3   Heat the oil and butter in a shallow frying-pan. When it is hot dip the chicken breasts, one at a time, in the beaten eggs, coating each side, and immediately lower into the hot fat.
4   Fry over moderate heat, turning once, 5–6 minutes each side, until golden and just cooked through. Drain on absorbent paper. Meanwhile, heat the grill to moderate.
5   Transfer the cooked chicken breasts to the grill rack, lay 3–4 drained asparagus spears on each and sprinkle with the remaining grated cheese. Grill gently for 2–3 minutes, until the cheese melts.
6   Arrange the chicken breasts on a heated serving dish. Garnish with lemon slices and parsley and serve at once.

Devilled chicken Delmonico

🔪 bringing to room temperature, then 1 hour

Serves 4
1.1 kg /2½ lb chicken
oil for greasing
50 g /2 oz fresh white breadcrumbs
bouquet of watercress, to garnish
For the devil mixture
65 g /2½ oz butter
15 ml /1 tbls curry powder
10 ml /2 tsp caster sugar
5 ml /1 tsp dry mustard
2.5 ml /½ tsp salt
2.5 ml /½ tsp paprika
5 ml /1 tsp Worcestershire sauce

1   Bring the chicken to room temperature, then joint it into 4 serving portions, removing the breasts from the bone. Remove the skin from all the pieces. Wipe dry with absorbent paper.
2   Heat the grill without the grid to high and the oven to 180C /350F /gas 4.
3   Prepare the devil mixture. In a small saucepan, melt the butter over a low heat. Stir in the remaining ingredients and mix until well blended.
4   Brush the grill grid with oil. Lay the chicken portions on the grid and brush both sides with a little of the devil mixture. Grill for 5 minutes on each side, 7.5 cm /3 in from the heat.
5   Transfer the chicken portions to a gratin dish large enough to take them in 1 layer.

Pour the juices from the grill pan into the remaining devil mixture. Add the breadcrumbs and stir to blend.
6   Spoon the mixture evenly over the chicken portions and bake for 30 minutes, or until cooked through and crisp.
7   Place the chicken portions on a heated serving dish, garnish with a bouquet of watercress and serve at once.

Chicken breasts Leoni

🔪 35 minutes

Serves 4
4 chicken breasts, boned and skinned
½ lemon
25 g /1 oz flour
salt and freshly ground black pepper
2 small eggs
50 g /2 oz Parmesan cheese or dry mature Cheddar, finely grated
30 ml /2 tbls oil
25 g /1 oz butter
12–16 cooked asparagus spears, frozen or canned
lemon slices and parsley, to garnish

1   Lay the chicken breasts between sheets of damp greaseproof paper and flatten them gently with a rolling pin until they are about 10 mm /½ in thick. Rub the chicken lightly with the cut side of the lemon, squeezing the lemon gently to extract a little of the juice.

Chicken breasts Leoni

Chicken cacciatore

🍴 1¼ hours

Serves 4

1.1–1.4 kg /2½–3 lb frying chicken, cut into
  8 pieces
60 ml /4 tbls olive oil
25 g /1 oz butter
2 medium-sized onions, cut into 5 mm /¼ in
  slices
2 garlic cloves, finely chopped
400 g /14 oz canned peeled plum tomatoes
150 ml /5 fl oz hot chicken stock, home-
  made or from a cube
30 ml /2 tbls tomato purée
2.5 ml /½ tsp celery seed
5 ml /1 tsp crushed dried oregano or basil
2 bay leaves
salt
freshly ground black pepper
60–90 ml /4–6 tbls dry white wine
275 g /10 oz spaghetti, to serve

1   Heat the oil in a large, thick-bottomed frying-pan. When it is hot, add the chicken pieces and sauté slowly, turning, until they are golden brown on all sides. With a slotted spoon remove the pieces to a flameproof casserole.
2   Add the butter to the pan and cook the onions and garlic in the oil and butter, stirring occasionally, until the onion is transparent, but not brown. Add the sautéed vegetables to the chicken in the casserole. Add the tomatoes, chicken stock, tomato purée, herbs and seasonings to the casserole, cover and simmer for 45 minutes.
3   Add the wine and cook gently, uncovered, turning occasionally, for a further 15 minutes, or until tender.
4   Meanwhile, add the spaghetti to a large saucepan of salted, boiling water and cook until *al dente*, tender but still firm – about 8 minutes. Drain thoroughly and arrange on a warmed serving platter.
5   Discard the bay leaves from the chicken sauce and skim off any excess fat. Spoon over the spaghetti and serve.

Turkey with barbecue sauce

🍴 1¼–1½ hours

Serves 4

4 small turkey wings or thighs
salt and freshly ground black pepper
30 ml /2 tbls olive oil
25 g /1 oz butter
1 Spanish onion, finely chopped
2 garlic cloves, finely chopped
125 ml /4 fl oz tomato ketchup
45 ml /3 tbls wine vinegar
45 ml /3 tbls brown sugar
15–30 ml /1–2 tbls Worcestershire sauce
15 ml /1 tbls Dijon mustard
1 green pepper, diced
2 celery stalks, diced
275 ml /10 fl oz boiling water

1   Heat the oven to 180C /350F /gas 4. Season the turkey with salt and pepper.
2   Heat the oil and butter in a large, heavy frying-pan and brown the turkey portions all over. Using a slotted spoon, transfer them to a casserole with a tight-fitting lid.
3   Add the onion and garlic to the fat remaining in the pan and cook gently, stirring, until soft. Add the remaining ingredients and bring to the boil. Season with salt and pepper.
4   Pour the sauce over the turkey. Cover and cook in the oven for 1–1¼ hours, or until the turkey is tender.

● If you wish to substitute chicken portions, cook them for 45–60 minutes.

Spicy stir-fried chicken

🍴 30 minutes

Serves 4

3 boned chicken breasts, cut in strips
45 ml /3 tbls oil
1 onion, thinly sliced
1 green pepper, sliced
250 g /8 oz button mushrooms, sliced
6 celery stalks, sliced
2.5 ml /½ tsp Worcestershire sauce
45 ml /3 tbls dry sherry
salt and freshly ground black pepper
boiled white rice, to serve

1   Heat half the oil in a wok or heavy-based frying-pan over a medium-high heat, add the chicken and cook, stirring, for 2–3 minutes. Remove the chicken with a slotted spoon.
2   Add the remaining oil to the pan and, when hot, add the sliced vegetables. Cook, stirring, for 2–3 minutes.
3   Return the chicken to the pan and add 200 ml /7 fl oz water, the Worcestershire sauce and sherry. Cook, stirring, for 2 minutes. Season with salt and pepper and serve at once, on a bed of rice.

LEFTOVER CHICKEN & TURKEY

So many excellent dishes can be created from small amounts of cold chicken and turkey that it is well worth cooking a larger bird than you need initially, just to ensure some delicious leftovers!

Leftover chicken and turkey need not be dull – the following five recipes suggest very different ways of using varying amounts of cooked poultry, ranging in weight from 50–700 g /2 oz–1½ lb. The quantities are not critical, however, so don't worry if you have a little more or less than the recipe states. And remember that you can happily substitute one for the other in these recipes.

Other uses for cooked poultry include salads, pancake and omelette fillings, croquettes, pilaffs, casseroles and fillings for sandwiches and pasta.

Cool leftover chicken and turkey quickly, and refrigerate them as soon as they are cold. If you can't use them within 3 days, allow the chicken or turkey to cool, then freeze for up to 3 months.

Chicken à la King

This dish, although fit for a king, was not named for a reigning monarch. It was created in the Brighton Beach Hotel (near Coney Island in Brooklyn, New York) by a chef named George Greenwald for his boss, E. Clarke King II. Serve with hot buttered toast, buttered noodles or rice.

🔪 35 minutes

Serves 4
450 g /1 lb cooked chicken, diced
75 g /3 oz butter
150 g /5 oz mushrooms, thinly sliced
30 ml /2 tbls flour
salt
freshly ground white pepper
250 ml /9 fl oz thin cream
3 medium-sized egg yolks
5 ml /1 tsp very finely chopped onion
30 ml /2 tbls lemon juice
30 ml /2 tbls dry sherry
50 g /2 oz pimento, chopped

1   Melt 25 g /1 oz butter in a large saucepan over medium-low heat. Sauté the mushrooms for 5 minutes, stirring. Stir in the flour and season well with salt and pepper.
2   Stir in the cream and cook, uncovered, over medium heat until the mixture thickens, stirring frequently. Add the chicken to the sauce and allow it to heat through thoroughly, stirring occasionally. Don't allow the mixture to boil.
3   Meanwhile, beat the remaining butter with a wooden spoon, then beat in the egg yolks. Add the onion, lemon juice and sherry. Add this slowly to the chicken mixture, stirring all the time. Continue to cook a few more moments, add the pimento, heat through without boiling and adjust the seasoning. Serve immediately.

Chicken and vegetable soup

Make stock from the carcass, then cook it with leftover shreds of chicken and fresh vegetables for this soup.

🔪 40 minutes

Serves 4
50 g /2 oz cooked chicken, shredded
1 L /1¾ pt chicken stock, preferably home-made
1 large carrot, coarsely grated
1 medium-sized turnip or swede, coarsely grated
2 leeks, finely shredded
100 g /4 oz firm cabbage, finely shredded
30 ml /2 tbls chopped fresh parsley
salt and freshly ground black pepper
grated Cheddar cheese, to serve
crusty bread, to serve

1   Bring the stock to the boil and add the carrot, turnip or swede, leeks and cabbage. Simmer for 15 minutes.
2   Add the chicken and parsley and simmer for 5 minutes or until the vegetables are cooked.
3   Season to taste with salt and freshly ground black pepper and serve in deep soup bowls, topped with grated cheese and accompanied by warm, crusty bread.

Chicken à la King

Curried turkey

 35 minutes

Serves 4
700 g /1½ lb cooked turkey, coarsely
   chopped
50 g /2 oz butter
1 Spanish onion, finely chopped
2 celery stalks, thinly sliced
1 small cooking apple, peeled and diced
1 garlic clove, finely chopped
15 ml /1 tbls flour
15–30 ml /1–2 tbls curry powder
425 ml /15 fl oz chicken stock, home-made
   or from a cube
salt and freshly ground black pepper
30 ml /2 tbls finely chopped fresh parsley
boiled rice, to serve

1   Melt the butter in a large saucepan and
sauté the onion and celery until the onion is
transparent. Add the apple, garlic, flour and
curry powder to taste. Continue to cook,
stirring, for a few minutes.
2   Gradually stir in the stock and bring to
the boil, then reduce the heat and simmer
for 5 minutes. Add salt and pepper to taste.
3   Add the turkey and parsley. Cover and
simmer gently for 10 minutes, then serve the
curried turkey in a ring of boiled rice.

Turkey plate pie

 1½ hours including cooling

Serves 4–5
225 g /8 oz cooked turkey, coarsely chopped
40 g /1½ oz butter
30 g /1¼ oz flour
300 ml /10 fl oz hot chicken or turkey stock,
   home-made or from a cube
150 ml /5 fl oz milk, plus extra for glazing
50 g /2 oz cooked ham or bacon, chopped
45 ml /3 tbls freshly chopped parsley
salt and freshly ground black pepper
575 g /21 oz shortcrust pastry, defrosted if
   frozen

1   Melt the butter in a saucepan, add the
flour, stir and cook gently for a minute. Add
the hot stock and stir briskly until blended,
then add the milk and stir until boiling.
Simmer gently for 3 minutes.
2   Stir in the turkey, ham or bacon and
parsley, season well and set aside to cool.
3   Heat the oven to 200C /400F /gas 6 and
preheat a baking sheet. Roll out half the
pastry and use it to line a greased 20–23 cm
/8–9 in diameter pie plate. Spread the cold
filling over the pastry up to within 20 mm /¾
in of the rim.
4   Roll out the remaining pastry and cover
the pie. Press the edges together to seal, then
trim and flute with your fingers. Brush the
top with a little milk and decorate with
leaves made from the pastry trimmings.
5   Stand the pie on the heated backing
sheet and bake in the top of the oven for
25–30 minutes, until the pastry is crisp and
golden. Serve the pie hot or cold.

Chicken vol-au-vent with prawns

 15 minutes,
 resting pastry, then 45 minutes

Serves 6
500 g /1 lb puff pastry
flour for dredging
1 large egg yolk, beaten with 15 ml /1 tbls
   water
For the filling
425 ml /15 fl oz milk
½ chicken stock cube, crumbled .
40 g /1½ oz butter
45 ml /3 tbls flour
salt and freshly ground black pepper
50 g /2 oz Cheddar cheese, grated
225 g /8 oz cooked chicken, diced
125 g /4 oz boiled, peeled prawns
a large pinch of paprika

1   On a lightly floured board, roll the
pastry into a 22 cm /8½ in square. Cut out a
20 cm /8 in circle and transfer it, turning it
upside down, to a dampened baking sheet.
Carefully brush off the surface flour. With a
sharp knife, mark the pastry in a circle 4 cm
/1½ in inside the circumference, but do not

Curried turkey

cut through. Score the top of the pastry.
2   Cover with cling film and leave in the
refrigerator to relax for at least 1 hour.
3   Meanwhile heat the oven to 220C /425F
/gas 7. Brush the vol-au-vent case with egg
glaze, being very careful not to go over the
incision or the edge of the pastry. Cook in
the oven for 30 minutes.
4   Meanwhile, make the filling: in a saucepan, bring the milk to the boil and add the
stock cube. In another saucepan melt the
butter; add the flour and stir over a low heat
for 2–3 minutes. Add the boiled milk
gradually, stirring with a wire whisk. Bring
to the boil, season with salt and pepper and
simmer until thickened.
5   Add the diced cooked chicken and
simmer for 2 minutes, then add the grated
Cheddar cheese, stirring until it melts.
6   Remove the vol-au-vent from the oven.
Carefully cut out and remove the lid and
reserve. Discard any uncooked dough from
the centre. Transfer to a heated serving
plate.
7   Add the prawns and paprika to the
filling. Simmer for 1–2 minutes to heat
through; adjust the seasoning and ladle the
filling into the vol-au-vent case. Replace the
lid and serve immediately.

STAR MENUS & RECIPE FILE

In the past, chicken was regarded as a symbol of prosperity, particularly during times of economic depression. Today, however, thanks to new breeding techniques and new methods of marketing, this former luxury has become an everyday dish, and it presents us with a challenge – imagination and skill are needed to give back to chicken dishes the splendour they once had when they graced only the tables of kings.

It was Naomi, my maid in Paris, who first revealed to me the many possibilities of chicken. Naomi was a really wonderful cook, and I will always remember her at work in my Paris kitchen where the walls were hung with saucepans in all shapes and sizes, and lined with shelves of earthenware and terracotta casseroles. She used to say that choosing the right casserole or saucepan was just as important as choosing the right ingredients for a dish.

One of her favourite ways of preparing chicken was Chicken with cucumber – *poulet aux concombres*. She roasted the chicken with buttered vegetables and served it with cucumber poached in cream. This is an excellent dish for a country-style luncheon or for an informal dinner party. Naomi accompanied it with a delicious Rice pilaff with mushrooms and raisins, and followed it with a salad of crisp lettuce leaves, tossed with a vinaigrette enlivened by chopped herbs, gherkins and hard-boiled egg. A bottle of lightly chilled Macon blanc is delicious with this main course.

Start the meal off with a pretty, cool pink and green combination of prawns and green beans, simple to prepare and easy to serve, and end with a super rich, moist Austrian chestnut cake, decorated with whipped cream and glacé chestnuts. There should be plenty of cake leftover but I guarantee it won't stay in the refrigerator for long!

Plan-ahead timetable

Early in the day
Austrian chestnut cake: make up the cake mixture and bake. Cool and place in an airtight tin or cover with foil.

Two hours before the meal
Prawn and green bean salad: prepare beans, make dressing.

One hour thirty minutes before the meal
Chicken with cucumber: prepare and roast the chicken. After fifteen minutes make additions to the chicken.

One hour before the meal
Rice pilaff with mushrooms and raisins: soak raisins, prepare rice, put in oven.
Prawns and green bean salad: cook and dress the beans; peel and dress prawns. Chill.

Thirty minutes before the meal
Austrian chestnut cake: decorate the cake.
Rice pilaff with mushrooms and raisins: prepare the garnish.

Fifteen minutes before the meal
Chicken with cucumber: prepare and blanch the cucumber; cook with butter and cream.
Prawn and green bean salad: combine green beans and prawns, arrange on serving dish.

Ten minutes before the meal
Rice pilaff with mushrooms and raisins: transfer rice to a serving dish, add the garnish, toss and keep warm.

Five minutes before the meal
Chicken with cucumber: dish up the chicken and vegetables. Finish the sauce. Arrange the cucumber shapes around the chicken and keep warm.

Prawn and green bean salad

Chicken with cucumber
Rice pilaff with mushrooms,
and raisins

Austrian chestnut cake

Wine: Macon blanc

Prawn and green bean salad

Serves 4
350 g /12 oz young green beans
salt
135 ml /9 tbls olive oil
45 ml /3 tbls wine vinegar
freshly ground black pepper
30 ml /2 tbls finely chopped fresh parsley
1 garlic clove, finely chopped
350 g /12 oz boiled prawns in their shells
60 ml /4 tbls coarsely chopped spring onions or shallots

1   Top and tail the green beans, cut into 25 mm /1 in lengths and cook in boiling salted water for about 5 minutes, until barely tender.
2   Meanwhile, make the dressing: put the olive oil, wine vinegar, and salt and freshly ground black pepper to taste, in a screw-topped jar and shake to mix.
3   Drain the beans well and toss immediately in half the dressing. Add the finely chopped parsley and garlic. Leave until cold, then chill in the refrigerator.
4   Peel the prawns and toss them in the remaining French dressing with the coarsely chopped spring onions or shallots. Chill.
5   When ready to serve, place the green bean and prawn mixture in a bowl. Toss until well mixed, correct the seasoning and pile into a serving dish.

🔪 30 minutes
plus cooling and chilling

Chicken with cucumber

Serves 4
1.6 kg /3½ lb chicken, with giblets
4 medium-sized carrots, thinly sliced
1 Spanish onion, thinly sliced
butter for greasing
90–120 ml /6–8 tbls melted butter
1.5 ml /¼ tsp powdered thyme
1 bay leaf, crumbled
salt and freshly ground black pepper
2 large firm tomatoes, blanched, skinned, juice and seeds removed
    and coarsely chopped
1 cucumber
75 g /3 oz butter
150 ml /5 fl oz thick cream
paprika

1   Bring the chicken to room temperature. Heat the oven to 180C /350F /gas 4. Chop the chicken giblets. Place the carrots, onions and giblets in the bottom of a well-buttered flameproof casserole and heat gently on top of the cooker for 5 minutes.
2   Brush the chicken all over with the melted butter, then place it on top of the carrot, onion and giblets. Roast in the oven for about 1 hour. Turn the chicken several times as it cooks, basting well each time.
3   Fifteen minutes after putting the chicken in the oven, add the powdered thyme and crumbled bay leaf, a sprinkling of salt and the coarsely chopped tomatoes.
4   Peel the cucumber, cut in half lengthways and remove the seeds with a pointed teaspoon. Cut into 5 cm /2 in lengths, and round off the edges to make attractive oval shapes. Blanch the cucumber pieces by placing them in boiling salted water for 3 minutes, then drain. Season the cucumber with salt and pepper.
5   Put the butter and thick cream in a small pan with a tight-fitting lid. Add the cucumber and simmer gently until tender – about 5 minutes. Remove from the heat and season with salt and paprika to taste.
6   When the chicken is cooked (when pierced with a sharp knife the juices run clear, not pink), transfer it, with the vegetables, to a warmed serving dish. Pour the remaining sauce from the cucumbers into the casserole and bring to the boil. Simmer for 2 minutes while you arrange the cucumber pieces round the chicken. Check the seasoning, strain the sauce over the chicken and serve immediately.

 bringing to room temperature, then 1½ hours   Mâcon blanc

Rice pilaff with mushrooms and raisins

Serves 4
boiling water
50 g /2 oz seedless raisins
100 g /4 oz butter
15 ml /1 tbls olive oil
½ Spanish onion, finely chopped
225 g /8 oz long-grain rice
1 chicken stock cube
salt and freshly ground black pepper
75 g /3 oz button mushrooms, sliced
25 g /1 oz pine nuts
sprig of parsley, to garnish

1   Pour boiling water over the raisins in a cup to plump them. Heat the oven to 180C /350F /gas 4. Heat 40 g /1½ oz of the butter and the olive oil in a heavy, flameproof casserole and cook the finely chopped onion gently for about 10 minutes, until soft.
2   Add the rice and stir over a moderate heat for 2–3 minutes, until the grains are thoroughly coated with butter.
3   Dissolve the stock cube in 450 ml /16 fl oz boiling water in a saucepan and bring back to the boil. Pour the boiling stock into the casserole (take care, as the stock will sizzle when it comes in contact with the hot butter). Season to taste with salt and freshly ground black pepper and quickly cover the casserole to prevent too much stock evaporating. Cook in the oven for 40 minutes, or until the rice grains are fluffy and separate, and the liquid has been absorbed.
4   Meanwhile, gently sauté the mushroom slices in 25 g /1 oz of the butter for 5 minutes. Sauté the pine nuts in 15 g /½ oz of the butter in a separate pan.
5   When the rice is cooked, transfer it to a serving dish. Add the sautéed mushrooms, drained plumped raisins, sautéed pine nuts and the remaining butter, and toss with a fork to mix them in lightly. Taste, and add more salt and freshly ground black pepper if necessary. Garnish with a sprig of parsley and serve immediately.

● If you cannot buy pine nuts, or find them too expensive, use blanched, halved almonds.

 1 hour

Austrian chestnut cake

Serves 12
butter for greasing
6 medium-sized egg yolks
175 g /6 oz caster sugar
700 g /1½ lb canned unsweetened chestnut purée
75 g /3 oz finely ground almonds
22.5 ml /1½ tbls dry breadcrumbs
10 ml /2 tsp vanilla essence
8 medium-sized egg whites
250 ml /9 fl oz thick cream
about 30 ml /2 tbls brandy
12 glacé chestnuts (marrons glacés)

1   Heat the oven to 180C /350F /gas 4 and butter a 23 cm /9 in cake tin.
2   In a large mixing bowl, beat the egg yolks with a wire whisk or rotary beater until light and fluffy. Add the caster sugar and beat thoroughly.
3   Add the chestnut purée to the egg yolk mixture, mixing well. Beat in the ground almonds, breadcrumbs and vanilla essence.
4   Whisk the egg whites until they form stiff peaks. Using a large metal spoon, carefully fold the egg whites into the chestnut mixture.
5   Spoon the mixture into the prepared cake tin, smoothing the surface with the back of a spoon. Place the tin in the oven and bake for 1½ hours, or until a metal skewer inserted into the centre of the cake comes out clean.
6   Leave the cake to cool in the tin for 15 minutes, then remove it from the tin and place it on a wire rack to cool completely.
7   In a medium-sized mixing bowl, whisk the thick cream until stiff. Fold in the brandy to taste.
8   Not more than 1 hour before serving, place the cake on a serving plate. Spread the cream over the top of the cake, making decorative swirls with a flat-bladed knife. Alternatively pipe the swirls using a small piping bag fitted with a 5 mm /¼ in star nozzle. Arrange glacé chestnuts on top. Serve as soon as possible.

● This is a most impressive cake, which makes a marvellous dinner party dessert. Store leftover cake in the refrigerator or freezer.

 2½ hours
plus cooling

STAR MENU 2

If you plan to invite two or three friends for lunch or supper during a busy holiday period and you want to entertain them without a lot of fuss and bother, then this light-hearted little menu of pâté, three salads and home-made ice cream is just the thing. The French liver pâté and Burnt honey ice cream can be prepared several days in advance and kept waiting in the refrigerator and the freezer respectively until they are called upon, while the turkey and ham salads can be made several hours or even the day before your planned meal.

The pâté is a bit of a cheat, actually – I make it with liver sausage combined with mayonnaise and cream, pack it into little crocks and decorate it prettily, then team it with crisp slices of hot toast spread with chilled butter and, for a change, thinly sliced sweet, ripe pears. But it looks very impressive and your guests will never imagine that it took only a few minutes to prepare.

Turkey and ham are popular Christmas and Easter fare, and two of my salads in this menu make imaginative use of the leftovers. You'll find that fresh orange segments and black olives will add interest as well as flavour to cold roast turkey in a rosemary-scented vinaigrette dressing. Team cubes of cooked ham with crisp slices of red apple and green pepper, toss in a mayonnaise-based dressing and sprinkle with crumbled blue cheese and chopped walnuts for Ham and apple salad. My Winter salad is a crunchy combination of red and white cabbage in a garlicky soured cream dressing. Accompany the three salads with a basket containing a variety of crusty breads, and a soft, light red wine from the Côte de Beaune area of Burgundy.

Burnt honey ice cream is made from a rich custard combined with caramelized honey, then topped with a little more burnt honey. Try a little brandied mincemeat as well, for an additional kick!

All these recipes for this easy-to-prepare-and-serve holiday meal can be multiplied to serve eight or twelve people or more, if you wish, and would make an ideal buffet supper.

French liver pâté
—
Turkey salad with orange
and black olives
Ham and apple salad
Winter salad
—
Burnt honey ice cream

Wine: Côte de Beaune

Plan-ahead timetable

The day before the meal
French liver pâté: make the pâté, and refrigerate.
Burnt honey ice cream: make the rich custard and cool. Make the burnt honey sauce and add to the custard. Freeze, whisking as directed in the recipe. Reserve the remaining sauce to serve with the ice cream.

Three hours before the meal
Turkey salad with oranges and black olives: dice the turkey, mix with the shallots and celery. Make the dressing, combine with the turkey and marinate. Peel the oranges and prepare the orange segments.
Winter salad: shred the white and red cabbages, cover and refrigerate.
Ham and apple salad: cube the ham, slice the green pepper and core and slice the apples. Combine the mayonnaise and cream with the ham, pepper and apples, toss.

Thirty minutes before the meal
Turkey salad with oranges and black olives: drain the turkey, add orange segments and remaining dressing and toss. Line a serving bowl with the lettuce leaves, fill with the salad and garnish with the olives and rosemary.
Winter salad: prepare dressing, add to shredded cabbage, toss and transfer to a serving dish.
Ham and apple salad: transfer to a serving dish, garnish with cheese, walnuts and apple.
French liver pâté: remove from the refrigerator, garnish with sieved hard-boiled egg yolk and parsley. Prepare the toast and butter.

Between the main course and the dessert
Burnt honey ice cream: scoop the ice cream into serving dishes, garnish and serve.

French liver pâté

Serves 4
225 g /8 oz liver sausage, diced
30 ml /2 tbls mayonnaise
30 ml /2 tbls thick cream
salt and freshly ground black pepper
lemon juice
sieved hard-boiled egg yolks and finely chopped fresh parsley, to garnish
toast and butter, to serve

1   Combine the diced liver sausage, mayonnaise and thick cream in a blender. Season with salt, freshly ground black pepper and lemon juice to taste and blend until smooth.
2   Put the liver pâté into small, individual crocks or a larger terrine. Refrigerate until needed. This pâté will keep for several days.
3   Decorate the crocks, or terrine, with sieved hard-boiled egg yolks and finely chopped parsley. Serve the liver pâté with toast and butter.

● Although not a 'true' liver pâté, this version using liver sausage is so quick and easy to prepare that it makes an invaluable standby recipe. To make it a little more special, try adding brandy instead of lemon juice.
● Try serving the pâté with thin slices of ripe pear and, instead of toast, thin slices of rye or pumpernickel bread.

15 minutes
plus chilling

Turkey salad with orange and black olives

Serves 4
700 g /1½ lb cold roasted turkey
4 shallots, finely chopped
2 celery stalks, sliced
90–135 ml /6–9 tbls olive oil
30–45 ml /2–3 tbls red wine vinegar
1.5–2.5 ml /¼–½ tsp chopped fresh rosemary leaves
salt and freshly ground black pepper
4 small oranges, peeled and separated into segments
1 lettuce, washed and dried
8–10 black olives, stoned
sprig of rosemary, to garnish

1   Dice the turkey into 10 mm /½ in cubes and place them in a large bowl. Sprinkle the finely chopped shallots and sliced celery over the top.
2   In a small bowl combine the olive oil, red wine vinegar and chopped rosemary leaves. Season with salt and freshly ground black pepper to taste and blend. Pour half of this dressing over the diced turkey. Toss well and leave to marinate, covered, for at least 2 hours in a cold place.
3   To serve, drain the diced turkey and transfer to a clean bowl. Add the orange segments and the remaining dressing and toss well. Line a salad bowl with the lettuce leaves; fill with the turkey salad, top with the stoned olives and garnish with a sprig of rosemary.

Ham and apple salad

Serves 4
3 red dessert apples
juice of 1 lemon
125 ml /4 fl oz mayonnaise
45 ml /3 tbls thick cream
350 g /12 oz cooked ham, cut into cubes
1 small green pepper, thinly sliced
salt and freshly ground black pepper
75 g /3 oz blue cheese, crumbled
45 ml /3 tbls chopped walnuts

1   Prepare acidulated water by putting 30 ml /2 tbls water and the juice of the lemon in a bowl. Core and slice the apples but do not peel them. Turn the apple slices in the acidulated water to prevent discoloration.
2   In a large bowl, combine the mayonnaise and thick cream. Drain most of the apple slices, leaving 16 in the acidulated water; they will be used later on for decoration.
3   Add the cubed ham, the thinly sliced green pepper and the apple slices to the mayonnaise and cream mixture. Season with salt and freshly ground black pepper to taste and toss with a fork until evenly coated.
4   To serve, spoon the salad onto a serving platter, sprinkle with the crumbled blue cheese and chopped walnuts and decorate with the reserved, drained apple slices.

20 minutes
plus 2 hours marinating   Côte de Beaune

30 minutes

Winter salad

Serves 4
250 g /8 oz white cabbage
250 g /8 oz red cabbage
150 ml /5 fl oz soured cream
90 ml /6 tbls chopped walnuts
1 small garlic clove, crushed
salt and freshly ground black pepper
sprig of flat-leaved parsley, to garnish

1   Thinly slice the white and red cabbages.
2   Pour the soured cream into a large bowl, add the chopped walnuts and crushed garlic and season with salt and freshly ground black pepper to taste. Add the thinly sliced cabbage and toss with a fork until evenly coated.
3   To serve, spoon the salad onto a serving platter and garnish with a sprig of flat-leaved parsley.

● This recipe is an economical way to enjoy a crisp, crunchy salad in the middle of winter. It is similar to coleslaw but the red cabbage adds colour and the soured cream and garlic add extra flavour.

25 minutes

Burnt honey ice cream

Serves 4
225 g /8 oz sugar
600 ml /1 pt milk
300 ml /10 fl oz thick cream
8 egg yolks
cracked ice for chilling
For the burnt honey sauce
225 g /8 oz sugar
120 ml /8 tbls clear honey

1   To make the rich custard, combine the sugar, milk and thick cream in a saucepan and bring to the boil. Remove the pan from the heat, cover and leave for 5–10 minutes.
2   Beat the egg yolks in the top pan of a double boiler, off the heat. Gradually pour on the hot milk mixture, stirring until foamy.
3   Put the pan over simmering water and cook, stirring constantly, until the custard coats the back of the spoon. Do not let the custard come to the boil or it will curdle.
4   Pour the custard into a bowl, cover, and set in a larger bowl filled with cracked ice. Leave until cold.
5   To make the burnt honey sauce, in a small saucepan bring the sugar and 60 ml /4 tbls water to the boil. Boil for 5 minutes, or until the caramel turns deep brown. Add another 60 ml /4 tbls water, covering your hand with a cloth as you do so to avoid being splashed. Blend with a wooden spoon and cook for a further 1–2 minutes until the syrup reaches 115C /240F; at this temperature a small amount dropped in cold water will form a soft ball. Stir in the clear honey, remove from the heat and allow to cool.
6   Stir half the cooled burnt honey sauce into the cooled custard and chill, covered, for 2 hours. Transfer the custard to a freezerproof container and put in the freezer until the mixture begins to harden to a depth of about 25 mm /1 in around the sides of the container, about 1–2 hours. Remove the mixture and beat briefly with a whisk or fork, return to the freezer and leave until frozen firm, about 2–3 hours.
7   About 30 minutes before serving, transfer the ice cream to the refrigerator to soften.
8   To serve, scoop the ice cream high into glass serving dishes and trickle over the remaining burnt honey sauce. Serve immediately.

● Try a topping of brandied mincemeat in addition to the burnt honey sauce.

40 minutes, cooling and chilling,
3–5 hours freezing plus softening

47

Tandoori chicken

Serves 4–6
2 × 1.1 kg /2½ lb roasting
    chickens, dressed weight
juice of ½ lemon
2.5 ml /½ tsp salt
2.5 ml /½ tsp Mexican chilli
    seasoning (see note)
For the garlic paste
1 small garlic clove, finely chopped
1 small piece fresh root ginger,
    finely chopped
2.5 ml /½ tsp salt
5 ml /1 tsp olive oil
For the marinade
150 ml /5 fl oz yoghurt

30 ml /2 tbls olive oil
15 ml /1 tbls Mexican chilli
    seasoning
15 ml /1 tbls ground cumin
15 ml /1 tbls ground coriander
15 ml /1 tbls ground allspice
2.5 ml /½ tsp grated nutmeg
2.5 ml /½ tsp ground mace
30 ml /2 tbls wine vinegar
a few drops of red food colouring
For the garnish
1 lettuce
1 Spanish onion, cut into rings
    and soaked in iced water
2 lemons, cut into wedges

1   Wipe the chickens with a damp cloth inside and out. With a
sharp knife, make 3 long cuts on each chicken breast and 2 cuts on
each thigh. In a small bowl, combine the lemon juice, salt and chilli
seasoning. Spoon the mixture into the incisions.
2   To make the garlic paste, combine the finely chopped garlic and
fresh root ginger with the salt and olive oil in a mortar, and work to
a smooth paste with a pestle.
3   Put all the marinade ingredients in a bowl and stir in the garlic
paste. Mix until well blended. Pour the mixture over the chickens
and leave to marinate in a cool place for at least 8 hours. Bring the
chickens to room temperature before you cook them.
4   Meanwhile, heat the oven to 200C /400F /gas 6.
5   Transfer the marinated chickens to a large ovenproof dish.
Spoon over the marinade and cook in the oven for 50–60 minutes or
until the chickens are tender, basting occasionally with the
marinade. To test that the chickens are cooked, push a skewer into
the thickest part of the inside leg. The juices should run clear.
6   Arrange a bed of lettuce leaves on a large serving platter. Drain
the onion rings. Place the chickens in the centre of the platter and
garnish with alternating lemon wedges and onion rings. Serve
immediately, accompanied by the defatted cooking juices in a sauce-
boat.

● Use Mexican chilli seasoning – a mixture of chilli pepper, garlic,
cumin, coriander and oregano – not the pure, very much hotter,
chilli powder.

 20 minutes, marinating,
then 1¼ hours

Creamed turkey au gratin

Serves 4
350 g /12 oz cold cooked turkey, in bite-sized pieces
65 g /2½ oz butter
60 ml /4 tbls flour
275 ml /10 fl oz milk
150 ml /5 fl oz thick cream
salt and freshly ground black pepper
cayenne pepper
1 egg, beaten
30 ml /2 tbls thick cream, whipped
90 ml /6 tbls fresh breadcrumbs
parsley sprig, to garnish

1   Melt 50 g /2 oz butter in a saucepan over low heat. Add the flour
and cook, stirring constantly with a wooden spoon, for 2 minutes.
2   Gradually whisk in the milk and bring to the boil. Lower the
heat to a gentle simmer and cook for about 5 minutes, whisking
frequently. Pour off slightly less than half the sauce and reserve.
3   Stir 150 ml /5 fl oz thick cream into the sauce left in the pan and
add the turkey. Cook, stirring, for 10 minutes or until the turkey is
heated through. Season to taste with a little salt, freshly ground
black pepper and cayenne pepper. Spoon the mixture into a
heatproof gratin dish. Heat the grill to medium.
4   Combine the reserved sauce with the beaten egg. Whisk in the
whipped cream and spread over the creamed turkey mixture.
5   Sprinkle with fresh breadcrumbs and dot with the remaining
butter. Brown under the grill, with the grid 7.5 cm /3 in from the
heat, for 10 minutes, or until heated through and browned on top.
Garnish with parsley and serve immediately.

● You can substitute leftover goose for the turkey in this recipe, if
wished.

40 minutes

Chicken liver brochettes

Serves 4
32 small chicken livers, about 450 g /1 lb
olive oil for greasing
8 large bacon slices
8 medium-sized tomatoes
salt and freshly ground black pepper
bay leaves, to garnish
For the dressing
120 ml /8 tbls olive oil
120 ml /8 tbls lemon juice
60 ml /4 tbls finely chopped fresh parsley
4 crumbled bay leaves
30 ml /2 tbls finely chopped onion, or 2 garlic cloves, finely chopped
salt and freshly ground black pepper

1   Remove any membranes or greenish patches from the chicken livers and rinse them. Drain them well on absorbent paper.
2   Remove the grid from the grill pan and grease the pan. Heat the grill without the grid to medium.
3   Cut each bacon slice into 4 even-sized pieces, then wrap 1 piece round each chicken liver.
4   Slice each tomato into quarters.
5   Thread 8 × 20 cm /8 in skewers with a piece of tomato, followed by a bacon-wrapped chicken liver, and repeat 3 times, making 4 sets on each skewer.
6   Season the brochettes to taste with salt and freshly ground black pepper.
7   Arrange the skewers side by side across the prepared grill pan, then grill 7.5 cm /3 in from the heat for 3–4 minutes on each side, or until the bacon is lightly coloured and the livers are cooked but still pink inside.
8   Meanwhile, in a bowl, combine the dressing ingredients, seasoning to taste with salt and freshly ground black pepper. Stir with a fork until the dressing emulsifies.
9   To serve, arrange the skewers on a heated serving platter or place 2 skewers on each of 4 heated individual plates. Garnish with bay leaves and spoon a little of the dressing over the brochettes. Serve immediately, accompanied by the remainder of the dressing.

 35 minutes

Polynesian chicken

Serves 4
1.6 kg /3½ lb roasting chicken or 8 small chicken portions
salt and freshly ground black pepper
flour
45 ml /3 tbls olive oil
225 g /8 oz canned pineapple rings in natural juice
425 ml /15 fl oz fresh orange juice
2.5 ml /½ tsp soy sauce
1.5 ml /¼ tsp ground cloves
1.5 ml /¼ tsp ground cinnamon
15–22.5 ml /1–1½ tbls cornflour
2 oranges, in segments
12 slices avocado, generously brushed with lemon juice
15–30 ml /1–2 tbls grated orange zest

1   If using a whole chicken, divide into 8 serving pieces, taking 2 portions from each leg and 2 from each breast. Season the chicken portions with freshly ground black pepper and bring to room temperature, then season with salt and more pepper and dust with flour.
2   Heat the olive oil in a heavy-based pan or flameproof casserole, add the chicken portions and sauté over a medium heat until golden brown on all sides. Drain off excess fat from the pan.
3   Drain the pineapple, reserving 75 ml /5 tbls juice. Heat the reserved pineapple juice and the orange juice. Cut each pineapple ring in half and add to the casserole with the heated juices, soy sauce, cloves and cinnamon. Mix well and cover the pan with a tightly fitting lid. Simmer for 45–55 minutes or until the chicken is tender.
4   With a slotted spoon, lift out the chicken portions and halved pineapple rings, allowing the juice to drain back into the pan. Arrange on a heated serving dish and keep hot.
5   In a small bowl, blend the cornflour with 30 ml /2 tbls cold water. Pour the mixture into the pan in a thin stream, stirring constantly. Bring to the boil and simmer, stirring, until the sauce is thick and translucent. Correct the seasoning if necessary.
6   Add the orange segments and avocado slices to the sauce and spoon over the chicken portions. Sprinkle with the grated orange zest and serve immediately.

● Pineapple and orange juice add a sweet touch to this chicken dish from the Polynesian islands.

bringing to room temperature,
then 1½ hours

Cold ginger chicken

Serves 4–6
4 chicken breasts
120 ml /8 tbls flour
salt
freshly ground black pepper
10 ml /2 tsp paprika
60 ml /4 tbls butter
30 ml /2 tbls vegetable oil
600 ml /1 pt chicken stock,
　home-made or from a cube

5 cm /2 in piece of fresh root ginger,
　finely chopped
90 ml /6 tbls Madeira
juice of 2 small oranges
5 ml /1 tsp soy sauce
For the garnish
3 × 10 mm /½ in pieces of preserved
　stem ginger, cut into fine batons
4–6 spring onion tassels (see note)

1　Cut the chicken breasts from the bone and remove the skin.
Remove the fillet (the loose piece of meat lying nearest the bone)
from each chicken breast and cut the remaining breast to make
strips the same size as the fillet.
2　Spread half the flour on a flat plate and season generously with
salt, freshly ground black pepper and paprika.
3　Toss the chicken strips in the seasoned flour, shaking off the
excess. Reserve the remaining flour.
4　In a large frying-pan, heat the butter and oil and sauté half the
chicken strips for 2–3 minutes each side, or until golden brown and
cooked through, turning them over with a spatula. Transfer them to
a plate with a slotted spoon. Repeat with the remaining chicken
strips, cool, cover closely and chill.
5　Spoon 60 ml /4 tbls of the butter and oil from the frying-pan
into a saucepan. Stir in the reserved flour and cook over a low heat
for 2–3 minutes to make a pale roux, stirring with a wooden spoon.
6　Add the chicken stock, stirring vigorously with a wire whisk to
prevent lumps forming. Stir in the finely chopped ginger and the
Madeira. Bring the sauce to the boil and boil over a high heat until
thick enough to coat the back of a wooden spoon.
7　Stir in the orange juice and soy sauce and season to taste with a
little salt and freshly ground black pepper to taste. Leave to cool
completely.
8　Arrange the chilled sautéed chicken pieces on individual dishes.
Spoon over enough cold sauce to coat them lightly and garnish with
batons of preserved ginger and a spring onion tassel at one end of
the dish. Serve the remaining sauce separately.

● To make the spring onion tassels, cut the green parts of the spring
onions into strips towards the base, leaving the whites intact. Soak
in chilled water until they open.

 45 minutes
plus chilling

Turkey scaloppine with lemon

Serves 4–6
700–900 g /1½–2 lb boned turkey breasts
salt and freshly ground black pepper
50 g /2 oz butter
30 ml /2 tbls olive oil
1 large Spanish onion, coarsely chopped
1 garlic clove, finely chopped
60–90 ml /4–6 tbls Madeira
juice of ½ lemon
300–425 ml /10–15 fl oz thick cream
6–8 thin lemon slices
60 ml /4 tbls halved blanched almonds, lightly toasted
1 lemon twist, to garnish
cooked rice or noodles, to serve

1　Cut the boned turkey breasts diagonally across the grain into
slices about 5 mm /¼ in thick. Season generously with salt and
freshly ground black pepper.
2　Heat 25 g /1 oz butter and 15 ml /1 tbls olive oil in a large,
shallow casserole over a medium heat. Add the chopped onion and
garlic to the pan and sauté until soft but not coloured. Using a
slotted spoon, remove the onion and garlic and reserve.
3　Add the remaining butter and oil to the pan. When the butter
has melted, add the turkey slices and sauté, stirring constantly, until
golden brown on all sides. Return the vegetables to the dish, stir
once and add the Madeira; cook over a high heat, stirring
constantly, until the Madeira is reduced to half its original quantity.
Reduce the heat to medium, add the lemon juice, stir once and add
the cream. Cook for a few minutes longer, stirring, until the sauce is
heated through. Add the lemon slices.
4　Scatter over the lightly toasted almonds, garnish with a lemon
twist and serve immediately, accompanied by cooked rice or noodles.

● This Italian-style dish can be made from boneless chicken breasts
instead of turkey.

25 minutes

Breast of chicken Valdostana

Serves 4
4 boned chicken breasts
salt and freshly ground black pepper
75 g /3 oz Philadelphia full-fat soft cheese
30 ml /2 tbls freshly grated Parmesan cheese
15 ml /1 tbls finely snipped chives
30–60 ml /2–4 tbls thick cream
4 slices prosciutto
flour for coating
25–50 g /1–2 oz butter
150 ml /5 fl oz dry white wine
sprigs of watercress, to garnish

1   Wrap the chicken breasts in a piece of cling film and pound them with a meat bat or rolling pin until they are very thin. Season to taste with salt and freshly ground black pepper.
2   In a bowl, combine the Philadelphia cheese, grated Parmesan cheese and finely snipped chives with enough thick cream to make a smooth, spreadable paste.
3   Leaving a narrow border, place a slice of prosciutto on each of the chicken breasts and spread generously with the cheese mixture. Fold the chicken breasts in half and pound the edges firmly together with the flat side of a knife.
4   Dip the chicken breasts in flour. Melt the butter in a large, shallow, flameproof casserole. When the foaming subsides, fry the chicken breasts until well browned on both sides. Add the dry white wine, cover and simmer very gently for 10–15 minutes or until the chicken breasts are tender. Transfer to a serving platter, garnish with watercress sprigs and serve at once.

● This luxurious chicken dish comes from the Val d'Aosta in the Alps on Italy's western border.

 40 minutes

Roast chicken with pineapple stuffing

Serves 4
1.4 kg /3 lb chicken, with giblets
salt and freshly ground black pepper
25 g /1 oz butter
300 ml /10 fl oz chicken stock, home-made or from a cube
For the stuffing
550 g /1 lb 4 oz canned pineapple rings, drained
40 g /1½ oz butter
grated zest of ½ lemon
50 g /2 oz fresh white breadcrumbs
75 g /3 oz walnuts, coarsely chopped
salt and freshly ground black pepper
For the garnish
50 g /2 oz walnuts, finely chopped
sprigs of watercress

1   Bring the chicken to room temperature. Heat the oven to 190C / 375F /gas 5.
2   Wipe the chicken inside and out with a damp cloth and season generously with salt and freshly ground black pepper.
3   To make the stuffing, reserve 4 pineapple rings for the garnish. Roughly chop the remaining rings.
4   Melt the butter in a saucepan. Stir in the grated lemon zest, fresh white breadcrumbs, chopped pineapple and walnuts. Season with salt and freshly ground black pepper to taste.
5   Fill the neck end of the bird with the stuffing and truss. Spread the butter over the chicken and cover with greaseproof paper.
6   Place the chicken in a roasting tin, surround with the giblets (reserving the liver) and roast in the oven for 1 hour.
7   Remove the greaseproof paper, put the liver in the tin and baste the chicken with the juices. Cook for a further 30 minutes.
8   Transfer the chicken to a heated serving platter and keep warm. Drain off the surplus fat from the pan and pour in the stock. Boil for 3 minutes over a high heat to reduce the liquid slightly, stirring occasionally with a wooden spoon. Correct the seasoning.
9 ' Chop the remaining pineapple into chunks, toss with the finely chopped walnuts and arrange round the chicken. Garnish with sprigs of watercress. Strain the sauce into a sauce-boat, discarding the liver and giblets, and serve with the chicken.

bringing to room temperature, then 2 hours

Turkey croquettes

Serves 4

350 g /12 oz cooked turkey, finely chopped
65 g /2½ oz butter
2 shallots, finely chopped
50 g /2 oz button mushrooms, finely chopped
60 ml /4 tbls finely chopped parsley
1.5 ml /¼ tsp paprika
a pinch of cayenne pepper
15 ml /1 tbls lemon juice
1.5 ml /¼ tsp grated lemon zest

salt and black pepper
90 ml /6 tbls flour
300 ml /10 fl oz hot milk
¼ chicken stock cube
1 egg, beaten
oil for deep frying
parsley, to garnish
For the coating
60–90 ml /4–6 tbls flour
salt and black pepper
1 egg
175 g /6 oz white breadcrumbs

1   Melt 15 g /½ oz of the butter and sauté the shallots for 5–7 minutes, until soft. Add the mushrooms and cook for 3–4 minutes. Leave to cool.
2   Mix the turkey with the parsley, paprika, cayenne, lemon juice and zest and sautéed shallots and mushrooms. Season with salt and freshly ground black pepper to taste.
3   Melt the remaining butter in a saucepan, blend in the flour and stir over low heat for 1–2 minutes. Gradually whisk in the hot milk. Bring slowly to the boil, stirring, and simmer gently for 3–4 minutes. Beat in the piece of stock cube and season to taste with black pepper. Off the heat, add the beaten egg in a stream, beating vigorously. Cool.
4   Fold the cool sauce into the turkey mixture and spread the mixture in a square tin about 20 × 20 cm /8 × 8 in lined with cling film. Cover with cling film and chill for at least 2 hours.
5   Prepare the coating: put the flour on a plate and season with salt and black pepper. Break the egg into a dish and beat it lightly with a fork. Spread the breadcrumbs on another plate.
6   Heat the oil in a deep-fat frier to 190C /375F. At this temperature a cube of day-old bread will turn crisp and golden in 50 seconds. Meanwhile, divide the turkey mixture into 12 and shape each portion into a croquette. One at a time, toss them in seasoned flour, shaking off the excess, dip them in beaten egg and roll in breadcrumbs. Pat the breadcrumbs firmly in place with a knife.
7   Lay half the croquettes in a wire frying basket and fry for 4–5 minutes, or until crisp and golden. Drain on absorbent paper and keep warm while you cook the rest. Pile the croquettes in a heated shallow serving dish, garnish with parsley and serve.

● Substitute chicken for turkey to make chicken croquettes.

⏲ 25 minutes, chilling, then 35 minutes

Chicken pot pie

Serves 4

1.4 kg /3 lb chicken, dressed weight
30 ml /2 tbls flour
salt and black pepper
30 ml /2 tbls olive oil
40 g /1½ oz butter
12 small onions
600 ml /1 pt hot chicken stock, home-made or from a cube

bouquet garni
juice of 1 lemon
24 button mushrooms, trimmed
15 ml /1 tbls flour
275 ml /10 fl oz thick cream
225 g /8 oz frozen peas, defrosted
225 g /8 oz shortcrust pastry, defrostedif frozen
1 egg yolk, beaten

1   Cut the chicken into 8 portions and bring to room temperature. Put the flour into a dish and season with salt and pepper. Toss each chicken portion in the seasoned flour, shaking off any excess.
2   Heat the olive oil and 15 g /½ oz of the butter in a large frying-pan. Sauté the chicken portions, in 2 batches, for 2–3 minutes on each side or until golden. Transfer to a casserole and keep warm.
3   In the same pan sauté the onions for 5–6 minutes, until lightly browned. Transfer with a slotted spoon to the casserole. Pour the hot chicken stock over the chicken and onions; add the bouquet garni and season with salt and pepper to taste. Cover the casserole and simmer gently for 1–1¼ hours, or until the chicken is tender. Remove the chicken and onions from the casserole. Strain and reserve 275 ml /10 fl oz stock; use the rest in another recipe.
4   Meanwhile, heat 15 g /½ oz butter in a large, clean frying-pan. Add the lemon juice and button mushrooms and cook, stirring, for 4–5 minutes, or until tender. Remove with a slotted spoon.
5   Melt the remaining butter in a heavy saucepan. Blend in the flour with a wooden spoon. Pour the reserved stock from the casserole into the pan, whisking continuously. Add the thick cream. Season with salt and pepper to taste, and cook for a further 10 minutes, or until the sauce thickens slightly.
6   Heat the oven to 190C /375F /gas 5. Place a pie funnel in the centre of a 1.4 L /2½ pt pie dish and arrange the chicken portions around it. Add the onions, mushrooms and peas; correct the seasoning and pour over the sauce. Leave to cool slightly.
7   Roll the pastry out a little larger than the pie dish. Moisten the rim of the dish with a little beaten egg yolk. Place the pastry over the dish and cut off any excess with a sharp knife. Flute the edges, make decorations from any scraps and attach to the pie with yolk. Cut vents in the pastry to allow steam to escape. Brush with beaten egg yolk and bake for 20 minutes, or until the pastry is golden. Serve the pie at once.

⏲ 2½ hours

Japanese marinated chicken

Serves 4
1.5 kg /3 lb 5 oz chicken, dressed weight
freshly ground black pepper
30 ml /2 tbls cornflour
60 ml /4 tbls peanut or olive oil
For the marinade
60 ml /4 tbls soy sauce
60 ml /4 tbls sake, or 30 ml /2 tbls each sherry and water
15 ml /1 tbls brown sugar
15 ml /1 tbls finely chopped fresh root ginger
2 shallots, finely chopped
4 lemon slices, coarsely chopped, unpeeled
1 clove garlic, finely chopped
For the garnish
1 lemon twist
1 spring onion flower (see note)

1 Cut the chicken into 4 portions and season generously with freshly ground black pepper.
2 Make the marinade. In a large bowl, combine the soy sauce, sake or sherry and water, brown sugar, finely chopped fresh root ginger, shallots, coarsely chopped lemon and finely chopped garlic. Stir until the mixture is well blended.
3 Sprinkle the cornflour onto a plate and toss each chicken portion in it to coat, shaking off the excess.
4 Transfer the coated chicken portions to the marinade and leave to marinate at room temperature for at least 4 hours, turning occasionally.
5 Meanwhile, heat the oven to 170C /325F /gas 3.
6 Arrange the chicken pieces in a shallow baking dish. Sprinkle with peanut or olive oil and bake uncovered, basting occasionally, for 1¼ hours, or until the chicken is cooked and the juices run clear when a skewer is inserted in the thickest part of the leg. Garnish with a lemon twist and a spring onion flower and serve immediately.

● To make a spring onion flower, remove the bulb. The stalk should measure 7.5 cm /3 in. Shred the green part, leaving 25 mm /1 in of the white stalk whole. Leave in iced water for 1 hour, drain and pat dry.

20 minutes, 4 hours or more marinating,
then 1¼ hours

Chicken in red wine

Serves 4
1.6 kg /3½ lb roasting chicken
about 45 ml /3 tbls flour
250 g /8 oz green bacon, in 1 piece
40 g /1½ oz butter
45 ml /3 tbls olive oil
3 large Spanish onions, coarsely chopped
150 ml /5 fl oz red wine
1–2 garlic cloves, crushed
1 strip dried orange zest
2 cloves
fresh bouquet garni made from 2 sprigs thyme,
*   4 sprigs parsley and 2 bay leaves*
coarse salt and freshly ground black pepper

1 Bring the chicken to room temperature. Heat the oven to 170C / 325F /gas 3. Cut the chicken into 8 pieces and dust with flour. Cut the green bacon into slices 15 mm /½ in thick.
2 In a large, flameproof casserole sauté the bacon in the butter and olive oil until the bacon is crisp and golden. Remove from the casserole with a slotted spoon and reserve.
3 Add the chopped onions to the casserole and sauté over a low heat, stirring constantly, until the onions are soft and transparent. Remove with a slotted spoon and reserve.
4 Add the chicken pieces to the casserole in 2 batches and sauté over medium heat, turning from time to time, until the chicken is golden on all sides.
5 Return the bacon pieces and onions to the casserole. Add the wine, garlic cloves, dried orange zest, cloves and bouquet garni and salt and freshly ground black pepper to taste. Bring to a simmer on top of the cooker, then cook in the oven for 35–45 minutes or until the chicken is tender.
6 If the sauce is too thin, remove the chicken and bacon pieces from the casserole with a slotted spoon and keep warm while you boil the cooking liquid quickly to reduce it.
7 Remove and discard the orange zest and bouquet garni and either return the chicken and bacon to the casserole and serve from the casserole, or pour the reduced sauce over the chicken and bacon on a serving platter.

bringing to room temperature,
then 1¾ hours

Chicken guacamole

Serves 4
4 boned chicken breasts
salt and freshly ground black pepper
25 g /1 oz butter
30 ml /2 tbls olive oil
For the guacamole sauce
2 ripe avocados
45 ml /3 tbls lemon or lime juice
60 ml /4 tbls chopped, cooked bacon
1 garlic clove, finely chopped
60 ml /4 tbls finely chopped onion
2 ripe tomatoes, blanched, skinned, seeded and chopped
2.5 ml /½ tsp ground coriander
30 ml /2 tbls finely chopped fresh parsley
45 ml /3 tbls olive oil
a pinch of chilli powder
salt and freshly ground black pepper

1   Slice each chicken breast in half horizontally through the middle to make 8 thin slices. Pound the slices between cling film until very thin and season generously with salt and freshly ground black pepper.
2   Heat the butter and olive oil in a large frying-pan and sauté half of the chicken slices for 3–4 minutes on each side or until golden, turning with a spatula. Drain on absorbent paper and transfer to a plate to cool. Sauté the remaining chicken slices in the same way.
3   Just before serving, make the guacamole sauce: cut the avocados in half and remove the stones. Scoop the avocado pulp into a bowl and mash it lightly with a fork. Stir in the lemon or lime juice, chopped cooked bacon, finely chopped garlic and onion, chopped tomatoes, ground coriander and finely chopped parsley. Beat in the olive oil. Season with a pinch of chilli powder and salt and freshly ground black pepper to taste.
4   Arrange the chicken slices, overlapping, on a serving dish. Spoon the guacamole sauce in the middle of the chicken slices and serve at once.

● This is a fine main course for a light luncheon.

Curried chicken réchauffé

Serves 2
225–275 g /8–10 oz cooked chicken, shredded
60 ml /4 tbls olive oil
½ Spanish onion, finely chopped
2 celery stalks, sliced
15 ml /1 tbls flour
15 ml /1 tbls curry powder
300 ml /10 fl oz well-flavoured chicken stock, home-made or from a cube
30 ml /2 tbls raisins
2 cloves
salt and freshly ground black pepper
juice and grated zest of ½ lemon
1 tart apple, peeled, cored and diced
boiled rice, to serve

1   Heat the olive oil in a heavy-based saucepan. Add the chopped onion and sliced celery. Sauté over a moderate heat for 10 minutes, or until the vegetables are soft, stirring occasionally with a wooden spoon.
2   Stir in the flour and reduce the heat. Cook for 3 minutes, stirring frequently, to make a pale roux. Stir in the curry powder and cook for a further minute.
3   Pour in the stock, stirring vigorously to prevent lumps forming. Add the raisins and cloves and season with salt and freshly ground black pepper to taste. Bring to the boil and simmer for 5 minutes, or until thickened, stirring frequently.
4   Stir the shredded cooked chicken, the lemon juice and zest and the prepared apple into the curry mixture. Simmer gently for 5 minutes, or until the chicken is heated through. Correct the seasoning.
5   Remove the cloves, transfer to a serving dish and serve immediately, with boiled rice as an accompaniment.

 30 minutes cooling,
then 20 minutes

30–40 minutes

Chicken liver terrine

Serves 6–8
500 g /1 lb chicken livers
90–120 ml /6–8 tbls port
2.5 ml /½ tsp dried thyme
4 bay leaves
3 large slices of bread, crusts
  removed
75 ml /3 fl oz milk
150 g /5 oz ham
350 g /12 oz sausage-meat
150 ml /5 fl oz dry white wine

1 garlic clove, finely chopped
salt and black pepper
225–350 g /8–12 oz thinly
  sliced streaky bacon
melted lard, to seal
For the garnish
3–4 thin orange slices, halved
sprigs of watercress
8 small orange segments,
  unpeeled
6 black olives, stoned

1   Place the chicken livers in a bowl; add the port to taste, dried thyme and 2 crumbled bay leaves. Leave to marinate for at least 6 hours in a cool place.
2   Heat the oven to 190C /375F /gas 5. Soak the bread in milk.
3   Put three-quarters of the marinated chicken livers through a mincer or food processor with the ham, sausage-meat and soaked bread slices. Stir in the dry white wine to make a rather wet mixture. Add the garlic, salt and black pepper to taste.
4   Line a 1.2 L /2¼ pt loaf tin with the bacon, reserving some bacon for the top of the mould. Spread half the minced liver mixture in the bottom of the mould, then tap the mould to fill any air pockets. Add the reserved whole chicken livers, cover these with the remaining minced liver mixture, and tap the mould again.
5   Top the mixture with the reserved slices of bacon and the remaining bay leaves. Cover the mould, place in a roasting tin which you have half filled with water, and bake for 1–1½ hours.
6   When cooked, drain the water from the tin and place a weight on top of the pâté while it is still in the roasting tin so that the excess liquid, which will pour over the edge of the mould, is caught in the tin. Allow to cool. When cold, coat the top of the pâté with a little melted lard. Refrigerate for 2–3 days.
7   Just before serving, remove the coating of lard and turn the terrine out onto a serving dish. Garnish the top with the halved orange slices, and the sides with watercress, orange segments and olives.

● For a more subtle flavour, line the mould with a mixture of bacon and pork fat. Ask your butcher to give you paper-thin strips of larding pork fat. Place the strips between 2 sheets of waxed paper and pound them as thinly as possible. Then alternate these with the strips of bacon when lining the mould.

 6 hours marinating, then 2–2½ hours
plus 2–3 days maturing

Italian chicken breasts with Parma ham

Serves 4
4 chicken breasts
25 g /1 oz butter
30 ml /2 tbls olive oil
salt and freshly ground black pepper
4 slices Parma ham
4 small tomatoes, blanched and skinned
60 ml /4 tbls freshly grated Parmesan cheese
sprigs of parsley, to garnish
For the marinade
60 ml /4 tbls olive oil
30 ml /2 tbls lemon juice
1 garlic clove, finely chopped
30 ml /2 tbls finely chopped onion
30 ml /2 tbls finely chopped fresh parsley
freshly ground black pepper

1   With a sharp knife, remove the bones and skin from each chicken breast. Discard the wing, if it is present. Place each breast between 2 sheets of cling film and beat with a meat bat or flatten with a rolling pin to approximately 20 × 18 cm /8 × 7 in.
2   In a bowl, combine the ingredients for the marinade, seasoning with freshly ground black pepper to taste. Beat with a fork until the mixture emulsifies.
3   Dip each chicken breast in the marinade and place in a flat dish. Pour over the remaining marinade, cover and leave for 4 hours.
4   Heat the grill without the grid to high.
5   Heat the butter and olive oil in a large frying-pan. Drain and pat each chicken breast dry with absorbent paper. Season each with a little salt and freshly ground black pepper. Sauté 2 at a time for 2 minutes each side, or until cooked, turning with a spatula.
6   Remove from the pan with a slotted spoon, drain on absorbent paper and arrange on a large ovenproof plate. Keep warm. Repeat with the remaining chicken breasts.
7   Cut the Parma ham to fit the sautéed chicken breasts and place a piece on top of each breast. Slice each tomato into 4 and arrange 4 overlapping slices over each piece of Parma ham.
8   Sprinkle with freshly grated Parmesan cheese and grill for 3 minutes, or until golden brown. Garnish with sprigs of parsley and serve immediately.

 30 minutes, 4 hours marinating,
then 30 minutes

Chicken liver risotto

Serves 4–6

175 g /6 oz chicken livers, sliced
100 g /4 oz butter
1½ large Spanish onions,
    finely chopped
350 g /12 oz medium-grain rice
90 ml /6 tbls dry white wine
1.2 L /2¼ pt chicken stock,
    home-made or from a cube
2.5 ml /½ tsp powdered saffron

50 g /2 oz prosciutto or other
    raw ham, coarsely shredded
salt and black pepper
175 g /6 oz button mushrooms,
    thinly sliced
15–30 ml /1–2 tbls finely
    chopped fresh parsley
flat-leaved parsley, to garnish
freshly grated Parmesan
    cheese, to serve

1   In a large, heavy saucepan melt 50 g /2 oz butter. Add half the onion and cook until soft and lightly golden, about 5 minutes.
2   Add the rice and cook over a moderately low heat for 2–3 minutes, stirring constantly with a wooden spoon. Moisten with the white wine and let it sizzle for 1–2 minutes.
3   In another saucepan, bring the chicken stock to the boil. Pour 600 ml /1 pt of stock over the rice, add the saffron and stir to blend. Simmer gently, uncovered, until most of the liquid has been absorbed. When the rice is moist but no longer wet, add another large ladleful of hot stock, stir to dislodge any rice stuck to the pan and simmer over a low heat until almost all the stock has been absorbed.
4   Meanwhile, melt the remaining butter in a medium-sized saucepan. Add the remaining onion and the prosciutto and sauté gently for 5 minutes. Add the chicken livers, season to taste with salt and freshly ground black pepper and cook over moderate heat for 1–2 minutes, turning the slices to brown them evenly, but leaving the centres pink. Remove the mixture from the pan with a slotted spoon and keep warm.
5   Add the mushrooms to the fat remaining in the pan and sauté over moderate heat for 2–3 minutes, until soft and golden. Keep warm.
6   Continue to add stock to the risotto, constantly stirring and scraping the bottom of the pan with a fork, taking care not to crush the grains. Stop adding stock when the rice is tender but not mushy. Total cooking time will be about 20–25 minutes.
7   Bring 150 ml /5 fl oz chicken stock to the boil again and add, with the reserved chicken liver mixture, to the mushrooms. Tip this mixture onto the cooked risotto, add the parsley and fold in.
8   To serve, mound the risotto on a heated serving dish, garnish with flat-leaved parsley, and serve immediately with a bowl of freshly grated Parmesan cheese.

 45 minutes

Arroz con pollo

Serves 4

1.6 kg /3½ lb roasting chicken
30 ml /2 tbls flour
7.5 ml /1½ tsp salt
1.5 ml /¼ tsp black peppercorns,
    cracked
2.5 ml /½ tsp dried thyme
30 ml /2 tbls olive oil
6 slices streaky bacon, chopped
2 Spanish onions, finely chopped
1 garlic clove, finely chopped

400 g /14 oz canned tomatoes
2 canned pimentos, drained
    and sliced
10 ml /2 tsp paprika
2.5 ml /½ tsp saffron
600 ml /1 pt boiling water
freshly ground black pepper,
    if needed
225 g /8 oz long-grain rice
100 g /4 oz frozen peas
30 ml /2 tbls chopped parsley

1   Bring the chicken to room temperature. Heat the oven to 180C / 350F /gas 4. Cut the chicken into 8 serving pieces.
2   Combine the flour, 2.5 ml /¼ tsp salt, cracked black peppercorns and dried thyme in a shallow dish. Toss the chicken pieces in this seasoned flour.
3   Heat the olive oil in a large flameproof casserole over a medium heat. Add the chopped bacon and sauté for about 5 minutes, until crisp. Remove the bacon with a slotted spoon and drain on absorbent paper. Reserve the bacon.
4   Sauté the seasoned chicken pieces on all sides in the remaining fat until the chicken is a light golden brown. Remove the chicken pieces from the casserole and reserve.
5   Add the finely chopped onions and garlic to the casserole and sauté over a moderate heat, stirring occasionally for 3–5 minutes, or until the vegetables are soft.
6   Remove any excess oil from the casserole. Place the chicken pieces on top of the vegetables and add the canned tomatoes with their juices, pimentos, paprika, saffron, 5 ml /1 tsp salt and the boiling water. Raise the heat and bring to the boil. Skim the froth from the top of the liquid, add the rice and the cooked bacon and stir well to mix. Cover the casserole and cook in the oven for about 35–40 minutes. Add a little more hot water if it seems dry.
7   Add the peas to the casserole and cook for a further 10 minutes, or until the chicken is tender. Season with pepper if wished, sprinkle with chopped parsley and serve immediately.

● A highly flavoured casserole from Spain, *arroz con pollo* combines chicken and rice with aromatics and spices.

bringing to room temperature,
then 1 hour 10 minutes

Duck, Goose & Guinea Fowl

ROASTING DUCK, GOOSE, GUINEA FOWL

Duck is prized for its pronounced flavour and succulence, but these are only achieved when duck is roasted properly. Roast goose or guinea fowl are also ideal for special occasions.

Duck, goose and guinea fowl, crisp and golden and roasted to perfection, make a refreshing change from chicken and turkey.

Duck

The duck is a web-footed water bird with dark succulent flesh. It has a strong flavour which varies according to what the bird has been fed. Domestic ducks have more meat and a less gamey flavour than wild ducks.

Ducks are available all the year, being at their best in spring. Ducklings until 7-8 weeks, the birds reach their prime at 9-12 weeks, when they weigh 2.3–3.2 kg /5–7 lb. A good duck for roasting is young, with a plump breast and well-rounded legs, but it should not be over-fattened.

Ducks are sold as either 'New York dressed' or 'oven-ready'.

New York dressed ducks are those seen hanging in butcher's shops with the head and feet attached. The selling weight of the bird includes the head and feet as well as the innards. The butcher will prepare your purchase after selection.

Oven-ready birds are cleaned, plucked and trussed, ready for the oven. Buy them, fresh or frozen, from butchers and supermarkets. Giblets may or may not be included. For thawing times see *page 105*.

Because duck contains a relatively high proportion of bone and fat to meat you will need a 2–2.3 kg /4–5 lb duck (dressed weight) to serve four people comfortably.

Preparing: make sure the duck is at room temperature. Remove the giblets, if there are any. If the duck has not been fully prepared by the butcher, pass it over a low gas flame to singe any visible small hairs. Then, using a pair of kitchen tweezers (or the point of a small knife and your thumb) remove any remaining pin feathers. Cut off the feet and the wings at the first joint.

Wash the duck, inside and out, and dry it with a clean cloth. Cut all visible fat from the openings of the duck before cooking.

Rub it generously, inside and out, with salt and freshly ground black pepper. Using a roasting fork or skewer, prick the skin all over to encourage the fat to run out during roasting. If you are using a stuffing, pack it into the duck through the vent or tail end. Truss the bird (see below).

Roast the duck on a rack in a roasting tin at 180C /350F /gas 4 (see chart on *page 106* for roasting times or follow individual recipes). Prick the skin every 30 minutes to release any melted fat. You will need to pour off the excess fat which accumulates.

To test that the duck is cooked, push a skewer through the thickest part of the leg, nearest the breast: the juices should run clear.

Goose

Geese are larger than ducks, but the proportion of bone to meat is even higher. Geese are also very fatty, with creamy white flesh which becomes light brown when cooked and has a faintly gamey flavour.

Goose is not seasonal, though it is best from December to March. A young goose has more tender flesh, and is recognized by its soft yellow feet and yellow bill. The fat should be yellow and the flesh pinkish.

Geese are sold, like ducks, either as New York dressed birds or oven-ready. Allow 700 g /1½ lb per serving.

Frozen: this is the cheapest way of buying a goose: it will cost only about half as much as a fresh one, though the quality may not be as high. Frozen birds must be totally thawed before cooking (see *page 105*).

Preparing: bring the bird to room temperature. Using tweezers or the point of a knife and your thumb, remove any pin feathers. Cut off the wing tips and feet at the first joint. Wash and dry and season the goose, inside and out, with salt and pepper. If using a stuffing, pack it in through the vent end. Remove any pieces of fat from around the vent, then, with the breast side up, pass a skewer through one wing, through the neck flap, then through the other wing. Prick the fatty parts with a fork.

Roasting: because goose is so fatty it requires a special initial cooking process to melt out excess fat and leave the meat juicy and tender. Cook the goose at 200C /400F / gas 6 for at least 45 minutes, pouring off the melted fat every 15 minutes, then either continue cooking at that temperature or reduce the heat to 170C /325F /gas 3 and roast until cooked. The thigh joint will move easily in its socket when the goose is cooked through.

Tip out the excess fat from the pan, strain it into jars, allow to cool, then refrigerate. It can be kept for several weeks in the refrigerator and makes a flavourful dripping for other dishes.

Guinea fowl

Guinea fowl are not seasonal, but are at their best from spring to early summer.

When choosing a guinea fowl, look out for a plump breast and smooth-skinned feet. An average-sized guinea fowl will serve two people. Guinea fowl are also available as New York dressed or oven-ready birds.

Guinea fowl are hung for several days, so that their flesh has a slight gameyness reminiscent of pheasant. When buying guinea fowl, tell the butcher when you intend to cook the bird, and ask for one that has been hung the appropriate length of time.

Prepare guinea fowl in the same way as chicken (*page 8*) and bring to room temperature before roasting.

Roasting: use plenty of fat when roasting guinea fowl or it will be dry. The best way is to bard the lean breast with slices of fat, unsmoked bacon or fat salt pork. Roast at 220C /425F /gas 7. See *page 106* or individual recipes for roasting times.

To test that the guinea fowl is cooked, push a skewer through the thickest part of the leg, nearest the breast: the juices should run clear.

Trussing a duck

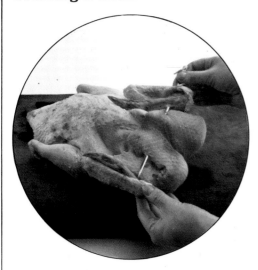

Lay the duck on its breast. Draw the neck skin over the back. Press the wings close to the body and insert a skewer through one wing, through the flap of the neck skin and out through the other wing.

Turn the duck onto its back and tie the legs together securely with fine string. Draw the string under the parson's nose and tie it tightly. The duck should be pricked all over with a skewer or fork before roasting.

Roast duckling with green pea sauce

Carving a goose or large duck

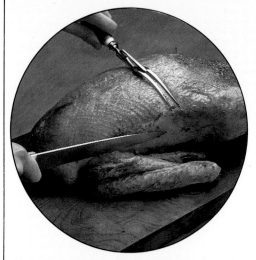

Carve one side before starting on the other side. With the bird placed breast uppermost, neck end facing you, ease a wing away from the body to locate the ball and socket joint. With a heavy knife, cut down through the joint and tough tendons. Lift the wing away.

Cut through a circle of skin around the leg and ease the thigh away from the body to expose the ball and socket joint. With a heavy knife, cut down firmly through the joint. Divide the leg into thigh and drumstick but do not slice.

With a long, thin, flexible knife, working from the neck and cutting to the shape of the breastbone, carve large, thin slices. Lift the slices away between the carving knife and fork to avoid piercing the meat. Carve the second side and serve.

Portioning medium-sized birds

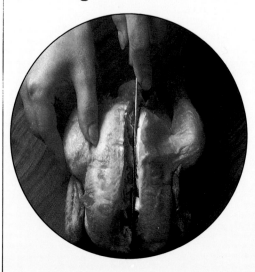

A small guinea fowl is simply divided in half to make two portions. Ducks are often halved again to make four portions from one duck.

To halve a small bird, position the bird, breast uppermost, on a wooden board. Using a heavy knife, cut firmly through the breastbone. Then, using a heavy knife, meat cleaver or game shears, cut firmly and cleanly through the backbone to make two portions.

To make four portions, halve as above then place each half flat on the wooden board. Insert, at an angle, a heavy, sharp knife between the leg and wing of one piece. Cut down firmly through the carcass to make two portions. Repeat this process with the other half.

Roast duckling with green pea sauce

bringing to room temperature, then 2–2½ hours

Serves 4

1.8 kg /4 lb duckling with giblets, completely defrosted if frozen
salt
25 g /1 oz flour
5 ml /1 tsp lemon juice
a large pinch of freshly grated nutmeg
200 g /7 oz shelled or frozen peas
a few outside leaves of lettuce, finely shredded
bouquet garni
fresh mint, for the sauce and garnish
15 ml /1 tbls thick cream
freshly ground black pepper

1 Bring the duckling to room temperature. Heat the oven to 180C /350F /gas 4. Put the giblets and 500 ml /18 fl oz water in a saucepan over medium-low heat and simmer for 45 minutes, remove from the heat, strain and reserve the stock – there should be about 400 ml /14 fl oz.
2 Meanwhile, begin roasting the duckling: prick the skin all over with a fork and rub the bird, inside and out, with salt. Place the duckling on a rack or trivet in a roasting tin and cook in the oven for 1½–2 hours, or until the skin is crisp and golden and the juices run quite clear when the thigh is pierced with the point of a sharp knife.
3 While the duck is roasting, prepare the sauce. Put 30 ml /2 tbls of the dripping and juices from the duckling into a saucepan and stir in the flour. Cook over gentle heat for 1 minute, then gradually add the reserved stock, lemon juice and nutmeg. Bring to the boil, stirring constantly, then add the peas,

lettuce, bouquet garni and a sprig of mint and bring back to the boil. Reduce the heat and simmer, stirring occasionally, for about 20 minutes, or until the peas and lettuce are quite tender.
4 Discard the bouquet garni and mint and blend the mixture to a purée or pass it through a sieve. Return the sauce to the rinsed-out pan. Stir in the cream, reheat and season to taste with salt and pepper. Garnish the duck with sprigs of mint and serve at once, handing the sauce round separately.

● If using a larger duck, increase the roasting time by 45 minutes per kg /20 minutes per lb.
● The perfect accompaniment to this dish would be tiny new potatoes, scrubbed and boiled with a sprig of mint in lightly salted water until just tender. Serve the duckling with a salad of lettuce hearts simply dressed with oil and lemon juice.

Plum-glazed duck

⏲ bringing to room temperature,
then 1 hour

Serves 4

1.8 kg /4 lb duck, dressed weight
olive oil
salt and freshly ground black pepper
½ Spanish onion, finely chopped
20 g /¾ oz butter
275 g /10 oz canned purple plums, stoned,
*   with juice reserved*
37.5 ml /2½ tbls soft light brown sugar
45 ml /3 tbls tomato ketchup
30 ml /2 tbls soy sauce
30 ml /2 tbls lemon juice
2.5 ml /½ tsp ground ginger
5 ml /1 tsp Dijon mustard
2.5 ml /½ tsp Worcestershire sauce
a few drops of Tabasco sauce

1 Bring the duck to room temperature. Heat the oven to 180C /350F /gas 4.
2 Joint the duck into quarters and cut away any excess fat. Prick the skin with a fork, rub with a little olive oil and season generously with salt and black pepper.
3 Place the duck portions in a roasting tin and roast for 45 minutes or until cooked.
4 Meanwhile, sauté the chopped onion in the butter over a moderate heat until soft.
5 In a blender combine the stoned plums, their juices, and the rest of the ingredients. Blend until smooth, then transfer the sauce to a saucepan and simmer gently for 20 minutes, stirring occasionally.
6 When the duck is cooked, brush with some of the sauce. Return it to the oven for a further 15 minutes or until it is glazed. Meanwhile, reheat the remaining sauce.
7 Transfer the cooked duck to a heated serving dish. Pour the sauce over the duck and serve at once.

Roast duck with beer

⏲ bringing to room temperature,
2½–2¾ hours, then 10 minutes or cooling

Serves 4

2–2.3 kg /4½–5 lb duck, dressed weight
salt and freshly ground black pepper
100 g /4 oz butter
30 ml /2 tbls olive oil
1 Spanish onion, finely chopped
1 garlic clove, finely chopped
2 celery stalks, trimmed and sliced
6 large slices crustless white bread, cubed
225 g /8 oz pork sausage-meat
2.5 ml /½ tsp crushed dried thyme
2.5 ml /½ tsp crushed dried rosemary
1 medium-sized cooking apple, peeled, cored
*   and diced*

For the basting sauce
600 ml /1 pt lager
50 g /2 oz soft light brown sugar
1.5 ml /¼ tsp ground cloves
15–30 ml /1–2 tbls soy sauce
15 ml /1 tbls lemon juice
5 ml /1 tsp dry mustard

For the beurre manié *(optional)*
15 ml /1 tbls flour
15 g /½ oz butter

1 Rinse the duck in warm water, and pat dry. Season inside and out with salt and black pepper. Prick the skin.
2 Melt 25 g /1 oz of the butter with the olive oil in a heavy-based frying-pan over a medium heat and sauté the finely chopped onion and garlic until transparent. Add the sliced celery and continue cooking until the vegetables begin to colour. Remove the vegetables with a slotted spoon and reserve.
3 Add another 25 g /1 oz of the butter to the pan. When it is foaming, add the cubes of bread and fry until golden on all sides.
4 In a large bowl, combine the sautéed vegetables and fried bread cubes with the sausage-meat, herbs and diced apple.
5 Heat the oven to 180C /350F /gas 4. Loosely pack the sausage-meat mixture into the duck through the tail end. Using a trussing needle and thread, sew up the neck.
6 Truss the duck. Melt the remaining 50 g /2 oz butter in a roasting tin over a low heat. Sauté the duck, turning it, until crisp and golden brown on all sides. Place the duck on a rack in the roasting tin.
7 Prepare the basting sauce. In a medium-sized, heavy-based saucepan, combine the lager with the soft brown sugar, ground cloves, soy sauce, lemon juice and dry mustard. Stir over a moderate heat until the sugar has dissolved, then strain the sauce over the duck.
8 Roast the duck in the oven for 1¾–2 hours until cooked, pricking the skin and basting every 30 minutes. To test that the duck is cooked, push a skewer through the thickest part of the leg, nearest the breast: the juices should run clear.
9 If serving the duck hot, remove the trussing skewer and string and the threads from the cooked duck and transfer the duck to a heated serving dish. Skim off the fat from the roasting tin. Stir the juices over a moderate heat, scraping the bits from the sides of the tin into the juices.
10 Mash together the flour and butter to make a beurre manié. Add this in pieces to the simmering juices, stirring. Bring to the boil and simmer for 3–4 minutes. Correct the seasoning, and pour into a heated sauceboat. Serve the duck immediately.
11 If serving the duck cold, skim off the fat from the juices in the roasting tin. Leave the duck on the rack and, as it cools, baste it frequently with the skimmed juices to build up a rich brown glaze.

Roast duck with beer

Roast duck with spiced Guinness gravy

⏸ bringing to room temperature, then 2 hours

Serves 4
1.8 kg /4 lb duck, dressed weight, giblets and
*   liver reserved*
salt
freshly ground black pepper
2 medium-sized oranges
1 large onion
50 g /2 oz butter
1 bay leaf
5 ml /1 tsp clear honey
orange slices, to garnish
For the basting sauce
225 ml /8 fl oz Guinness
5 ml /1 tsp Dijon mustard
3 cloves
15 ml /1 tbls brown sugar
25 mm /1 in piece cinnamon stick

1   Bring the duck to room temperature, then season the outside with salt and freshly ground black pepper, and prick the skin all over with a fork.
2   Heat the oven to 180C /350F /gas 4.
3   Cut the oranges in half and the onion into quarters. Stuff these inside the duck (this is to flavour the bird, not a stuffing to eat) then truss it. Melt the butter in a deep roasting tin over a medium heat and turn the duck in the butter until it is crisp and golden all over, about 10 minutes.
4   Remove the duck from the tin, season again outside with salt and freshly ground black pepper and place it on a rack in the roasting tin.
5   Combine the Guinness, mustard, cloves, sugar and cinnamon stick in a jug and pour over the duck. Put into the oven and roast for 1¼ hours, basting with the Guinness mixture and pricking the skin with a fork every 20 minutes.
6   Meanwhile, rinse the giblets and duck liver carefully, making sure there are no yellowish traces on the liver. Put in a small saucepan with the bay leaf and water to cover, bring to the boil and simmer gently for 5–7 minutes. Drain, chop the giblet meat and liver and reserve.
7   Remove the duck from the oven, take off the trussings and remove and discard the pieces of orange and onion from inside the duck. Keep the duck warm while you finish the gravy.
8   Pour off all the fat and discard the cloves and cinnamon. Add the honey, reserved chopped giblets and liver and 125 ml /4 fl oz water. Put the roasting tin over a medium heat and bring to the boil, stirring in all the crusty bits from the sides and bottom of the tin. Boil for 2–3 minutes, then pour 60 ml /4 tbls gravy over the duck. Garnish the duck with orange slices and serve immediately, with the rest of the gravy handed round separately in a sauce-boat.

Orange-glazed duck with pineapple

Orange-glazed duck with pineapple

In this recipe a duck is cut into portions, given a curry-flavour coating, then roasted until tender and served with slices of juicy caramelized pineapple.

⏸ bringing to room temperature, then 45 minutes

Serves 4
1.8 kg /4 lb duck, dressed weight
45 ml /3 tbls flour
10 ml /2 tsp curry powder
2.5 ml /½ tsp salt
freshly ground black pepper
a pinch of cayenne pepper
45–60 ml /3–4 tbls olive oil
425 ml /15 fl oz chicken stock, home-made
*   or from a cube*
juice and grated zest of 2 oranges
30 ml /2 tbls cognac
16 small white onions, peeled
8 slices canned pineapple, drained
40 g /1½ oz butter
15 ml /1 tbls Demerara sugar
15 ml /1 tbls cornflour
To garnish
sprigs of fresh watercress
4–6 clusters white grapes
4–6 thin unpeeled orange slices formed into
*   twists*

1   Bring the duck to room temperature. Heat the oven to 200C /400F /gas 6.
2   Cut the duck into 4 serving pieces, removing the backbone. Combine the flour, 5 ml /1 tsp of the curry powder, salt, freshly ground black pepper and cayenne pepper in a flat dish. Coat the duck portions with the flour mixture and sauté in the olive oil in a frying-pan for 2 minutes on each side or until golden.
3   Transfer the duck portions to a roasting tin. Place in the oven and roast for 40–45 minutes or until done. To test that the duck is cooked, push a skewer through the thickest part of the leg: the juices should run clear.
4   Make the sauce while the duck is cooking. Put the chicken stock, grated orange zest, remaining curry powder and the cognac in a saucepan. Bring to the boil, add the small white onions and simmer for 10–15 minutes or until the onions are tender but still firm.
5   In a frying-pan sauté the pineapple slices in butter until lightly brown on each side. Sprinkle with Demerara sugar and continue to cook to caramelize the sugar.
6   Remove the duck from the oven and transfer the portions to a heated serving dish. Arrange the caramelized pineapple slices on either side. Keep warm.
7   Blend the cornflour with the orange juice, add to the sauce and bring to the boil. Cook the sauce for 2 minutes or until it is thickened. Spoon the sauce over the duck and garnish with sprigs of watercress, 4–6 clusters of white grapes and 4–6 thin, unpeeled orange slices formed into twists. Serve immediately.

Roast duck stuffed with apricots

⏸ bringing to room temperature, then 2¼–2½ hours

Serves 4
2.3 kg /5 lb duck, dressed weight
salt and freshly ground black pepper
150 ml /5 fl oz canned
*   beef consommé*
For the stuffing
60 ml /4 tbls olive oil
2 slices lean bacon, chopped
1 Spanish onion, chopped
350 g /12 oz crustless white bread, cut into
*   cubes*
225 g /8 oz dried apricots, chopped
a large pinch of grated nutmeg
50 g /2 oz butter, melted
1 medium-sized egg, beaten
salt
freshly ground black pepper
For the honey glaze
30 ml /2 tbls thin honey
15 ml /1 tbls soy sauce or liquid gravy
*   browning*
For the sauce
90 ml /6 tbls port or orange juice
10 ml /2 tsp cornflour

1   Bring the duck to room temperature, then sprinkle the body and cavity liberally with salt and freshly ground black pepper. Heat the oven to 170C /325F /gas 3.
2   Make the stuffing. Heat half the oil in a frying-pan, add the bacon and onion and sauté until the onion is transparent. Using a slotted spoon, transfer to a large bowl. Add the remaining oil to the pan and sauté the bread cubes until golden. Add to the bacon mixture with the apricots and nutmeg, stirring well. Beat together the melted butter and egg and stir into the stuffing mixture with salt and pepper to taste. Leave to cool.
3   Loosely pack the stuffing into the neck and body cavity of the duck through the tail end. Fold the neck skin over the opening and secure to the back with a skewer. Truss the duck and lightly prick the skin all over with a fork to encourage the fat to run out.
4   Place the duck on a rack in a roasting tin and pour over the beef consommé. Roast for 1½ hours, frequently pouring off excess fat.
5   Make the honey glaze: in a bowl, blend together the honey, soy sauce or gravy browning and 15 ml /1 tbls of the pan juices. Increase the oven temperature to 200C / 400F /gas 6 and brush the duck with the honey glaze. Roast for a further 15–30 minutes, basting the duck occasionally, until the juices run clear when the duck is pierced. Remove the trussings from the cooked duck, transfer to a heated serving dish and keep warm.
6   Pour off all but 150 ml /5 fl oz of the drippings in the roasting tin. Stir the port or orange juice into the reserved juices. Blend the cornflour with 60 ml /4 tbls water and stir into the sauce. Bring the sauce to the boil, reduce the heat and simmer, stirring, until thickened; strain, pour over the duck and serve at once.

Roast goose with apple stuffing

🍴 bringing to room temperature, then 3¼ hours

Serves 6
3.6 kg /8 lb goose, dressed weight
salt and freshly ground black pepper
275 ml /10 fl oz chicken stock, home-made or from a cube
beurre manié made from 15 g /½ oz butter and 15 ml /1 tbls flour
celery curls and leaves, to garnish
For the stuffing
100 g /4 oz bacon, chopped
50 g /2 oz butter
4 medium-sized onions, chopped
4 celery stalks, chopped
8 cooking apples, peeled and sliced
175 g /6 oz fresh white breadcrumbs
90 ml /6 tbls freshly chopped parsley
sugar
salt and freshly ground black pepper

1   Bring the goose to room temperature. Heat the oven to 200C /400F /gas 6. To make the stuffing, fry the bacon in the butter in a frying-pan for 2–3 minutes until golden brown, then remove it from the pan with a slotted spoon. Sauté the onion and celery in the pan until soft, then remove them with a slotted spoon.
2   Add the apple to the pan and fry for 2–3 minutes or until soft. Add to the bacon, onion and celery, along with the breadcrumbs, parsley, sugar, salt and freshly ground black pepper to taste. Let cool.
3   Place the cooled stuffing inside the goose, not packed too tightly and with the majority of it at the neck end. Pass a skewer through one wing, then through the body and out through the other wing. Prick the fatty parts of the goose and sprinkle with salt and freshly ground black pepper.
4   Put the goose in a baking tin on a rack and cook for 2½–2¾ hours, basting frequently. From time to time, drain off the fat that collects in the baking tin. If the breast of the goose begins to brown too quickly, cover with a buttered paper.
5   When the goose is cooked remove it from the tin and keep warm. Drain off excess fat from the tin, place it over a moderate heat and add the stock. Bring to the boil, stirring, then lower the heat. Blend the butter and flour to make a *beurre manié* and add it, in tiny pieces, to the liquid, stirring until the gravy thickens. Season to taste and strain into a heated sauce-boat. Garnish the goose with celery curls and leaves and serve at once, with the gravy.

Calvados goose

🕐🍴 overnight soaking, 1½ hours, then 1½–2¼ hours roasting

Serves 4–6
2.7–4 kg /6–9 lb goose, dressed weight
175 g /6 oz prunes
100 g /4 oz sultanas or seedless raisins
150 ml /5 fl oz port
3 slices back bacon, rinds removed
37.5 ml /2½ tbls olive oil
65 g /2½ oz butter
1 Spanish onion, finely chopped
2 celery stalks, sliced
125 g /4 oz stale white bread, cut into 10 mm /½ in cubes
350 g /12 oz sausage-meat
1 goose liver, chopped
2 small cooking apples, peeled, cored and diced
1 egg, beaten
15 ml /1 tbls finely chopped fresh parsley
2.5 ml /½ tsp dried thyme
salt and freshly ground black pepper
60–90 ml /4–6 tbls calvados or cognac
60–75 ml /4–5 tbls dry white breadcrumbs
275 ml /10 fl oz hot chicken stock (preferably made from giblets)
beurre manié made from 15 g /½ oz butter and 15 ml /1 tbls flour

Roast goose with apple stuffing

1   The night before you intend to cook the goose, place the prunes in a bowl and cover them with cold water. Put the sultanas or seedless raisins in a separate bowl and pour in the port. Soak them overnight.
2   Bring the goose to room temperature. Heat the oven to 200C /400F /gas 6. Cut off the goose's wing tips and feet at the first joint. Remove any pieces of fat from around the vent, then, with the breast side up, pass a skewer through one wing, through the neck flap, then through the other wing.
3   Prick the fatty parts of the goose with a fork, place the bird on a rack set over a roasting tin and cook in the oven for 15 minutes, or until the fat begins to run. Remove the goose from the oven and tip the fat from the body cavity into a dish. Return to the oven for a further 30–45 minutes and carry out this draining process 2 or 3 more times, then remove the goose from the oven, pour off the fat and leave to cool while you make the stuffing. Reduce the oven temperature to 170C/325F /gas 3.
4   To make the stuffing, drain and stone the soaked prunes. Fry the bacon slices in 7.5 ml /½ tbls oil until they are crisp and dark golden. Remove the bacon slices from the pan and crumble them into a large bowl.
5   Add 15 ml /1 tbls of the oil and 15 g /½

oz butter to the fat remaining in the frying-pan. Add the finely chopped onion and sauté over a moderate heat for 6–8 minutes, or until soft, stirring frequently. Remove the onion from the pan with a slotted spoon and add to the bacon.
6   Add the remaining olive oil to the frying-pan, add the sliced celery and sauté for 5 minutes, until the celery is slightly softened. Remove the celery from the pan with a slotted spoon and add it to the bacon and onion mixture.
7   Add the remaining butter to the frying-pan and heat until frothy. Add the bread cubes, and toss over a medium heat until they have absorbed all the fat and are crisp. Add to the bowl.
8   Add the sausage-meat to the frying-pan and sauté for 10–12 minutes, stirring and crumbling it with a fork, until it is lightly and evenly browned. Add the sausage-meat to the bowl of stuffing ingredients.
9   Place the sultanas or raisins, the port and prunes in the frying-pan. Bring slowly to the boil, stirring and scraping the base and sides of the frying-pan with a wooden spoon to dislodge any crusty bits. Add the contents of the pan to the bowl of stuffing.
10 Add the chopped goose liver, diced apple, beaten egg, finely chopped parsley and dried thyme to the bowl and mix until the ingredients are thoroughly blended. Season to taste with salt and freshly ground black pepper.
11 Generously season the goose, inside and out, with salt and freshly ground black pepper. Stuff the goose through the vent end, then sew up the vent securely and tie the legs together. If you have any stuffing left over, put it in a buttered ovenproof dish, cover the dish with foil and plan to put it in the oven with the goose for the last 30–45 minutes cooking time.
12 Place the stuffed goose, breast side up, on a rack set over a roasting tin and roast for 1¼–2 hours, depending on the size of the bird. Prick the bird occasionally during the cooking time to release the excess fat, and turn the bird over halfway through the cooking time. Ten to fifteen minutes before the goose is cooked, turn it breast side up on the rack. Heat the calvados or cognac in a small pan, set it alight with a taper and pour the burning liquid over the goose. Sprinkle the breadcrumbs over the goose, then roast for a further 10–15 minutes.
13 When the goose is cooked (the thigh joint will move easily in its socket) remove it from the oven. Lift the goose onto a heated serving dish and keep warm.
14 Make the gravy: skim the excess fat from the roasting tin, place the tin over a moderate heat and add the stock. Bring to the boil, stirring and scraping the base and sides of the tin with a wooden spoon to dislodge any crusty bits.
15 Blend the butter with the flour to make a *beurre manié*. Add this to the simmering liquid in tiny pieces, then continue to simmer, stirring constantly, until the gravy has thickened. Season to taste with salt and freshly ground black pepper, skim any excess fat from the surface and strain into a heated sauce-boat. Serve the gravy immediately, with the roast goose.

Guinea fowl with pine nuts

bringing to room temperature, then 1¾ hours

Serves 2
1 kg /2 lb 3 oz guinea fowl
salt
freshly ground black pepper
100 g /4 oz chicken livers
75–100 g /3–4 oz butter
1 medium-sized onion, chopped
25 g /1 oz pine nuts
75 g /3 oz long-grain rice
15 ml /1 tbls chopped fresh mint
50 g /2 oz butter, softened
4 slices streaky bacon
90 ml /6 tbls red wine
black grapes, to garnish
sprigs of mint, to garnish

1   Bring the guinea fowl to room temperature, then season it, inside and out, with salt and freshly ground black pepper.
2   Rinse the chicken livers, cutting out and discarding any yellowish parts. Melt 75 g /3 oz butter in a large frying-pan over medium-high heat. Sauté the chopped onion until soft and golden, about 10–15 minutes.
3   Remove the onion with a slotted spoon and place in a large bowl. Add the pine nuts to the pan and sauté for 3–4 minutes. Remove from the pan and add to the bowl. Put the chicken livers into the pan and sauté for 2–3 minutes – they should be pink in the middle but not raw. Remove from the pan, chop coarsely and add to the bowl.
4   Add the rice to the pan, with another 25 g /1 oz butter if necessary, and sauté for 2 minutes, stirring constantly to coat all the grains. Pour in 75 ml /3 fl oz water, bring to the boil, then turn down the heat and simmer until all the water has been absorbed, about 7–8 minutes.
5   Heat the oven to 220C /425F /gas 7. Tip the rice into the bowl, add the chopped mint, season with salt and freshly ground black pepper and mix everything well. Let the stuffing cool.
6   Put the stuffing into the cavity of the guinea fowl, pushing in well. Coat the breast of the bird with the softened butter and cover with the bacon slices. Fix them with skewers and tie the legs.
7   Place the bird in a roasting tin and roast for 35 minutes, basting every 10 minutes.
8   Remove the bacon slices and reserve. Roast the guinea fowl for a further 10 minutes to brown the breast. Take out of the oven, place on a heated serving platter and keep warm.
9   Skim off any excess fat from the roasting tin; place the tin on top of the stove over medium heat. Crumble the reserved bacon slices into the pan, add about 150–175 ml / 5–6 fl oz water and the wine, and bring to the boil. Boil for 3–4 minutes until the gravy is slightly reduced. Pour into a warmed sauce-boat. Garnish the guinea fowl with the black grapes and the sprigs of mint and serve at once, with the gravy handed round separately.

GRILLING DUCK & GUINEA FOWL

Duck and guinea fowl, marinated in herbs and spices or given a delicious coating, are simple to grill, but are elegant enough for even the most special dinner party dish.

Duck grills to perfection: its fatty skin and rich, tasty flesh give a crisp and crusty outside and a pink and succulent centre. Guinea fowl, spatchcocked (opened out flat and held in place with skewers) can be grilled and served with Maitre d'hotel butter for a really special dish.

Choosing duck and guinea fowl
The only part of duck which is suitable for grilling is the breast, which gives a good portion of tender meat. The legs and wings tend to burn before they are cooked through. If you buy a whole duck, remove the breasts from the carcass – without any bone – and use the rest of the meat left on the bird for a duck terrine or pie.

Whole guinea fowl can be spatchcocked and grilled: split the bird down the backbone, remove the backbone and open the bird out. A skewer through the legs holds it flat during cooking and another through the wings keeps them close to the body.

Preparing for grilling
Remember to remove the bird from the refrigerator well before you intend to cook it, to allow it to come to room temperature. Wipe it dry with absorbent paper and season with freshly ground black pepper before leaving it to stand. Just before cooking, season with salt and a little more pepper, if wished, and brush with oil and melted butter to keep it moist.

Alternatively, give the meat extra flavour by marinating it for at least 4 hours in a marinade of olive oil, wine or fruit juice and herbs or spices. Sliced onion, carrot or shallots can be added to give extra flavour. Don't marinate in the refrigerator unless it has to be for a long time, or if it is a particularly hot day and, even then, try to remove it from the refrigerator in time to bring the meat to room temperature.

How to grill duck and guinea fowl
Heat the grill to maximum before starting to cook, but remove the grid from the grill pan so that the grid itself doesn't get hot. When you are ready to cook, brush the grid with a little oil to prevent the meat from sticking to it.

Arrange the bird on the grid with the side that will be served uppermost on top. This usually means skin side upward. This is because the side grilled first always has the better appearance.

A duck breast is at its best if it is crisp and brown on the outside but still pink in the middle. This comes as a shock to people who think duck should be well cooked all the way through. But try it this way and you will be pleasantly surprised. You can, of course, cook it a little longer if you prefer, until the juices run clear, but avoid prolonged cooking as this will invariably toughen the meat.

Guinea fowl also becomes tough and dry if overcooked. To test when it is cooked, insert a skewer or knife in the thickest part of the meat, nearest to the bone – the juices should run clear. If you overcook the guinea fowl the juices will cease to flow altogether.

Spatchcocked guinea fowl

66

Grilled duck breasts with soy and honey

⏱ 15 minutes, 4 hours marinating, then 20–25 minutes

Serves 4
4 boneless duck breasts without wings,
weighing 225 g /8 oz each
olive oil
For the soy-honey marinade
30 ml /2 tbls soy sauce
120 ml /8 tbls dry sherry
45 ml /3 tbls clear honey
45 ml /3 tbls oil
a little finely chopped root ginger
finely grated zest of 1 orange
½ Spanish onion, finely chopped
freshly ground black pepper
spring onions, to garnish

1 Wipe the duck breasts with absorbent paper. With a sharp knife make several parallel diagonal cuts through the skin and fat of each duck breast, then cut in the same way at a 45° angle to the first cuts, to make a diamond pattern.
2 In a shallow dish, combine the ingredients for the soy-honey marinade. Add the duck breasts and turn them to coat well. Cover and leave to marinate for 4 hours, turning the breasts from time to time.
3 Heat the grill without the grid to high.
4 Brush the grill grid with olive oil. Place the duck breasts on the grid, skin side up. Grill, with the grid 7.5 cm /3 in from the heat, for 15–20 minutes, turning once and brushing frequently with the marinade. The breasts should be crisp on the outside but still pink in the centre.
5 Transfer to a heated serving dish, garnish with spring onions and serve.

Spatchcocked guinea fowl

⏱ 30 minutes, 1 hour chilling, standing, making garnishes, then 30 minutes

Serves 4
2 × 700 g /1½ lb guinea fowl, dressed weight
salt and freshly ground black pepper
30 ml /2 tbls finely chopped parsley
30 ml /2 tbls finely chopped shallots
olive oil
30 ml /2 tbls melted butter
5 ml /1 tsp crushed juniper berries
watercress, to garnish
game chips or crisps, to serve
For the Maitre d'hotel butter
50 g /2 oz butter, softened
15 ml /1 tbls finely chopped parsley
15 ml /1 tbls lemon juice
salt and freshly ground black pepper

1 Make the Maitre d'hotel butter: cream the butter, parsley and lemon juice and season with salt and pepper. Roll into a sausage shape in greaseproof paper, chill.
2 Prepare the guinea fowl, one at a time, in the following way: using a sharp knife,

Grilled duck breasts with soy and honey

cut off the wing tips at the first joint. Cut down both sides of the backbone to remove the backbone without separating the 2 halves of the bird. Open the bird like a book. Slip out the breastbone, being careful not to snip through the skin. Cut down the breastbone, then open out really flat. Now cut the breastbone out completely, but leave the rib cage in place.
3 To spatchcock the bird, thread a skewer across the bird, leg to leg and wing to wing.
4 Season the guinea fowl with pepper and sprinkle with chopped parsley and shallots. Leave to come to room temperature. Heat the grill without the grid to high.
5 Brush the grill grid with olive oil and lay the birds, skin side up, on the grid. Brush with some of the melted butter and season generously with salt, pepper and crushed juniper berries. Grill, with the grid 12.5 cm / 5 in from the heat, for 15 minutes, turning once and brushing frequently with butter.
6 Remove one skewer from the guinea fowl to release the legs. Cover the breasts with foil and fold back the legs to allow the insides of the legs to be cooked for a further 5 minutes, or until done.
7 Remove the remaining skewer, then the rib bones from the guinea fowl. Place the birds on a heated serving dish. Cut the Maitre d'hotel butter into 4 and arrange on top of the guinea fowl with the watercress. Serve with game chips or crisps.

Grapefruit duck

⏱ 25 minutes, 4 hours marinating, then 20–25 minutes

Serves 4
4 boneless duck breasts without wings,
weighing 225 g /8 oz each
olive oil
2.5 ml /½ tsp cornflour mixed with 15 ml /1 tbls water
½ grapefruit, sliced
For the marinade
30 ml /2 tbls oil
juice of ½ grapefruit
1 garlic clove, crushed
2.5 ml /½ tsp ground allspice
2.5 ml /½ tsp salt
freshly ground black pepper
15 ml /1 tbls chopped fresh herbs
1 bay leaf

1 Wipe the duck breasts with absorbent paper, then make cuts through the skin and fat to make a diamond pattern.
2 In a shallow dish, combine the marinade ingredients. Add the duck and turn to coat well. Cover and leave to marinate for 4 hours, turning the breasts from time to time.
3 Heat the grill without the grid to high.
4 Brush the grill grid with olive oil. Place the duck on the grid, skin side up. Grill, with the grid 7.5 cm /3 in from the heat, for 15-20 minutes, turning once and brushing frequently with marinade, until crisp on the outside but still pink in the centre.
5 Meanwhile, begin making the sauce: cut 2 of the grapefruit slices into quarters and reserve. Peel and chop the remaining slices. Mix the remaining marinade with the cornflour and water and bring to the boil in a small saucepan, then simmer for 2 minutes. Stir in the chopped grapefruit.
6 Transfer the duck to a heated serving dish, pour over the sauce and garnish with the reserved grapefruit slices.

PAN FRYING DUCK & GUINEA FOWL

Succulent duck, cooked to perfection and elegantly presented, or guinea fowl combined with the flavours of the East: for elegant and unusual dishes pan frying is the cooking method to choose.

Pan frying is a simple but effective cooking method, and by using duck and guinea fowl you can create some sophisticated dishes.

Goose is not suitable for pan frying; it is much better reserved for a special-occasion roast. Both duck and duckling are delicious quartered and pan fried. There is very little meat on the legs of a duck, so the bird is best divided by halving it first, then dividing each half in two as evenly as possible, leaving a portion of the breast with each leg.

Guinea fowl, which weigh 1–1.4 kg /2–3 lb, can also be pan fried. One bird is usually halved or quartered to serve two people. As the flesh is inclined to be dry, you must be sure to sear the guinea fowl portions well on all sides initially, to keep the juices inside.

Pan frying duck and guinea fowl is the basis of some delicious *nouvelle cuisine* style dishes. This new style of cooking has emerged out of France and works on the adage 'make it simple'.

Gone are the heavy sauces and the rich seasoning. The emphasis is on the freshness and quality of the ingredients and on maintaining all the natural tastes. As in the Magrets de canard au cassis, duck breasts with blackcurrant sauce (see recipe), the meat is cooked until just done, preserving its full flavour and juiciness. Accompanying sauces are no longer designed to mask any of the flavours of the other ingredients, they are a light combination of pan juices, stock and wine, thickened by reduction and finished perhaps with cream or butter. Finally, the presentation of the dish is almost as important as the taste itself. The food is simply but artistically arranged to please the eye as much as the taste buds.

Nouvelle cuisine has its roots in the culinary traditions of many countries: of France itself, of Japan – masters of the art of presentation, and of China, which bases much of its cuisine on fast cooking and crisp textures.

In China, duck, especially smoked (see recipe), is a popular ingredient in stir-fry dishes, a delicious method of pan frying which combines small strips of meat with other ingredients.

Magrets de canard au cassis

 1¾ hours

Serves 4
*4 boneless duck breasts, about 150–175 g /
5–6 oz each*
salt
freshly ground black pepper
40–50 g /1½–2 oz butter
15 ml /1 tbls olive oil
2 tart dessert apples
60 ml /4 tbls blackcurrants
sprigs of watercress, to garnish
For the glaze
75 g /3 oz butter
¼ chicken stock cube
15 ml /1 tbls tomato purée
1 carrot, finely chopped
½ Spanish onion, finely chopped
150 ml /5 fl oz dry white wine
freshly ground black pepper
30 ml /2 tbls crème de cassis

1 Prepare the glaze: melt the butter in a saucepan, add the ¼ chicken stock cube and tomato purée with the finely chopped carrot and onion and sauté until the ingredients are well browned. Stir in 600 ml /1 pt water and the white wine and cook, skimming the surface of the sauce from time to time, until the liquid is reduced to half its original quantity.
2 Strain the sauce into a small saucepan, pressing the carrot and onion to extract all the juice. Continue to cook the sauce over a low heat until it is reduced to about 150 ml /

5 fl oz. Season with freshly ground black pepper, add the *crème de cassis* and keep warm over a low heat.

3 With a sharp knife, slash the skin on each duck breast diagonally at 5 mm /¼ in intervals in both directions to form a lattice pattern all over the skin.

4 Season the duck breasts with salt and freshly ground black pepper. Heat 15 g /½ oz butter and the oil in a large, heavy-based pan over a high heat. Sear the skin side of each breast for 30 seconds to brown, then remove from the pan and pour off the fat.

5 Return the breasts to the pan, skin side down, cover and cook over a low heat for 10–12 minutes, turning once during cooking. The duck should be slightly pink in the middle.

6 Remove the duck from the pan and, using a knife, or a kitchen towel to protect your hands, remove the skin.

7 Place the duck breasts in a shallow, flameproof serving dish or shallow casserole (an enamelled gratin dish is good for this).

8 Peel, quarter and core the apples and slice them thinly. Melt 25 g /1 oz of the butter in a small frying-pan, add the apple slices and sauté gently until golden brown, adding a little more butter if necessary. Make a new skin for each breast of duck by carefully covering it with overlapping slices of sautéed apple.

9 Place the serving dish over a medium heat to reheat the duck breasts; brush the apple slices with a little of the glaze. Add the blackcurrants to the remaining glaze and

Magrets de canard au cassis

pour it around the duck breasts in the serving dish. Garnish with sprigs of watercress and serve immediately.

Stir-fried duck with ginger and leeks

⏱ 25 minutes

Serves 2–3, or 5–6 as part of a larger meal
500 g /1 lb boned smoked or cold roast duck, cut into matchstick strips
20 ml /4 tsp salted black beans
60 ml /4 tbls oil
3 garlic cloves, roughly chopped
4 slices root ginger, cut into thin slivers
1 small red pepper, cut into matchstick strips
2 medium-sized leeks, cut into matchstick strips
30 ml /2 tbls lard
60 ml /4 tbls good stock
30 ml /2 tbls soy sauce
30 ml /2 tbls white wine vinegar
10 ml /2 tsp sugar
10 ml /2 tsp chilli sauce
boiled rice, to serve

1 Soak the black beans in water to cover for 10 minutes and drain.

2 Heat the oil in a wok or a large, heavy-based frying-pan over high heat. Add the beans, garlic, ginger, pepper and leeks; stir-fry for 2 minutes, then push to sides of pan.

3 Melt the lard in the centre of the wok or pan. Add the duck and all the other ingredients and stir-fry vigorously for 2 minutes. Bring the pepper and leek mixture back into the centre of the pan and stir-fry them with the duck mixture for 1½ minutes. Serve immediately with boiled rice.

Duck with black cherry sauce

⏱ 45 minutes

Serves 4
2.3 kg /5 lb duck, quartered
15 ml /1 tbls lemon juice
salt and freshly ground black pepper
15 g /½ oz butter
225 g /8 oz black cherries, stoned
50 g /2 oz blanched almonds
30 ml /2 tbls brandy
1 onion, sliced
1 bay leaf
125 ml /4 fl oz red wine
15 ml /1 tbls cornflour
30 ml /2 tbls cherry brandy

1 Blot the duck quarters with absorbent paper, then sprinkle them with lemon juice. Season generously with salt and pepper.

2 Heat the butter in a large, heavy-based frying-pan for which you have a close-fitting lid. When the foaming subsides, fry the duck, skin side down, turning the pieces with

with a fish slice or tongs, until they are browned on all sides. Remove the breast pieces and pour off any excess fat. Cook the legs for a further 5 minutes on their own and then return the breasts to the pan.

3 Cover the pan and cook the duck over a low heat for 25 minutes, turning once.

4 Meanwhile, stuff each stoned black cherry with a blanched almond.

5 Heat the brandy in a ladle. When the duck is tender ignite the brandy and pour over the duck in the pan. When the flames have subsided, remove the duck to a heated serving platter and keep warm.

6 Sauté the onion in the pan juices until transparent. Pour off any excess fat, then add the bay leaf and the red wine and boil rapidly for 2–3 minutes, to reduce slightly.

7 Blend the cornflour with the cherry brandy and stir into the wine sauce. Reduce the heat and simmer the sauce for 1–2 minutes until it thickens. Add the stuffed cherries to the pan and warm them through. Do not cook the cherries for too long, or they will discolour.

8 Discard the bay leaf, pour the sauce over the duck and serve.

Oriental pan-fried guinea fowl

⏱ 1 hour, then 35 minutes

Serves 4
2 guinea fowl, quartered
30 ml /2 tbls coriander seeds
5 ml /1 tsp black peppercorns
30 ml /2 tbls thick honey
30 ml /2 tbls soy sauce
salt and freshly ground black pepper
60 ml /4 tbls peanut oil
1 Spanish onion, finely chopped
425 ml /15 fl oz hot chicken stock, home-made or from a cube
1.5 ml /¼ tsp ground cinnamon
1.5 ml /¼ tsp ground cloves

1 Dry fry the coriander seeds for a few seconds in a frying-pan without any fat.

2 Pound the coriander seeds and black peppercorns in a mortar until powdered. Add the honey, soy sauce and salt to taste. Rub this mixture into the guinea fowl and leave for 1 hour to absorb the flavours.

3 Heat the oil in a large heavy-based frying-pan and sauté the onion until transparent. Remove with a slotted spoon and reserve. Increase the heat to high and sear the guinea fowl quarters on all sides. Reduce the heat slightly, return the onions to the pan and cook for 20–25 minutes, turning the guinea fowl once. Be careful not to overcook or they will become very tough.

4 Transfer the guinea fowl to a heated serving dish and keep warm. Add the hot chicken stock to the pan and stir to deglaze the pan. Boil over a high heat, until the stock has reduced by half.

5 Season the sauce with the ground cinnamon and cloves, and salt and freshly ground black pepper to taste. Pour the sauce over the guinea fowl and serve immediately.

CASSEROLING DUCK & GUINEA FOWL

Duck and guinea fowl make succulent casseroles which can be flavoured with a range of ingredients, from Oriental spices and coconut for a duck curry to truffles and pâté for the extra-special Guinea fowl à la Souvaroff.

Casseroling, pot-roasting and braising are ancient methods of cooking, left over from the days when there were few domestic ovens. The only alternative to the open spit was a covered pot on the fire. The difference between a casserole and a braise or pot-roast was in the quality of the meat used and the quantity of liquid added. For a casserole the bird would be cut up into portions and well covered with liquid; cooking might be for many hours, which meant that even a tough old bird would emerge tender. For a pot-roast or braise, the bird would often be left whole and just a small amount of liquid would be added, the bird cooking in its own juices for a comparatively short time.

Nowadays we may have more modern equipment but the principles are still the same and the results just as delicious.

Duck, though usually roasted, is also good casseroled, pot-roasted or braised. Bred for tenderness these days, and nearly always killed very young, they are invariably tender. Though they are a little fatty it is possible to deal with this by pricking the skin all over before you start cooking, and carefully removing all the excess fat that appears in the pan at the end.

The little guinea fowl is also a favourite of mine. Although farmyard bred these days, guinea fowl retain some of their 'gamey' flavour. Lean, small and tender, they are excellent birds for the pot.

Cooking the bird

First wipe the bird, which should be at room temperature, with a damp cloth and season it well with salt and pepper. If you are cooking the bird whole you can stuff it, then truss it to keep it neat.

Heat a little duck fat, olive oil, butter or a mixture in a flameproof casserole, just large enough for the bird to fit snugly. Brown on all sides, turning with two spoons – a fork would pierce the skin, allowing the precious juices to seep out and making the meat dry and tough.

Remove the browned bird from the casserole and sauté any flavouring vegetables in the remaining fat. If there is much fat left at the end of this process pour it off.

Return the bird to the casserole and add stock, wine, herbs, spices or other flavourings. Be sure the stock you add is very hot, as bringing the liquid to the boil from cold will extract flavour from the bird – making a lovely stock, but leaving the meat less tasty. Wine can be either at warm room temperature or gently heated. Cover the casserole tightly, using a luting paste of flour and water, if necessary, to seal the lid. Simmer it very gently on top of the stove or in the oven. The bird is cooked if the juices run clear when you pierce the inside of the thigh with a thin skewer or sharp knife.

Serving the bird

Although most casseroles make good oven-to-table ware, you need to dish up a pot-roasted or braised bird on a carving dish for serving. Take the cooked bird from the pot, draining the juices well from the cavity. Place it on a heated serving dish, remove the trussing strings and keep it hot while you finish the sauce.

Skim any fat from the sauce and, if necessary, reduce it over a high heat to concentrate the flavour. Thicken the sauce or not, according to the recipe, and serve it in a heated sauce-boat, spooning a little over the bird to glaze the breast, if you wish. Garnish simply with a few sprigs of watercress, some parsley or other fresh herbs, and carve the bird at the table.

Duck with figs

Duck breasts in piquant sauce

In the Gascony region of France, this would be made with the breasts of ducks specially fattened for their livers.

 1¼ hours

Serves 2
2 plump duck breasts, boned, with excess fat removed and reserved; skin well pricked
75 ml /3 fl oz armagnac
40 g /1½ oz flour
5 ml /1 tsp tomato purée
150 ml /5 fl oz dry white wine
100 ml /3½ fl oz hot chicken stock, home-made or from a cube
salt
100 ml /3½ fl oz thick cream
20 preserved green peppercorns, drained

1 Heat the oven to 180C /350F /gas 4. In a small saucepan, over a low heat, render the reserved duck fat to produce 30 ml /2 tbls liquid fat.
2 Transfer the fat to a heavy frying-pan and brown the breasts over medium heat, skin side first, for 4–5 minutes each side. Pour off the fat (the skin will make at least 15 ml /1 tbls extra fat) and reserve. Transfer the duck to an ovenproof serving dish.
3 Warm the armagnac in a ladle, ignite and pour over the breasts.
4 Return 45 ml /3 tbls of the reserved duck fat to the pan over medium heat. When sizzling, stir in the flour and allow it to colour well but not burn. Stir in the tomato purée, the wine and hot chicken stock and season to taste with salt. Simmer the mixture for 5 minutes.
5 Pour the sauce over the duck breasts, cover the dish tightly with foil, and cook in the oven for 25 minutes.
6 Remove the dish from the oven, add the thick cream and the preserved green peppercorns to the sauce and check the seasoning. Return the dish, uncovered, to the oven for a further 5–10 minutes for the sauce to heat through. Serve immediately, from the dish.

Guinea fowl with almond sauce

⏱ 1¼ hours

Serves 4
2 × 700 g /1½ lb guinea fowl
salt and freshly ground black pepper
5 ml /1 tsp dried marjoram
75 g /3 oz butter
8 streaky bacon slices
1 garlic clove, finely chopped
50 g /2 oz flaked almonds
15 ml /1 tbls dry sherry
225 ml /8 fl oz thick cream

1 Season the guinea fowl inside and out with salt, freshly ground black pepper and dried marjoram. Rub 15 g /½ oz butter over each bird and wrap 4 slices of bacon around each bird, tying them on with string.
2 In a large, heavy flameproof casserole, melt the remaining butter. Place the birds on their sides in the butter and cook, covered, over a low heat for 20 minutes.
3 Roll the birds onto the other side and

cook for another 20 minutes, basting.
4 Turn the birds on their backs and cook for a further 20 minutes, basting frequently, or until the juices run clear when the thickest parts of the legs are pierced by a skewer.
5 Remove the birds from the casserole and remove and discard the trussings and bacon. Place on a serving dish and keep warm.
6 Pour off all but 15 ml /1 tbls fat from the casserole. Add the garlic and flaked almonds and cook until the almonds are lightly browned. Stir in the sherry, thick cream and 60 ml /4 tbls water. Boil the sauce, stirring constantly, for 2–3 minutes or until thick and creamy. Season with salt and freshly ground black pepper. Pour a little sauce over the birds and serve, with the remaining sauce in a sauce-boat.

Duck with figs

⏱ 1 hour,
then 1½–2 hours cooking

Serves 4
1.8 kg /4 lb duck, giblets reserved
salt and freshly ground black pepper
1 garlic clove, sliced
2 bay leaves
1 orange, quartered
15 ml /1 tbls olive oil
425 ml /15 fl oz dry white wine
250 g /8 oz fresh figs, quartered
sprigs of fresh thyme, to garnish
For the stock
duck giblets (see above)
½ Spanish onion, sliced
2 carrots, thickly sliced
2 garlic cloves, crushed
2.5 ml /½ tsp dried marjoram
2.5 ml /½ tsp dried thyme
2.5 ml /½ tsp salt
4 black peppercorns

1 Place the duck stock ingredients in a saucepan, cover with 425 ml /15 fl oz water and bring to the boil. Lower the heat, cover and simmer for 45 minutes, skimming regularly, until the liquid is reduced to half its original quantity. Strain.
2 Heat the oven to 170C /325F /gas 3. Rub the cavity of the duck with salt and freshly ground black pepper. Put the garlic, bay leaves and orange inside the cavity. Truss the duck and prick the skin all over.
3 In a flameproof casserole, heat the olive oil and lightly brown the duck all over. Pour off the excess fat.
4 Pour the dry white wine and duck stock into a saucepan. Bring to the boil and pour it into the casserole, cover and cook the duck in the oven for 1½–2 hours or until the juices run clear when the inside of the leg is pierced with a skewer.
5 Transfer the duck to a warmed serving plate and remove the string. Keep warm.
6 Skim as much fat as possible from the sauce. Add the quartered figs and bring the sauce back to the boil. Correct the seasoning. As soon as the figs are heated through and the sauce is thick, pour it over the duck. Garnish with sprigs of fresh thyme, then serve immediately.

Guinea fowl à la Souvaroff

Seal the lid tightly with luting paste and break the seal when you present the dish at table; the heady aroma is delicious, and the bird will be tender and moist.

 1½ hours

Serves 4
2 small guinea fowl, cut into serving pieces
400 g /14 oz good-quality canned beef consommé (not concentrated)
1 onion, finely chopped
1 carrot, finely chopped
5 ml /1 tsp tomato purée
bouquet garni
beurre manié, made with 15 ml /1 tbls flour and 15 g /½ oz butter
salt and freshly ground black pepper
25 g /1 oz butter
30 ml /2 tbls olive oil
30 ml /2 tbls cognac
60 ml /4 tbls Madeira
30 ml /2 tbls dry white wine
125 g /4 oz pâté de foie gras, diced
1 large truffle, diced
45 ml /3 tbls truffle juice from the can
luting paste, made with 50 g /2 oz flour and 50 ml /2 fl oz water

1 Heat the oven to 190C /375F /gas 5.
2 Pour the consommé into a saucepan and add the chopped onion and carrot, tomato purée and bouquet garni. Bring to the boil and continue to boil until reduced to half its original quantity.
3 Gradually whisk in the beurre manié, a little piece at a time, and boil the sauce until it thickens.
4 Skin the guinea fowl and season with salt and freshly ground black pepper.
5 Heat the butter and oil in a flameproof casserole. When foaming subsides, add enough guinea fowl pieces to cover the base of the casserole and sauté until they are golden brown on all sides. Remove from the casserole. Repeat with the remaining pieces.
6 Pour off the excess fat; pour in the cognac and ignite it. When the flames die down, add the reduced consommé and vegetables, the Madeira and white wine. Bring it to the boil, stir to remove the sediment from the base of the pan and simmer for 5 minutes. Season the sauce to taste with salt and pepper.
7 Add the guinea fowl pieces to the sauce; scatter the diced foie gras and truffle over the guinea fowl. Remove from the heat and stir in the truffle juice.
8 Cover the casserole and seal with luting paste. Cook in the oven for 30–35 minutes.
9 Remove the casserole from the oven, break the luting paste seal open and serve the guinea fowl immediately.

Duck with olives

 45 minutes, then 1¾ hours cooking

Serves 4
2 kg /4½ lb duckling
salt
30 ml /2 tbls olive oil
25 g /1 oz butter
1 medium-sized onion, chopped
15 ml /1 tbls tomato purée
2.5 ml /½ tsp dried thyme
2.5 ml /½ tsp dried rosemary
1 bay leaf
freshly ground black pepper
275 ml /10 fl oz dry white wine
250 g /9 oz green olives, stoned
200 g /7 oz mushrooms, halved

1 Prick the skin of the duck all over with a fork and sprinkle generously, inside and out, with salt.
2 Heat the olive oil and butter in a flameproof casserole. Brown the duck evenly on all sides for about 20 minutes, until the skin is evenly browned and crisp.
3 Remove the duck from the casserole, put it on a heated plate and keep it hot. Drain off the excess fat from the casserole, keeping only 15 ml /1 tbls.
4 Fry the onion in the reserved duck fat until soft. Then add the tomato purée,

Duck with olives

thyme, rosemary, bay leaf, pepper and 225 ml /8 fl oz white wine. Boil until the mixture reduces and thickens slightly.
5   Return the duck to the casserole, cover and simmer for about 1¼ hours, turning and basting it occasionally. Add the olives and mushrooms and cook for a further 30 minutes, adding a little water if necessary.
6   Joint the duck and arrange on a serving dish with the olives and mushrooms. Add the remaining wine to the casserole, stir and bring to the boil. Strain into a sauce-boat and serve at once, with the duck.

Duck curry

 2 hours

Serves 4
1.8 kg /4 lb duck, cut into 4 serving
    pieces
30 ml /2 tbls olive oil
5 ml /1 tsp black mustard seeds
1 Spanish onion, finely chopped
2 garlic cloves, finely chopped
4 cm /1½ in piece root ginger, finely
    chopped
1 green chilli, seeded and finely chopped
5 ml /1 tsp ground cumin
5 ml /1 tsp chilli powder
5 ml /1 tsp ground coriander
5 ml /1 tsp ground turmeric
salt and freshly ground black pepper
45 ml /3 tbls vinegar
50 g /2 oz desiccated coconut
saffron rice (page 30), to serve

1   In a flameproof casserole, heat the olive oil. Prick the duck skin all over with a fork and sauté the pieces in the oil for 4–5 minutes on each side or until they are golden brown. Remove the duck from the casserole and pour off the excess fat.
2   Add the mustard seeds to the casserole, cover the pan and fry them for 2 minutes. Add the onion and sauté for 20 minutes or until golden brown, stirring occasionally. Add the chopped garlic, ginger and green chilli and fry, stirring constantly, for 2–3 minutes.
3   In a small bowl, mix the ground cumin, chilli powder, ground coriander, turmeric and 2.5 ml /½ tsp salt. Add the vinegar and mix to form a paste.
4   Add the spice paste to the casserole and fry, stirring constantly, for 8 minutes.
5   Add the duck pieces and turn them over several times so they are coated with the spices. Continue frying for 2–3 minutes.
6   Bring 300 ml /10 fl oz water to the boil and stir in the desiccated coconut. Pour the coconut milk over the duck pieces in the pan and stir to mix into the spices. Cover and simmer for 40–50 minutes or until the duck is tender and the sauce has thickened.
7   Skim off any excess fat, correct the seasoning with salt and freshly ground black pepper and serve immediately, on a bed of saffron rice.

Duck curry

Braised guinea fowl with brandy and soured cream

 1¾ hours

Serves 4
1.4 kg /3 lb guinea fowl, jointed
75 g /3 oz butter
75 g /3 oz thickly sliced streaky bacon, rind
    removed and cubed
salt and freshly ground black pepper
500 g /1 lb button onions
60 ml /4 tbls brandy
2 cloves garlic, crushed
600 ml /1 pt hot chicken stock, home-made
    or from a cube
15 ml /1 tbls tomato purée
5 ml /1 tsp sugar
15 ml /1 tbls chopped fresh basil or 5 ml /1
    tsp dried basil
100 g /4 oz button mushrooms
15 ml /1 tbls flour
1.5 ml /¼ tsp freshly grated nutmeg
75 ml /3 fl oz soured cream
For the garnish
croûtons
freshly chopped parsley

1   Melt 25 g /1 oz of the butter in a flameproof casserole and fry the bacon cubes until golden. Remove the bacon from the casserole with a slotted spoon.
2   Season the guinea fowl joints with salt and pepper. Add to the fat in the casserole and fry gently until browned all over. Return the bacon to the casserole; add the onions. Continue frying until the onions begin to colour. Pour the brandy into the casserole and set alight.
3   When the flames subside, add the garlic, hot stock, tomato purée, sugar and basil, and stir well. Bring to the boil, cover and simmer over a low heat for about 40 minutes, or until the guinea fowl is tender.
4   Transfer the guinea fowl and onions to a warm serving dish and keep hot. Boil the liquid in the pan until reduced to about 500 ml /18 fl oz, then remove from the heat.
5   Meanwhile, melt the remaining butter in a frying-pan and sauté the mushrooms for about 2 minutes. In a bowl, blend together the flour, nutmeg, 30 ml /2 tbls water and the soured cream. Add the mushrooms and the soured cream mixture to the liquid in the casserole and stir. Bring to the boil, stirring constantly, and simmer for 3 minutes.
6   Adjust the seasoning if necessary and pour over the guinea fowl in the dish. Serve at once, garnished with croûtons and freshly chopped parsley.

STAR MENUS & RECIPE FILE

Roulade of tuna fish

Duck with orange jelly
Tossed green salad
with crisp mushroom slices

Praline chocolate mould

Wine: Deidesheimer or
another Rheinpfalz wine

Plan-ahead timetable

On the day before
Praline chocolate mould: make the praline and the coffee ice
cream and combine. Add to the mould and freeze overnight.
Duck with orange jelly: cook and bone the duck and refrigerate;
strain and chill the stock.

On the morning of the meal
Duck with orange jelly: reheat the stock and make the aspic.
Decorate and coat the duck, then arrange on a platter with the
garnishes. Refrigerate.

In the summer it is so much nicer to have most of your meal prepared ahead of time, rather than getting hot and bothered doing
last-minute chores in the kitchen just as your guests are arriving.
Cold food, of course, is appealing in this kind of weather, but every
meal – unless it is a picnic or a buffet spread – is rather more
interesting if it includes one hot dish. Make life easier by choosing a
menu which is as simple as possible, or where a lot of the hard work
can be done on the day before the party. Like this you will not have
to spend hours over a hot stove when you want to be at your sparkling best.

The combination I have given here fits the bill for a sweltering
day. The first course, Roulade of tuna fish, consists of a light-
textured green-tinted spinach 'sponge', which is spread with a
creamy pink filling of tuna fish, and then rolled up Swiss-roll style.
The effect of the pink tuna filling against the green roulade is most
appealing and certainly starts off our meal with a flourish.

Easy-to-serve portions of cold duck masked with a glittering coat
of wine and citrus aspic set the scene for the glamorous main course.
I like to accompany the shimmering platter of Duck with orange jelly
with a traditional garnish of chopped or diced aspic, large cubes of
bacon and whole button onions and mushrooms. A refreshing green
salad with crisp mushroom slices, tossed in a tangy fennel dressing, is
a simple but perfect accompaniment to this elegant main course.

Finish the meal in style with Praline chocolate mould. This is a
really luscious dessert of ice cream encased in a firm chocolate crust.
The ice cream is coffee flavoured, with crushed praline added to give
a slightly crunchy texture. Similar to a traditional bombe, yet much
easier to make and just as ritzy, this dessert is guaranteed to surprise
and delight your guests. The combination of the crisp, semi-sweet
chocolate shell and the rich ice cream is quite divine and totally
irresistible!

Tossed green salad with crisp mushroom slices: thoroughly wash and dry the lettuce leaves and refrigerate.

One hour thirty minutes before the meal
Roulade of tuna fish: prepare the tin, cook the spinach and make and cook the spinach roulade.

Thirty minutes before the meal
Roulade of tuna fish: prepare the tuna fish filling. Keep warm.
Tossed green salad with crisp mushroom slices: slice the mushrooms and soak in acidulated water. Prepare the French dressing.

Fifteen minutes before the meal
Roulade of tuna fish: roll up the hot roulade in a damp tea-towel lined with greaseproof paper, then unroll, add the tuna fish filling and roll up again.

Five minutes before the meal
Roulade of tuna fish: brush with melted butter and heat through. Serve accompanied by soured cream.
Praline chocolate mould: dip the mould in hot water and invert onto a plate. Refrigerate until ready to serve, then decorate.
Tossed green salad with crisp mushroom slices: drain the mushrooms and assemble the salad.

Roulade of tuna fish

Serves 6–8
oil for greasing
100 g /3½ oz butter
700 g /1½ lb fresh spinach
30 ml /2 tbls chicken stock, home-
made or from a cube
1 Spanish onion, chopped
almost to a purée
60 ml /4 tbls flour
150 ml /5 fl oz hot milk
4 egg yolks
30 ml /2 tbls freshly grated
Parmesan cheese
salt and ground black pepper

a big pinch of freshly grated
nutmeg
6 egg whites
30 ml /2 tbls melted butter
soured cream, to serve
For the filling
25 g /1 oz butter
25 g /1 oz flour
175 ml /6 fl oz milk
200 g /7 oz canned tuna fish,
drained and flaked
a dash of Tabasco sauce
a big pinch of paprika
salt and ground black pepper

1   Lightly oil a 23 × 36 cm /9 × 14 in Swiss-roll tin and line it with
a sheet of greaseproof paper. Grease the paper with 15 g /½ oz
butter. Heat the oven to 200C /400F /gas 6.
2   Cook the spinach in the stock and 50 g /2 oz butter until soft.
3   Drain the spinach and purée it in a blender, or chop it finely and
rub through a sieve. Press out as much liquid as possible.
4   Sauté the onion in 25 g /1 oz butter until softened. Blend in the
flour with a wooden spoon, then gradually stir in the hot milk. Stir
over a low heat for 3–4 minutes until the mixture is very stiff.
5   Beat the egg yolks with the cheese. Add to the hot sauce together
with the spinach. Mix well and season with salt, pepper and nutmeg.
6   Whisk the egg whites until stiff but not dry, and fold into the
spinach mixture with a metal spoon. Adjust seasoning if necessary,
and spread in the tin. Smooth over and bake for 20–25 minutes or
until springy to the touch. If it starts to brown, cover it with foil.
7   Prepare the filling: melt the butter, add the flour and cook for a
few minutes. Whisk in the milk and cook until thickened. Fold in
the tuna, Tabasco, paprika and salt and pepper to taste.
8   Leaving the oven on, turn the spinach roulade out onto a damp
tea-towel lined with a lightly greased sheet of greaseproof paper.
Carefully remove the paper from the spinach roulade, edges first,
and allow steam to escape for about 1 minute. Then roll up,
including the towel, starting from a long side. Leave for a minute.
9   Unroll the spinach roulade and spread it with the tuna sauce,
leaving a 25 mm /1 in margin free at each long side. Roll it up on its
own from the long side and lay on a heated, ovenproof dish with the
join underneath. Brush with melted butter and return to the oven
for 5 minutes. Serve with soured cream.

 1½ hours

Duck with orange jelly

Serves 8
2 × 2 kg /4½ lb ducks
75 g /3 oz butter
30 ml /2 tbls olive oil
275 ml /10 fl oz dry white wine
850 ml /1½ pt chicken stock,
preferably home-made
salt and ground black pepper
bouquet garni
8–10 × 10 mm /½ in cubes of
bacon
8–10 button onions

175 g /6 oz button mushrooms
30 ml /2 tbls powdered gelatine
50 ml /2 fl oz Madeira or port
grated zest and strained juice
of 1 orange and ½ lemon
a pinch of cayenne pepper
fennel leaves and thin strips of
green leek, dipped in boiling
water, to garnish
hard-boiled egg white cut into
flower shapes, to garnish

1   Cut the duck into quarters, removing the backbone. Sauté the
quarters, a few at a time, in 50 g /2 oz butter and the olive oil in a
large flameproof casserole until golden on all sides. Return all the
duck portions to the casserole, add the wine and stock and bring to
the boil. Add salt, pepper and the bouquet garni, reduce the heat
and simmer for 30 minutes.
2   Sauté the bacon in the remaining butter until golden then
transfer to the casserole. Sauté the onions in the resulting fat until
golden; add to the casserole with the mushrooms. Cover and simmer
for 30 minutes or until tender, basting occasionally.
3   While the cooked duck pieces are still hot, carefully remove the
bones, using a sharp knife, and leaving the pieces whole. Put aside
to cool on a rack. Reserve the bacon, mushrooms and onions.
4   Strain the cooking stock through a sieve lined with fine muslin
until clear, then leave until cold. Remove any fat that sets on the
surface. Place the gelatine in a small bowl with 60 ml /4 tbls cold
water. Leave for 5 minutes to soften. Bring the cold stock almost to
the boil. Add the gelatine and stir until it dissolves. Cool, then add
the Madeira or port and zest and juice of the orange and lemon.
5   Test the aspic for set: pour a 15 mm /½ in layer into a small dish
and put in the refrigerator for 15 minutes, turn out and cut into
small pieces. They should remain set after 10 minutes at room
temperature. If they don't, reheat the aspic and add a little more
dissolved gelatine. Chill until syrupy and just beginning to set.
6   Put the duck pieces on a wire rack over a board or dish and
sprinkle with cayenne pepper to taste. Dip the fennel, green leek and
egg white shapes in aspic and garnish the duck. Use a spoon to pour
the aspic over the duck pieces until coated, then chill. Repeat
coating once or twice. Chop any leftover aspic. Garnish with
chopped aspic, bacon, onions, mushrooms and fennel leaves.

 3¼ hours
plus cooling

Deidesheimer or
another Rheinpfalz wine

Tossed green salad with crisp mushroom slices

Serves 8
2 lettuces
50 g /2 oz mushrooms
15 ml /1 tbls lemon juice
For the French dressing
15 ml /1 tbls lemon juice
15–30 ml /1–2 tbls wine vinegar
1.5 ml /¼ tsp dry mustard
30 ml /2 tbls chopped fennel leaves
coarse salt
freshly ground black pepper
90–120 ml /6–8 tbls olive oil

1   Separate the lettuce leaves and wash well in a large quantity of water.
2   Drain the leaves well and dry thoroughly in a cloth or a salad basket so that there is no water left on them to dilute the dressing. Wrap in a dry tea-towel and refrigerate until ready to use.
3   To make the French dressing, combine the lemon juice, wine vinegar, dry mustard and 15 ml /1 tbls chopped fennel in a bowl.
4   Season to taste with coarse salt and freshly ground black pepper. Add the olive oil and beat with a fork until the mixture emulsifies.
5   Shortly before serving, slice the mushrooms thinly and soak in 30 ml /2 tbls water mixed with lemon juice to prevent discoloration.
6   To serve, put the lettuce leaves in a salad bowl. Drain and pat dry the mushroom slices, then add to the lettuce. Pour over the French dressing, and toss so that the lettuce glistens. Correct the seasoning and sprinkle with the remaining chopped fennel. Serve immediately.

20 minutes plus chilling

Praline chocolate mould

Serves 6–8
flavourless oil for greasing
75 g /3 oz sugar
1.5 ml /¼ tsp lemon juice
25 g /1 oz toasted blanched almonds
225 g /8 oz semi-sweet chocolate, melted
50 g /2 oz coffee beans
425 ml /15 fl oz thick cream
5 ml /1 tsp vanilla essence
3 eggs, separated
To decorate
orange segments
whipped cream

1   Make the praline: lightly brush a cool surface with oil. In a heavy pan, melt 25 g /1 oz sugar with the lemon juice and 15 ml /1 tbls water over a low heat. Increase heat and boil the syrup to a golden caramel (170C /340F on a sugar thermometer). Remove from heat and mix in the almonds. Pour on the oiled surface and leave to set.
2   Lightly grease a 1L /2 pt metal mould with oil, then chill.
3   Pour the melted chocolate into the mould. Tip and rotate to coat the inside completely. Place over ice and continue rotating until set.
4   To make the ice cream, scald the coffee beans and half the cream over a low heat. Remove from the heat, cover and infuse for 20 minutes. Strain into a bowl. Discard the coffee beans. Cool, then stir in the remaining cream and the vanilla essence. Whisk the egg yolks until they are well blended. Set aside.
5   In a small saucepan, dissolve the remaining sugar in 75 ml /3 fl oz water over low heat, then increase the heat to moderate and boil until the temperature reaches 105C /220F on a sugar thermometer or until the surface of the syrup forms bubbles that resemble small pearls. Remove from the heat and let stand for 1 minute.
6   Pour the syrup over the egg yolks in a steady stream, whisking constantly. Continue until thick and fluffy. Mix in the cooled cream.
7   Whisk the egg whites until stiff, then fold into the cream mixture. Pour into freezer trays and freeze for 30 minutes.
8   Lift the praline off the surface. Break it up, lay it between 2 sheets of greaseproof paper and crush with a rolling pin.
9   Spoon the ice cream into a chilled bowl. Whisk well and stir in the crushed praline. Spoon the ice cream into the chocolate-lined mould. Smooth the top and freeze overnight.
10   Remove the mould from the freezer and dip quickly into hot water. Invert a chilled serving plate over the mould and reverse. Place the mould in the refrigerator for 15–30 minutes before serving. Decorate with orange segments and cream to serve.

 2¾ hours plus overnight freezing

Plan-ahead timetable

On the day before the meal
Orange snaps: make and shape the biscuits and store in an airtight container.

On the morning of the meal
Guinea fowl with pears: prepare the syrup and poach the pears. Remove the pears with a slotted spoon and reserve.

Two hours before the meal
Shrimp timbales with champagne sauce: prepare the fish mousseline. Chill. Prepare moulds and make shrimp mixture. Fill the moulds and refrigerate.

Forty minutes before the meal
Guinea fowl with pears: sauté guinea fowl and onion, return guinea fowl to casserole, cover and cook.

Thirty minutes before the meal
Yellow rice striped with pimento: cook the rice.
Shrimp timbales with champagne sauce: cook moulds. Prepare the champagne sauce and keep hot.

Ten minutes before the meal
Guinea fowl with pears: add wine, port and pears. Finish cooking, then season and keep hot.

STAR MENU 2

Shrimp timbales with champagne sauce

*Guinea fowl with pears
Yellow rice striped with pimento*

Orange snaps

Wine: Meursault

This elegant dinner party menu could easily be called a gourmet's delight. Shrimp timbales with champagne sauce, which start our meal, are sophistication itself. The word timbale originally described an individual drinking vessel but now, as in this recipe, it describes a little mould. Tiny turrets of fish *mousseline* are here filled with shrimps in thick cream flavoured with chopped fennel leaves, then baked in a *bain marie*. Turned out carefully, the shrimp timbales are served with a cream sauce, luxurious as only champagne can make it.

You can buy small quarter bottles of champagne – more than enough for your sauce. Why not buy a whole bottle instead, take out what you need for the sauce and drink the rest with your guests as an aperitif? It will get your evening off to a sparkling start. If you are worried about the champagne going a little flat while you are finishing off the sauce, serve it as the base for a cocktail – mixed, for instance, with a little blackcurrant-flavoured crème de cassis for a delicious Kir royale.

Guinea fowl with pears, which follows, is an 18th century style dish of poultry braised in white wine and port with fruit. Cook the guinea fowl very lightly so as not to toughen it, then serve it quartered and decorated with the poached pear halves. The delicately flavoured sauce which is poured over to serve nicely completes this tempting dish. The flavour and delicate colour is fully complemented by the Yellow rice striped with pimento, gently flavoured with a touch of saffron.

To complete this meal serve a simple but elegant dessert, delicately shaped Orange snaps – tasty crisp biscuits flavoured with tangy orange marmalade. To follow such a luscious meal you may prefer to serve these biscuits simply as they are; alternatively you can add the finishing touch by piping whipped cream into them. Either way would make a fitting end to a glorious meal.

Just before the meal
Shrimp timbales with champagne sauce: turn out, spoon over the sauce, garnish and serve.

Between the first and the main course
Guinea fowl with pears: thicken sauce, cut guinea fowl into portions, spoon the sauce over, garnish and serve.
Yellow rice striped with pimento: garnish and serve.

Between the main course and the dessert
Orange snaps: whip cream and pipe into the snaps, if using.

Shrimp timbales with champagne sauce

Serves 4

175 g /6 oz sole or turbot fillets	**For the champagne sauce**
45 ml /3 tbls egg white	5 ml /1 tsp butter
salt and freshly ground white pepper	2 shallots, finely diced
275 ml /10 fl oz thick cream	4 mushrooms, roughly chopped
softened butter for greasing	a sprig of fresh tarragon
75 g /3 oz boiled, peeled shrimps	1.5 ml /¼ tsp tomato purée
25 ml /1½ tbls chopped fennel leaves	90 ml /6 tbls dry white wine
4 fennel sprigs, to garnish	90 ml /6 tbls champagne
	275 ml /10 fl oz thick cream

1 Put the fish through the finest blade of a mincer 3 times, then place in a bowl. Add the egg white, salt and pepper to taste and blend with a wooden spoon. Or blend in a food processor, then add the egg white and seasoning and mix for several short bursts.
2 Reserving 15 ml /1 tbls cream, add the rest to the fish mixture and beat with the spoon until slightly thickened. Alternatively, mix in the cream for a few seconds in the food processor, taking care not to overbeat, then transfer to a bowl. Correct the seasoning, cover and chill for 20 minutes. Heat the oven to 170C /325F /gas 3.
3 Brush 4 × 150 ml /5 fl oz dariole moulds with softened butter. Cut 4 circles of greaseproof paper to fit the base of the moulds and put them in position. Brush with softened butter.
4 In a small bowl, mix the shrimps with the reserved cream and the chopped fennel. Season to taste with salt and freshly ground white pepper. Line the base and sides of each mould with the fish mixture, then spoon the shrimp mixture into the centre and cover with the remaining fish mixture, taking care not to overfill, as the mixture will puff up during cooking. Tap each mould on the work surface to eliminate any air bubbles and smooth the top. Cover with foil and place in a roasting tin. Add boiling water to come halfway up the sides of the moulds and cook for 20 minutes.
5 Meanwhile, make the champagne sauce. In a small saucepan, melt the butter, then add the shallots, mushrooms, tarragon and tomato purée. Simmer gently for 10 minutes, or until the shallots are soft. Add the wine and champagne, raise the heat and cook until reduced to a quarter of the original quantity. Stir in the cream and simmer until the sauce has the consistency of bechamel.
6 Turn the timbales out onto a heated serving dish. Strain the sauce over them, garnish with fennel sprigs and serve.

 about 2 hours

Guinea fowl with pears

Serves 4

900 g /2 lb guinea fowl, dressed weight	125 ml /4 fl oz port
2 firm pears, peeled, cored and halved	5–10 ml /1–2 tsp lemon juice
50–75 g /2–3 oz butter	15 ml /1 tbls cornflour
1 medium-sized onion, thinly sliced	a bunch of watercress, to garnish
salt and ground white pepper	**For the syrup**
150 ml /5 fl oz dry white wine	225 g /8 oz sugar
	juice and pared zest of 1 lemon

1 Prepare the syrup. In a saucepan, combine the sugar, lemon juice and zest with 425 ml /15 fl oz water and stir over a low heat with a wooden spoon until the sugar is dissolved. Increase the heat and boil for 10 minutes, then remove the lemon zest.
2 Add the prepared pears and poach gently for 10 minutes, or until slightly softened. Remove with a slotted spoon and drain. Discard the syrup.
3 In a flameproof casserole, heat the butter and sauté the guinea fowl until golden on all sides. Remove from the pan.
4 Sauté the onion slices in the hot fat until transparent, stirring with a wooden spoon.
5 Return the guinea fowl to the casserole. Season generously with salt and freshly ground white pepper, then cover and cook over a medium heat for 10–15 minutes, turning the guinea fowl frequently.
6 Add the white wine, port and poached pears. Simmer for a further 10–15 minutes, or until the guinea fowl is tender and cooked through. The juice should run clear when a skewer is inserted in the thickest part of the inside leg. Add salt, white pepper and a little lemon juice to taste. Remove the guinea fowl from the casserole and keep hot.
7 In a small bowl, blend the cornflour with 30 ml /2 tbls cold water, then stir in 30 ml /2 tbls hot sauce. Return the cornflour mixture to the sauce and simmer for 1–2 minutes, or until the sauce thickens, stirring constantly with a wooden spoon. Keep hot.
8 To serve, cut the guinea fowl into quarters, arrange on a heated serving dish, garnished with pear halves. Spoon the sauce over the guinea fowl pieces and the pears and garnish with a bunch of watercress in the centre. Serve immediately.

 1½ hours   Meursault

Yellow rice striped with pimento

Serves 4
25 g /1 oz butter
½ Spanish onion, finely chopped
175 g /6 oz long-grain rice
425 ml /15 fl oz chicken stock, home-made or from a cube
1.5 ml /¼ tsp turmeric
a pinch of powdered saffron
1.5 ml /¼ tsp paprika
a pinch of cayenne pepper
salt and freshly ground black pepper
1 canned pimento, drained and thinly sliced

1   In a heavy-based saucepan, melt the butter. Stir the finely
chopped onion in the hot butter and sauté over a moderate heat for
7–10 minutes, or until the onion is softened, stirring occasionally
with a wooden spoon.
2   Stir in the rice and cook for few minutes, until transparent,
stirring occasionally.
3   Pour in the stock and bring to the boil. Reduce the heat to a
simmer and stir in the turmeric, powdered saffron, paprika, cayenne
pepper and salt and freshly ground black pepper to taste.
4   Cover and simmer gently for 15–20 minutes, or until the rice is
tender but not mushy.
5   Transfer the rice to a heated serving dish and arrange the thinly
sliced pimento in a fine lattice over the top. Serve immediately.

 45 minutes

Orange snaps

Makes 14
50 g /2 oz butter, plus extra for greasing
75 g /3 oz caster sugar
65 g /2½ oz thin-cut orange marmalade
60 ml /4 tbls flour
a pinch of salt
5 ml /1 tsp grated orange zest
whipped cream, to serve (optional)

1   In a small heavy-based saucepan, melt 50 g /2 oz butter with the
sugar and the marmalade, stirring with a wooden spoon over a low
heat until the syrup is quite smooth. Remove from the heat.
2   Sift the flour and pinch of salt into the orange butter mixture
and beat well. Beat in the grated orange zest. Leave to cool.
3   Refrigerate for 30–45 minutes, or until the mixture has
hardened enough to roll into balls. Heat the oven to 180C /350F /
gas 4.
4   Grease 2 or 3 baking sheets with a little butter. Roll the
hardened biscuit mixture into 14 balls and place 4–5 balls on each
baking sheet, 5 cm /2 in apart. Bake 1 sheet at a time, keeping the
remainder in the refrigerator until required, for 8 minutes or until
the orange snaps are lightly golden, bubbling discs.
5   Remove the baking sheet from the oven and allow the snaps to
set for a few seconds until very slightly hardened.
6   Run a palette knife quickly under each snap and transfer onto
the greased handle of a wooden spoon. Roll it round to shape it into
a cylinder. Leave to harden on the handle for 1–2 minutes, then slip
it onto a cooling rack. Repeat with the remaining balls, using
several spoons and rolling 1 as another sets. When cold, store in an
airtight container.
7   If you wish you can fill the snaps with whipped cream, using a
piping bag, just before serving.

● Rolling the snaps round the handle can be tricky. If they begin to
harden and crack as you roll them, return the backing sheet to the
oven for a few seconds to soften.

10 minutes, cooling and chilling,
then 45 minutes plus cooling

French duck and bean casserole

Serves 4
1.8–2.3 kg /4–5 lb duckling
250 g /8 oz dried haricot beans
salt and freshly ground black pepper
30 ml /2 tbls olive oil
25 g /1 oz butter
2 medium-sized onions, finely chopped
2 garlic cloves, finely chopped
400 g /14 oz canned peeled tomatoes
175 g /6 oz canned pimentos, drained and chopped

1   Put the beans in a saucepan and cover with about 1.7 L /3 pt water. Bring to the boil and remove from the heat. Cover and allow to stand for 1 hour.
2   Drain the beans and replenish with fresh water to cover. Replace the pan on the heat, bring to the boil and simmer for 1–2 hours until tender. Add more water to the beans during cooking if necessary.
3   Heat the oven to 170C /325F /gas 3.
4   Cut the duckling into 4 serving portions. Season them generously with salt and freshly ground black pepper.
5   Heat the olive oil and butter in a frying-pan large enough to take the duckling portions in 1 layer. Sauté the portions for 4–5 minutes on each side or until browned all over. Remove with a slotted spoon and keep warm.
6   Add the finely chopped onions and garlic to the frying-pan and sauté for 10 minutes or until browned, stirring constantly with a wooden spoon. Remove with a slotted spoon to a separate plate and keep warm.
7   Drain the beans and put them into a large casserole. Stir in the canned tomatoes with their juice, the chopped pimentos and cooked onions and garlic. Season with salt and freshly ground black pepper to taste. Arrange the duck portions on top, cover and bake for 1¼ hours.
8   Uncover and bake for a further 30 minutes or until the duck is tender.
9   Skim the excess fat from the cooking juices and correct the seasoning. Serve immediately, from the casserole or in a heated serving dish.

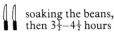 soaking the beans,
then 3½–4½ hours

Pan fried guinea fowl au vinaigre

Serves 4
1.4 kg /3 lb guinea fowl
salt and freshly ground black pepper
butter
30 ml /2 tbls olive oil
bouquet garni
15 ml /1 tbls wine vinegar
15 ml /1 tbls brandy
15 ml /1 tbls Dijon mustard
5 ml /1 tsp tomato purée
50 ml /2 fl oz dry white wine
50 ml /2 fl oz thick cream
flat-leaved parsley, to garnish

1   Cut the guinea fowl into 4 serving pieces and reserve the backbone. Season generously with salt and freshly ground black pepper.
2   In a large heavy frying-pan, melt 25 g /1 oz butter and the olive oil. When the foaming subsides, add the guinea fowl portions, flesh side down, and pan fry, turning with a fish slice or tongs, until they are browned on all sides.
3   Add the bouquet garni and the reserved backbone. Cover with a lid and cook over a gentle heat for 20 minutes.
4   Add the wine vinegar, cover and continue cooking, allowing the vinegar to evaporate and completely reduce, for an additional 20–30 minutes. Check the guinea fowl is cooked by making sure the juices from the thickest part of the leg run clear when pierced with a knife, then remove the portions to a heated serving platter and keep warm. Discard the backbone.
5   Add the brandy to the pan juices and stir over high heat for 1–2 minutes. Add the Dijon mustard, tomato purée and dry white wine. Simmer until reduced to half its original quantity.
6   Add the thick cream, correct the seasoning and heat the sauce through. Spoon the sauce over the guinea fowl portions, garnish with flat-leaved parsley, and serve immediately.

 45 minutes

Potted duck

Serves 4 as a main course
1 plump duck, 2–2.3 kg /4½–5 lb
5 ml /1 tsp salt
5 ml /1 tsp powdered mixed spice
1.5 ml /¼ tsp crushed thyme
50 g /2 oz saltpetre
225 g /8 oz duck or chicken fat
about 500 g /1 lb lard

1   Cut the duck into 4 portions, removing and reserving the 2 lumps of fat on either side of the vent.
2   Pound the salt, mixed spice and crushed thyme in a mortar, rub the duck portions with this mixture and place them, with the fat, in a large casserole. Sprinkle the saltpetre over the duck, cover and leave in the refrigerator for 24–36 hours.
3   Dice the duck or chicken fat and the reserved fat and place it in a saucepan with 1 L /2 pt water. Melt the fat over a gentle heat. Brush the saltpetre from the duck portions and add the duck to the saucepan. Simmer gently for about 1 hour, or until the duck is tender. Remove the duck portions with a slotted spoon. Set aside.
4   Choose an earthenware or ovenproof straight-sided container just large enough to take the portions packed tightly together, rinse out with boiling water and dry well. Pack in the duck tightly.
5   Continue to cook the fat and remaining broth until a froth forms on the surface, about 30 minutes. Skim off the impurities thoroughly; remove from the heat, cool and chill. When the fat has solidified, discard or reserve for another recipe any remaining stock.
6   Melt and strain the fat through a fine sieve and pour over the duck portions. Melt enough lard to cover the top of the fat completely. Pour over the duck portions and fat and allow to cool. Cover the container with a lid or foil. Keep the *confit* in the refrigerator for a week before serving. (A well-prepared *confit* will keep in a cold place for several months.)
7   Serve cold with salads as a main course, or with toast as an appetizer for a larger number.

● This method of preserving duck, goose, turkey or pork is used often in France where it is called a *confit*, a preserve.
● The saltpetre in this recipe is used to give the meat a beautifully rosy colour. It is not, however, a preservative. If you cannot obtain it, the dish can safely be made without it.

  15 minutes, then 1–2 days,
3¾ hours, then 1 week

Braised duck à l'orange

Serves 4
1.8 kg /4 lb duck, dressed weight
salt and freshly ground black pepper
25 g /1 oz butter
150 ml /5 fl oz Cointreau
15 ml /1 tbls wine vinegar
juice of 1 orange
150 ml /5 fl oz beef stock, home-made or from a cube
10 ml /2 tsp cornflour
4 medium-sized oranges, peeled and cut into segments
watercress sprigs, to garnish

1   Sprinkle the cavity of the duck with salt and freshly ground black pepper and prick the skin all over with a skewer.
2   Melt the butter in a deep, flameproof casserole, just large enough to contain the duck, and sauté the bird until golden on all sides. Reduce the heat and continue cooking gently, covered, for 30 minutes, turning the duck from time to time. Add two-thirds of the Cointreau and allow to simmer for a few more minutes.
3   Remove the duck from the casserole. Skim the fat from the juices, then return the duck to the casserole. Add the wine vinegar, orange juice and beef stock and bring to the boil. Cover, lower the heat and simmer gently until the duck is tender, about 1 hour.
4   Remove the duck from the casserole, place it on a heated serving dish and keep it warm. Place the casserole over a high heat and bring the liquid to the boil, stirring constantly and scraping all the crusty bits on the bottom and sides of the casserole into the sauce. Then reduce the heat and simmer gently for 10 minutes. Skim the fat from the surface and pass the sauce through a fine sieve. Season generously with salt and freshly ground black pepper and add the remaining Cointreau.
5   In a small bowl blend the cornflour with 15 ml /1 tbls water until smooth. Stir into the sauce and bring to the boil, whisking constantly, then lower the heat and simmer for 4–5 minutes or until slightly thickened. Add half the orange segments and simmer a little longer to heat them through.
6   To serve, pour a little of the sauce around the duck and garnish with the remaining orange segments and sprigs of watercress. Serve the orange segments in the remaining sauce in a sauce-boat.

  2¼ hours

North African guinea fowl

Serves 2
1.1 kg /2½ lb guinea fowl
salt and freshly ground black pepper
15 ml /1 tbls freshly chopped parsley
15 ml /1 tbls freshly chopped chervil
½ Spanish onion, finely chopped
75 g /3 oz butter
5 ml /1 tsp powdered cumin
1.5 ml /¼ tsp cayenne pepper
7.5–15 ml /½–1 tbls flour
sprigs of parsley, to garnish

1   Heat the oven to 220C /425F /gas 7. Bring the guinea fowl to room temperature, then season the cavity with salt and freshly ground black pepper.
2   Using a mortar and pestle, pound the parsley, chervil, chopped onion, butter, cumin, 2.5 ml /½ tsp salt and the cayenne pepper to a smooth paste. Spread the paste carefully all over the guinea fowl using a palette knife.
3   Pass a skewer through the wings to secure them closely to the sides of the bird.
4   Lay the guinea fowl on 1 side of the breast in a roasting tin and roast in the oven for 20 minutes, basting occasionally with the pan juices, until lightly browned. Turn the bird onto its other side and roast for a further 15–20 minutes, continuing to baste. Remove the bird from the oven.
5   Reduce the oven temperature to 180C /350F /gas 4.
6   Turn the bird on its back and sift a dusting of flour over the breast. Baste with the pan juices, and continue to roast for about 1 hour or until the guinea fowl is tender, basting frequently. If you push a skewer through the thickest part of the inside leg, the juices should run clear.
7   When the guinea fowl is cooked, remove the skewer and transfer it to a wooden board. With a sharp knife, cut the bird into halves or quarters, arrange the portions on a warmed serving platter, garnish with sprigs of parsley and serve immediately.

 bringing to room temperature,
then 2 hours

Roast duck with fruit stuffing

Serves 4
1.8 kg /4 lb duck, dressed weight
1 garlic clove, halved
salt and freshly ground black pepper
juice and grated zest of 2 oranges
50 g /2 oz butter, melted
1.5 ml /¼ tsp dried thyme
1 large orange, to garnish
flat-leaved parsley, to garnish
For the stuffing
500 g /1 lb dessert apples
225 g /8 oz prunes, soaked overnight
30 ml /2 tbls finely chopped onion
1 garlic clove, finely chopped

1   Bring the duck to room temperature, then remove any visible fat from the neck and vent of the duck. Rub the halved garlic clove over the skin and then season generously, inside and out, with salt and freshly ground black pepper. Prick the duck all over with a skewer or fork.
2   Heat the oven to 180C /350F /gas 4.
3   To make the stuffing, peel, core and slice each apple into 6. Stone the prunes and combine the flesh in a bowl with the apple, finely chopped onion and garlic. Stuff the body cavity of the duck with the mixture.
4   To truss the duck, pass a skewer through 1 wing of the duck, then through the neck flap and then the other wing. Tie the legs together. Place the duck on a wire rack standing in a roasting tin.
5   Spoon the juice and grated zest of 2 oranges and the melted butter over the duck. Sprinkle it with dried thyme. Roast in the oven, basting with the pan juices and pricking every 30 minutes, until the skin is crisp and the duck is cooked through, about 1½–2 hours. To test it, push a skewer through the thickest part of the leg, nearest the breast: the juices which run out should be clear.
6   Meanwhile make the garnish. With a vegetable peeler, pare the zest from the whole orange and cut into short, fine strips. Place the julienne strips in a saucepan of cold water and bring to the boil. Reduce the heat and simmer for 2–3 minutes. Drain and refresh under cold running water. Drain again.
7   Remove the string and skewer from the duck and transfer to a heated serving dish. Skim off the fat from the pan juices then pour the juices over the duck. Sprinkle with the julienne strips of orange, garnish with flat-leaved parsley and serve immediately.

soaking prunes overnight,
then 2–2½ hours

Game

ROASTING GAME

A simple roast of game, with traditional accompaniments, is a delightful way to revive the cooking of bygone days and at the same time do justice to some particularly fine meat.

Game is much prized for its distinctive flavour. Grouse, partridge, pheasant, wood pigeon, wild duck, snipe and woodcock all feed on food not available to farm-raised birds; this gives their flesh a gamey taste.

Venison, rabbit and hare (collectively called furred game) were an everyday sight on medieval dining tables. Nowadays they are not as common, though venison and rabbit are increasingly being raised commercially, thus becoming more available.

Only the finest, most tender young game should be roasted. If in doubt, forget about roasting and instead think in terms of pot-roast, casserole, pie or terrine as these methods provide a built-in safeguard against drying out the juices.

Game birds

The red grouse is Britain's best-known game bird, with a strong gamey flavour. The male has a red mark round the eyes, a dark back and white breast going down to give a trouser effect over the legs. The female has brownish plumage with dark bars.

Pheasants, the most handsome of the large game birds, have a strong flavour. They are often sold as a 'brace' – a pair. The cock has russet feathers, a long tail and a bright green top to his head. The smaller hen has muted brown plumage.

A partridge is slightly smaller in size than a pheasant and the flavour is more delicate – nearer to that of a chicken. Both sexes have greyish breasts, barred wings and a chestnut-coloured head.

Of the wild ducks, mallard is perhaps the most familiar. The male has brilliant green head feathers; the female is less conspicuous with brownish feathers. Teal is much smaller and is also beautifully coloured, while widgeon is between the mallard and the teal in size.

Wood pigeons are small, grey-brown birds, often shot as farm pests. Strictly speaking they are the only pigeons that count as game. On the other hand, conservationists are trying to protect snipe, woodcock and plovers. These are all small birds with long bills, and when cooked they are served whole. Quail, which are commercially farmed, are also served whole.

Venison

The term venison used to cover any wild animal hunted for food but now applies only to deer: antelope, elk, reindeer, roe, fallow and red deer. The male, or buck, is better for eating then the female, but neither should be more than three years old, the prime animals being between 18 months and two years old.

Rabbit and hare

Commercially bred rabbit, known as tame rabbit, is widely available and is ideal for roasting. It is more delicate in taste than wild rabbit, which is best used for making casseroles and pies.

Hares look similar but are bigger, with longer ears and hind legs. Young hares can be recognized by their short necks, long joints and thin saddle. A leveret is a hare less than one year old. It has a small, bony knob near the foot which disappears as the animal grows older. Only leverets and young hares are suitable for roasting.

Buying and storing game birds

A good poulterer will classify birds as 'young' and suitable for roasting, or as 'casserole' birds. Generally speaking you can identify a young bird by its relatively smooth legs, moist, supple feet and tender pinions (the long wing-tip feathers). If your poulterer specializes in game he should be able to stock quail (which are farmed) and pigeon throughout the year. He may also have frozen birds out of season. Grouse, partridge, pheasant and wild duck may be in stock in season; snipe and woodcock, on the other hand, will always need to be ordered.

Hanging tenderizes the flesh and intensifies the flavour. Hanging times differ from one game bird to another. Pigeon and quail are never hung and young game birds, shot early in the season, require minimum hanging. Young grouse shot on the opening day of the season, 'the glorious twelfth', are traditionally cooked that day.

If you are given game birds still in feather, your best plan is to take them to the poulterer who, for a fee, will hang, pluck, draw and truss them for you. If you are buying ready-prepared birds, tell the poulterer when you want to eat them and ask him for birds that have been hung the correct length of time. After hanging, the birds are plucked, drawn and trussed; the head is cut off and the crop removed. Woodcock, snipe and quail are traditionally cooked undrawn.

Plucked game birds can be kept, loosely wrapped, in the refrigerator for up to 2 days.

Buying and storing venison

Unless your local retailer specializes in game, you will probably have to order venison. The haunch and the saddle are the best parts to roast. Specify whether you want the meat well hung or not. This depends on how high you like it (see *page 110* for hanging times). Venison is very rich so 175 g /6 oz boneless meat (225 g /8 oz on the bone) per person should be adequate.

Store venison in the refrigerator in a marinade which should contain wine, some port or brandy, an onion, herbs and spices and a little olive oil. The meat should be turned regularly to soak it thoroughly in the marinade, which will later form the sauce or gravy. It can be kept for up to 3 days, providing it is completely submerged.

Buying and storing rabbit and hare

Tame rabbit is available all year round, both fresh and frozen. If buying fresh, the butcher will skin it for you. Rabbits are not normally hung, but drawn immediately on killing. Tame rabbit should be cooked within 24 hours of purchase.

You will probably have to order hare and specify whether you want it hung. After hanging, the meat may be kept in a marinade for up to 3 days, provided it is completely submerged. The liver, kidneys and heart must be submerged as well. Add 5 ml /1 tsp vinegar to the blood and refrigerate, uncovered.

Preparing and roasting game

Wipe game birds inside and out with a damp cloth, bring to room temperature, then pack stuffing, if using, into the body cavity. Sew up the cavity with a trussing needle and fine string, then truss the bird in the same way as a chicken (*page 10*).

The most important task in the preparation of hare is the removal of the bluish, thin membrane which holds the joints together.

Barding or larding is advisable for all game, from a tiny quail to a large haunch of venison, to keep it moist during cooking. For barding, use thin pieces of fat salt pork, fresh pork fat or fat, unsmoked bacon, and wrap them all around the bird or joint, tying them in position with string. As the fat melts it runs down the sides of the meat, making it almost self-basting, though you can also baste with the juices in the roasting tin.

Joints which are too thick for a barding strip need larding, which is slightly more difficult. Strips of fat (pork, salt pork or bacon) are pushed through the length of the joint (with the grain) using a special larding needle, or, if the structure of the joint does not allow this, pushed down into the meat as deeply as possible from either end, so that melting fat provides constant basting.

Game birds should be roasted as quickly as possible at a high temperature, so they have little opportunity to dry out. Conversely, larger game, which requires longer in the oven anyway, should be taken more slowly, otherwise the joint will be dry and fibrous on the outside by the time it has cooked through to the centre. For roasting times and oven temperatures see page 110. For small birds, use a small roasting tin so the juices do not spread out too much. Take care not to overcook; game quickly becomes tough if cooked for too long.

Serving roast game

Serve roast game (except for hare which should always be well cooked) very lightly cooked, unless you really dislike rare meat. If well done, the meat is likely to be tough. Game is usually served with certain traditional garnishes and accompaniments. Bread sauce and browned breadcrumbs are among these, and sharp fruit relishes such as redcurrant jelly or cranberry sauce are excellent with gamey meat. Game chips are a favourite accompaniment, and a full-bodied red wine will go perfectly.

Roast pheasant

Roast pheasant

bringing to room temperature, then 1¾ hours

Serves 4

1 plump young cock pheasant, dressed
salt and freshly ground black pepper
thin strips of fat salt pork or unsmoked fat
  bacon
15 g /½ oz butter, softened
175 ml /6 fl oz red wine
175 ml /6 fl oz chicken stock
15 ml /1 tbls redcurrant jelly
30 ml /2 tbls fresh white breadcrumbs
1 green dessert apple, to garnish
lemon juice
watercress sprigs, to garnish

For the stuffing

15 ml /1 tbls olive oil
30 ml /2 tbls finely chopped onion
1 medium-sized cooking apple
5 ml /1 tsp lemon juice
50 g /2 oz butter, softened
salt and freshly ground black pepper

1 Bring the pheasant to room temperature. Heat the oven to 220C /425F /gas 7.
2 Make the stuffing: in a small pan heat the olive oil, add the finely chopped onion and sauté until soft and lightly coloured. Remove the onion with a slotted spoon and transfer to a bowl.
3 Peel and core the cooking apple and grate it coarsely into the bowl with the onion. Quickly add the lemon juice and toss.

4 Add the softened butter. Blend the stuffing ingredients together and season.
5 Wipe the pheasant clean inside and out with a damp cloth or absorbent paper. Pack the stuffing into the body cavity, pushing it right in – the handle of a wooden spoon makes a good utensil. Sew up the stuffed cavity with a trussing needle and fine string.
6 Sprinkle the bird lightly with pepper. Cover the breast of the bird with strips of thinly pounded salt pork or slices of unsmoked bacon, then truss.
7 Spread the pheasant with softened butter and place it in a small roasting tin.
8 Mix 90 ml /6 tbls red wine and 90 ml /6 tbls chicken stock together in a small jug.
9 Roast the bird in the oven for 50–60 minutes, basting every 10 minutes, the first time with some of the wine and stock mixture, then alternately with pan juices and more wine and stock. The pheasant is ready once the juices run clear when you pierce the thickest part of the inside leg with a skewer. Do not overcook it.
10 Lift the pheasant out of the roasting tin, letting the juices from the body cavity drain back into the tin. Place it on a heated serving dish. Remove the trussing strings, skewer and the remains of the barding fat. Keep warm while you finish the gravy.
11 Skim the roasting juices of all fat. Place the tin over a moderate heat, add the remaining stock and red wine and bring to simmering point, stirring and scraping the tin clean with a wooden spoon.
12 Stir in the redcurrant jelly and breadcrumbs and continue to simmer, stir-

ring constantly, until the sauce has thickened slightly. Taste and season with salt and pepper, if necessary. Pour into a heated sauce-boat and keep warm.
13 To make the apple garnish, cut a slice off the side of the apple so it will stand firmly. On the side directly opposite that slice, using a very sharp knife, cut a small V into the apple without going right down to the core. Leave the cut piece in place. Now cut 2 more, larger Vs outside the first, making the third cut right to the core. Place the apple on the serving dish and push the cut pieces forward. Brush with lemon juice, garnish with watercress sprigs and serve.

Roast mallard with port sauce

bringing to room temperature, then 1¾ hours

Serves 4

2 mallards, dressed
salt and freshly ground black pepper
10 ml /2 tsp dried thyme
1 orange
1 tart apple
1 large onion
8 thin slices bacon
300 ml /10 fl oz port
orange slices, to garnish
sprigs of watercress, to garnish

Roast mallard with port sauce

For the sauce
30 ml /2 tbls flour
juice of 2 oranges
juice of 2 lemons
90–120 ml /6–8 tbls port
salt and freshly ground black pepper

1 Bring the mallards to room temperature. Heat the oven to 230C /450F /gas 8.
2 Wipe the ducks clean inside and out with a damp cloth or absorbent paper. Rub the cavities with salt, pepper and thyme.
3 Chop the orange (with its peel), unpeeled apple and onion coarsely and stuff the ducks with some of this mixture, keeping the remainder for the roasting tin. Sew up the stuffed cavity with a trussing needle and fine string and then truss.
4 Place the ducks, breast side up, on a rack in a roasting tin. Cover the breasts with bacon slices and pour the port into the tin, add the reserved orange, onion and apple. Roast the duck in the oven for 20 minutes, basting several times with the port.
5 Remove the bacon; baste the duck well with the pan juices and continue roasting until the duck is cooked (a total of 40–50 minutes). The juices should run clear when you pierce the inside of the leg with a skewer. Remove the trussing strings and skewers, and the flavouring mixture from inside the birds. Transfer the ducks to a heated serving dish and keep warm.
6 To make the sauce, skim most of the fat from the pan juices and discard. In a small bowl, blend the flour to a smooth paste with the orange and lemon juices. Stir the mixture into the roasting juices and place over high heat, stirring until all the crusty bits from the bottom and sides of the tin are incorporated into the sauce and the sauce thickens. Then add the port, and salt and pepper if necessary. Heat through and strain into a heated sauce-boat.
7 When ready to serve, place on a serving dish and garnish with the orange slices and sprigs of watercress. Serve with the sauce.

Roast venison in juniper cream sauce

overnight marinating,
then 1 hour 40 minutes

Serves 6–8
½ saddle well-hung venison, 1.6–1.8 kg /
  3½–4 lb dressed weight
thin strips of fat salt pork
150 ml /5 fl oz olive oil
juice of 1 lemon
5 ml /1 tsp juniper berries
salt and freshly ground black pepper
1 medium-sized onion, sliced
7.5 cm /3 in strip of lemon zest
30 ml /2 tbls wine vinegar
60 ml /4 tbls melted butter
350 ml /12 fl oz whipping cream, or half
  thick and half thin cream
15 ml /1 tbls cornflour
new potatoes, to serve
flat-leaved parsley, to garnish

Roast venison in juniper cream sauce

1 Ask your butcher to remove the tough outer membrane from the saddle of venison, cut away the sinews and bard along the length of the saddle with strips of fat salt pork, allowing 2 rows of barding on each side.
2 In a large bowl, beat the olive oil and lemon juice together with a fork. Add the saddle of venison and turn it until thoroughly coated. Leave, covered, to marinate overnight in the refrigerator.
3 Bring the venison to room temperature. Heat the oven to 180C /350F /gas 4.
4 Drain the venison thoroughly and pat dry with absorbent paper.
5 In a mortar, crush the juniper berries and 5 ml /1 tsp salt with a pestle. Rub the mixture into the venison.
6 Place the saddle, meaty side upwards, in a roasting tin. Scatter the sliced onion around it and add the strip of lemon zest. Pour the wine vinegar and the butter over the venison and put it in the oven.
7 Meanwhile, put 300 ml /10 fl oz of the cream in a small saucepan and warm it gently, stirring.
8 When the venison has been roasting for 15 minutes, baste with half of the warmed cream. Return it to the oven for a further 20–30 minutes, basting once or twice during this time with the pan juices.
9 Turn the saddle so that the rib bones face upwards. Pour over the remainder of the warmed cream and continue to roast for a further 15 minutes.
10 Remove the roasting tin from the oven. Increase the temperature to 220C /425F / gas 7. Turn the saddle meaty side up again and return it to the oven for 10 minutes longer.
11 Check the venison by inserting a sharp knife next to the bone. If it is too rare for your taste, add water (no more than 45 ml / 3 tbls) to the roasting tin and return to the oven for 10 minutes, or until the venison is cooked to your liking.
12 Transfer the venison to a heated serving dish and return it to the turned-off oven to keep hot while you make a sauce.
13 Strain the sauce from the roasting tin into a medium-sized saucepan, reserving the onions. In a small bowl, blend the cornflour with 30 ml /2 tbls cold water, stir in 30 ml /2 tbls sauce, return it to the saucepan and bring to the boil, simmer for 1–2 minutes. Add the remaining cream, season to taste with salt and freshly ground black pepper and simmer gently.
14 Discard the lemon zest, spread the onion on top of the saddle and garnish with new potatoes and flat-leaved parsley. Pour the sauce into a heated sauce-boat and serve.

CASSEROLING GAME

Game birds and animals make excellent casseroles. First cooked in peasant and farm kitchens, many of them have been developed by great chefs over the centuries into exquisite masterpieces.

Game birds and animals, even if they are too old and tough to roast, take well to being casseroled. Flavoured with herbs and vegetables, moistened with stock or wine and cooked slowly until tender, game becomes a luxury dish for a winter dinner.

Take, for instance, Chartreuse of partridge. I have given you a simple version close to those used in the farm kitchens of France for centuries. Two not-so-young partridges are browned in goose fat or lard and are then tucked inside a leafy cabbage. Bacon and sausage are added for extra depth of flavour, along with the usual pot vegetables, and the whole is cooked in a rich beef stock until meltingly tender. For the *haute cuisine* version of this, an old partridge would be used to flavour the cabbage, then that would be discarded and replaced at the table by young roasted birds, tender and in their prime. It is reputed that this dish was the ingenious invention of the monks of the Grande Chartreuse. These self-denying Carthusians are, supposedly, forbidden the flesh of bird or beast – so the partridges were concealed in a leafy cabbage to keep up appearances!

Delicious jugged hare is another classic dish, rich and dark and thickened with blood. This is a technique that has largely disappeared from our kitchens, owing to modern slaughtering practices that distance the killing from the kitchen by such a long way. Nowadays we thicken sauces with flour, or with cream or egg. Cooking with game is one of the rare occasions when the blood is available, and a wise cook will make use of this ancient practice that gives considerable extra flavour to the dish. Take care, though, not to let the sauce boil – if it boils it will curdle.

Game birds

Pheasants are amongst the most beautiful of wild birds, with the brilliant plumage of the cock and the soft muted browns of the hen making a handsome sight when they are paired together in a brace.

A young cock bird will have short, rounded spurs which lengthen and sharpen with age. The hen is an altogether rounder, plumper creature. A young one will have soft, pliable feet and her plumage will be a shade lighter than that of an old bird. The feathers under the wing should be soft and downy, and the flight feathers round rather than pointed. A young pheasant makes a superb roast, but if you are in any doubt about its age play safe with a casserole; this moist method of cooking ensures that the flesh cooks to tenderness without becoming dry and stringy.

The king of the moor, grouse has a subtle yet distinct flavour of the heather on which it feeds. Gourmets eagerly await the start of the season when the first birds are rushed by

road, rail and air to the tables of the grand restaurants all over the world. A great deal of the aura that surrounds grouse stems from its rarity. Although many different birds around the world are described as 'grouse', the red or Scottish grouse has so far defied all attempts to transplant it from the British Isles. Only young grouse should be roasted – the others fare best in casseroles, pies and terrines.

For those who are not over-enthusiastic about the strong flavours of game, partridge is the answer. The flavour of a young, plump partridge is quite exquisite, delicate like chicken, yet with a fullness and richness no farmyard bird would have. A young partridge will have pale, yellow-brown feet and, when plucked, the flesh will be a shade paler than that of an older bird.

Snipe is a tiny bird with an excellent flavour. Although it is often roasted without being drawn (that is, with its innards still inside), it should be drawn before being casseroled.

Woodcock resembles snipe, with a long pronounced bill, but it is slightly larger.

Wood pigeon is not strictly game but 'rough shooting'. It is always cooked like game, though, and is best casseroled.

Venison

Venison makes excellent eating, but care must be taken when cooking it, as it tends to be dry by nature. All venison improves with marinating. The leg, loin and saddle make superb roasts; the remainder of the carcass should be casseroled or put into a pie.

Ideally the animal is skinned and cleaned immediately after shooting. The butcher will then hang it in a cold, airy place. The longer it is left, the 'riper' it will become.

Hare and rabbit

Hare is considered by many to be on a par with venison and, like venison, it tends to be dry unless precautions are taken, such as barding, larding and steeping in a marinade.

When ordering hare, ask your butcher or poulterer to save the blood for you. Ask him to skin the animal carefully and remove the intestines without disturbing the liver, heart and kidneys. Because hare is hung by the hind feet, the blood collects round the rib cage, so that little should escape during paunching. Take the skinned hare home in a watertight plastic bag. At home, suspend the hare head downwards over a large bowl and leave it until most of the blood has dripped off. Cover the bowl tightly and store in the refrigerator. Add 15 ml /1 tbls vinegar to it if you are not cooking it within 24 hours, or the blood will clot.

Rabbit, like pigeon, is not actually game, as it is not protected by law. Indeed, much of the rabbit in the shops has never even seen the wild but has been bred specially for the

table – this tame or 'hutch' rabbit is a much milder meat than hare, with a flavour more akin to chicken than to most game, though wild rabbit often has a gamey flavour.

Frozen tame rabbit, on the bone or in boneless blocks, is widely available and is best casseroled or used in pies.

Casseroling game

Game birds can be casseroled whole – they can be stuffed in this case – or cut into joints, depending on their size, while hare and rabbit are usually portioned. Venison can be boned and cubed, or a shoulder or haunch can be rolled and tied.

Before cutting up the bird or animal, wipe it thoroughly, inside and out, with a damp cloth or absorbent paper.

Marinating is particularly useful for making older game birds and animals tender and juicy, but will also improve the taste of younger game wonderfully. If you don't marinate, season the game well with salt and freshly ground black pepper, or dredge with seasoned flour.

The game to be casseroled is usually first browned in butter, olive oil or bacon fat, then cooked, with flavouring herbs and vegetables, in stock, wine or water (stock or water should be very hot when it is added to the casserole, otherwise flavour will be extracted from the game). Cooking time depends on what you are casseroling, but it should be slow so that the game emerges deliciously tender.

Salmis

A salmis is a traditional dish in which a game bird — woodcock, pheasant, grouse, partridge, wild duck or wood pigeon — is part-roasted to sear it and seal in its juices, then portioned. The skin and some of the bones are removed. A rich sauce is made using the carcass and trimmings along with red or white wine, chicken or beef stock, herbs and flavouring vegetables, and the cooking is completed in the sauce — the classic method is to finish it in style in a chafing dish at the table, but it can also be done in a frying-pan in the kitchen.

Baked rabbit in lemon sauce

1 hour 10 minutes

Serves 4
900 g /2 lb rabbit, jointed
salt and freshly ground black pepper
15 ml /1 tbls olive oil
30 ml /2 tbls lemon juice
75 g /3 oz softened butter
5 ml /1 tsp dried tarragon
2.5 ml /½ tsp dried oregano
1 large lemon, thinly sliced
50 g /2 oz butter
15 ml /1 tbls flour
125 ml /4 fl oz chicken, home-made or from a cube
25 ml /1 fl oz dry white wine
150 ml /5 fl oz thick cream
thin slices of lemon, to garnish
sprigs of watercress, to garnish

Moroccan grouse

1 Heat the oven to 190C /375F /gas 5. Season the rabbit joints well with salt and freshly ground black pepper. Place them in a roasting tin.
2 Mix the olive oil with 15 ml /1 tbls lemon juice and pour over the rabbit. Mix together the softened butter, tarragon and oregano. Spread this paste evenly over the rabbit joints, place 2 lemon slices on each joint and bake for 30–40 minutes or until the rabbit is tender, basting from time to time.
3 Meanwhile, make the sauce. Melt the butter in a small saucepan and stir in the flour. Add the stock and wine gradually, stirring constantly. Add the remaining lemon juice and bring to a simmer. Simmer for 4 minutes, stirring, then add the cream, blend and heat through gently.
4 Remove the rabbit from the oven and arrange on a warmed serving platter, garnishing with the lemon slices and watercress sprigs. Keep warm. Pour any juices from the roasting tin into the sauce and stir thoroughly. Pour over the rabbit and serve.

Moroccan grouse

This is a very different way to serve grouse. The spicy marinade ensures that the bird absorbs all the flavours.

24 hours marinating, then 1¼ hours

Serves 4
2 grouse, 350 g /12 oz each dressed weight
1 Spanish onion, sliced
225 ml /8 fl oz olive oil
4 ml /¾ tsp ground ginger
4 ml /¾ tsp ground turmeric
4 ml /¾ tsp ground coriander
4 ml /¾ tsp ground cumin
45 ml /3 tbls finely chopped fresh coriander
salt and freshly ground black pepper
300 ml /10 fl oz boiling water
350 g /12 oz potatoes
4 medium-sized tomatoes, blanched, skinned, seeded and quartered

1 Cut each grouse into 4 serving pieces, removing the back- and breastbones. Lay the pieces in a shallow dish and cover with the onion slices.
2 In a measuring jug, mix the olive oil, ginger, turmeric, ground coriander, cumin, finely chopped fresh coriander and salt and freshly ground black pepper to taste. Pour over the grouse and turn them to ensure they are well coated. Cover and leave to marinate for 24 hours in the refrigerator.
3 Bring the grouse to room temperature.
4 In a flameproof casserole, heat 60 ml /4 tbls of the marinade and brown the grouse and onions. Add the remaining marinade and the boiling water. Cover the casserole and simmer gently for 40 minutes.
5 Cut the potatoes into even-sized wedge shapes. After 40 minutes, place the potatoes and the tomatoes on top of the grouse. Cook, covered, for 20 minutes. Correct the seasoning and serve immediately.

Venison hot pot

overnight marinating,
then 2¾ hours

Serves 4–6

1 kg /2 lb shoulder or haunch of venison,
  rolled and tied
600 ml /1 pt strong beef stock, home-made
  or from a cube
500 g /1 lb pickling onions
500 g /1 lb button mushrooms
225 g /8 oz canned artichoke hearts, drained
beurre manié, made with 15 g /½ oz flour
  and 15 g /½ oz butter

For the marinade

600 ml /1 pt red wine
30 ml /2 tbls red wine vinegar
4 garlic cloves, crushed
5 ml /1 tsp ground allspice
5 ml /1 tsp dried basil
2 bay leaves
2 anchovies, pounded
salt
freshly ground black pepper

Venison hot pot

1   Combine the wine, wine vinegar, garlic, allspice, basil, bay leaves, anchovies and salt and freshly ground black pepper to taste in a deep bowl. Add the shoulder or haunch of venison and leave to marinate in a cool place for 24 hours, turning occasionally.
2   Heat the oven to 150C /300F /gas 2. Transfer the venison and its marinade to a large, flameproof casserole. Add the beef stock and the pickling onions and stir well. Cover with foil and then the lid, and cook in the oven for 2 hours.
3   Add the button mushrooms and drained artichoke hearts to the casserole and return to the oven for another 30 minutes or until the venison is very tender – you should be able to pierce it easily with a fork.
4   To serve, transfer the venison to a warmed serving platter and carve it. Add the vegetables, using a slotted spoon, and keep warm while you finish the sauce. Over a low heat, add about 15 ml /1 tbls *beurre manié* to the casserole, stirring it in in small pieces until the sauce has thickened slightly. Pour over the venison and serve at once.

● Serve this simple but rich casserole with buttered noodles or boiled potatoes.

Wood pigeons with grapes

This makes an impressive dinner party dish, yet it requires the minimum of last-minute attention.

45 minutes, 1¼–1½ hours cooking, then 10 minutes

Serves 4

4 young wood pigeons, cleaned and dressed
100 g /4 oz softened butter
salt
freshly ground black pepper
8 thin slices of unsmoked streaky bacon
200 ml /7 fl oz hot chicken stock, home-
  made or from a cube
450 g /1 lb seedless grapes
15 ml /1 tbls flour
150 ml /5 fl oz thick cream
30 ml /2 tbls brandy (optional)
sprigs of watercress, to garnish

To serve

croûtons
creamed potatoes

1 Heat the oven to 180C /350F /gas 4. Rub the pigeons all over with butter and put a little into the cavity of each bird, using about 40 g /1½ oz in all. Season the birds inside and out with salt and freshly ground black pepper, wrap them in the thin slices of streaky bacon and tie them with fine string.

2 Melt about 40 g /1½ oz of the remaining butter in a large flameproof casserole over a medium heat and fry the pigeons on all sides for about 15 minutes, until the bacon is almost crisp.

3 Arrange the pigeons neatly, breast side up, in the casserole and pour on the hot chicken stock. Season with salt and freshly ground black pepper and bring to the boil. Put the lid on the casserole (over a piece of aluminium foil if necessary) and transfer it to the oven. Cook for 1 hour.

4 Add the grapes and cook for a further 15–30 minutes, or until the pigeons feel tender when they are pierced in the thickest part of the leg with a fine skewer.

5 Remove the pigeons from the casserole and remove and discard the string and the bacon. Arrange them on a warmed serving dish. Remove the grapes with a slotted spoon, arrange them around the pigeons and cover the dish with foil to keep warm.

6 Mix the remaining butter with the flour to make a *beurre manié*. Place the casserole over a moderate heat, add the beurre manié in small pieces and stir until the sauce thickens. Stir in the thick cream and, if you are using it, the brandy. Pour the sauce over the pigeons, scatter with the croûtons, garnish with sprigs of watercress and serve at once, accompanied by creamed potatoes.

Rabbit with tarragon and garlic sauce

Tarragon, garlic, mustard and tomatoes are combined here to make an aromatic sauce for rabbit. Use defrosted frozen rabbit pieces instead of a whole one if you wish.

 2 hours

Serves 4
1 kg /2 lb rabbit, dressed weight
10–15 ml /2–3 tsp finely chopped fresh tarragon or 5 ml /1 tsp dried tarragon
15 ml /1 tbls Dijon mustard
salt
freshly ground black pepper
about 50 g /2 oz thinly sliced fat salt pork
butter for greasing
2 medium-sized onions, sliced
4 medium-sized tomatoes, sliced
2 garlic cloves, chopped
1.5 ml /¼ tsp dried thyme
1 bay leaf, crumbled
150 ml /5 fl oz dry white wine
10–15 ml /2–3 tsp cornflour
hot buttered noodles, to serve

1 If fresh tarragon is not available, use dried tarragon instead: put it in a small

bowl, then pour over 15 ml /1 tbls boiling water and leave to infuse for a few minutes (as you would tea-leaves).

2 Meanwhile, joint the rabbit: cut off the front of the rabbit at the ribs and divide it in half. Cut off the legs at the thigh. Chop the saddle across into 2.

3 Heat the oven to 230C /450F /gas 8.

4 Drain the infused tarragon if using. Mix the fresh or infused tarragon with the mustard.

5 Season each piece of rabbit with salt and freshly ground black pepper, and spread lightly with tarragon mustard.

6 Wrap each piece of rabbit in fat salt pork, securing it with string.

7 Select a large casserole that will take the rabbit pieces in a single layer. Grease it with butter and cover the base with a layer of sliced onions and tomatoes. Sprinkle with chopped garlic, thyme, crumbled bay leaf and a little salt and black pepper. Lay the rabbit pieces on the bed of vegetables.

8 Bake, uncovered, for 10 minutes, or until the rabbit pieces are lightly coloured.

Rabbit with tarragon and garlic sauce

9 Remove the casserole from the oven and turn the heat down to 170C /325F /gas 3.

10 Moisten the casserole with the dry white wine, cover tightly and return to the oven for a further 40–45 minutes, or until the rabbit is tender.

11 Untie the rabbit joints and discard the pork fat. Arrange the joints in a shallow, ovenproof serving dish and return them to the oven to keep hot.

12 Strain the contents of the casserole through a fine sieve into a saucepan, pressing the vegetables against the sides of the sieve with the back of a spoon to extract their juices without rubbing them through.

13 Mix the cornflour to a smooth paste with 30 ml /2 tbls cold water, then blend in 30–45 ml /2–3 tbls of the sauce. Stir into the remaining sauce, bring to the boil and simmer, stirring, for 2–3 minutes, or until the sauce has thickened.

14 Spoon the sauce over the rabbit joints and serve with hot buttered noodles.

Jugged hare

🔪 40 minutes, 3 hours cooking,
then 15 minutes

Serves 6–8
1 hare, jointed, blood reserved
seasoned flour
50 g /2 oz bacon fat
2 medium-sized onions, chopped
2 carrots, chopped
1 celery stalk, chopped
850 ml /1½ pt hot beef or game stock
bouquet garni
salt and freshly ground black pepper
150 ml /5 fl oz port
15 ml /1 tbls redcurrant jelly

1   Coat the hare pieces in the seasoned flour, shaking off any excess. Heat the oven to 180C /350F /gas 4.
2   In a large flameproof casserole over a moderate heat, melt the bacon fat. Add the portions of hare and brown them evenly. Add the onions, carrots and celery and cook for a further 5 minutes.
3   Add the hot stock, bouquet garni and salt and pepper to taste. Cover and cook in the oven for 3 hours, or until the meat parts easily from the bone.
4   Remove the casserole from the oven. Put the blood in a bowl and carefully stir in 45 ml /3 tbls of the cooking liquid. Gradually add the blood to the casserole, stirring. Stir in the port and redcurrant jelly.
5   Place over a very gentle heat and reheat carefully, without bringing to the boil, for 5 minutes, then serve.

Venison stew

This stew is especially good when served with boiled rice or noodles and redcurrant jelly spiced with cinnamon and cloves.

🔪 45 minutes,
then 3 hours cooking

Serves 6–8
1.5 kg /3¼ lb boned venison, in large cubes
seasoned flour
bacon fat or olive oil
3 large celery stalks, thinly sliced
3 large carrots, thinly sliced
2 medium-sized onions, coarsely chopped
1 small garlic clove, finely chopped
1 small green pepper, diced
salt and freshly ground black pepper

1   Toss the venison cubes in the seasoned flour. Heat the bacon fat or olive oil in a large, deep, heavy-bottomed frying-pan over medium-high heat and fry the meat cubes, in batches, until brown on all sides.
2   Return the meat the pan. Add the celery, carrots, onions, garlic, green pepper and salt and freshly ground black pepper to taste. Cook for a few minutes, stirring, pour in 400 ml /14 fl oz hot water and bring to the boil, then lower the heat and simmer, tightly covered, for about 3 hours, or until tender.
3   Adjust the seasoning and serve at once.

Chartreuse of partridge

🔪🔪 1 hour,
then 1½–1¾ hours cooking

Serves 4
2 partridges, dressed
1.1 kg /2½ lb whole green cabbage
salt
freshly ground black pepper
60 ml /4 tbls goose fat or 50 g /2 oz lard
1 Spanish onion, sliced
2 carrots, thinly sliced
225 g /8 oz slice of ham sausage
350 g /12 oz smoked bacon joint, such as collar
425–600 ml /15 fl oz–1 pt, hot beef stock, home-made or from a cube

1   Heat the oven to 150C /300F /gas 2.
2   Hollow out the thick core from the base of the cabbage with a potato peeler – otherwise the middle will still be hard when the outside is cooked.
3   Select a large, deep, flameproof casserole that will hold the whole head of cabbage with room to spare. Fill the casserole about two-thirds full with salted water and bring to the boil. As soon as the water boils, duck the cabbage in. Making sure it is immersed, cover and boil for 5 minutes.
4   Drain the cabbage and quickly immerse it in a bowl of cold water. Leave under the cold tap to cool.
5   Cut the partridges into 4 joints each and season generously with salt and freshly ground black pepper. Rinse out and dry the casserole. Melt the goose fat or lard in it and brown the partridge pieces all over. Transfer the pieces to a plate.
6   In the same fat, sauté the onion and carrots for about 5 minutes, until golden.
7   Cut the ham sausage into 4 equal chunks. Add to the casserole and continue to sauté for a further 5 minutes, until coloured all over. Remove the sausage chunks to the plate with the partridges.
8   Strip 3–4 of the large outer leaves from the cabbage. Lay them over the vegetables.
9   Drain the cabbage thoroughly and carefully ease apart its leaves. Tuck the pieces of partridge deep down among the leaves. Fit the cabbage into the pot. If you can't fit all the partridge pieces inside the cabbage, nestle them round the outside.
10   Cut the bacon into 4 equal slices and lay them around the cabbage, together with the sausage chunks. Pour in half the hot stock and sprinkle with salt and freshly ground black pepper.
11   Cover the casserole tightly and cook in the oven for 40 minutes. Then moisten with the remaining hot stock and continue to cook for a further 50–65 minutes.
12   To serve, lift out the whole cabbage onto a large, deep serving dish. Lift any extra pieces of partridge out, lay them on top and surround with bacon slices and sausage chunks. Moisten the dish generously with about three-quarters of the strained cooking juices (use the remainder for a soup), and serve immediately.

Pheasant in red wine

🔪🔪 about 3 hours

Serves 4
1 tender pheasant, dressed, liver reserved
salt
freshly ground black pepper
2 shallots, finely chopped
40 g /1½ oz butter
15 ml /1 tbls olive oil
8 button mushrooms
275 ml /10 fl oz burgundy or other red wine
beurre manié, made with 7.5 g /¼ oz butter and 7.5 ml /½ tbls flour
8 button onions
15 ml /1 tbls sugar
15 ml /½ tsp lemon juice
chicken stock, home-made or from a cube (if needed)

1 Season the pheasant inside and out with salt and freshly ground black pepper. Stuff the body cavity of the bird with the finely chopped shallots and its own liver. Sew up the cavity with a trussing needle and fine string and then truss the bird.
2 In a sauté pan or deep frying-pan, melt 15 g /½ oz butter with the olive oil. Over a moderate heat, brown the pheasant thoroughly all over for 15–20 minutes. Transfer the pheasant to a medium-sized, flameproof casserole with a tight-fitting lid. Cover and keep warm.
3 Trim the stalks from the button mushrooms. Put the mushroom caps aside and add the stalks to the sauté pan, together with the red wine. Bring to the boil over a high heat, stirring and scraping the bottom and sides of the pan clean with a wooden spoon. Boil the sauce until it has reduced to half its original quantity. Remove from heat.
4 Add the *beurre manié* to the hot wine sauce in small pieces, stirring until it has completely dissolved. Return the pan to the heat, bring to the boil again and simmer, stirring, for 2–3 minutes longer, until the sauce has thickened.
5 Strain the sauce over the pheasant. Replace the lid and put aside.
6 Heat the oven to 140C /275F /gas 1.
7 Bring to the boil a small saucepan of salted water. Add the button onions and simmer for 10 minutes, then drain thoroughly. Add 15 g /½ oz butter to the pan and swirl over a low heat until melted. Then sprinkle with the sugar, turn the heat up to moderate and sauté the onions for about 10 minutes or until they are coated with a rich caramel glaze. Add them to the casserole.
8 Melt 15 g /½ oz butter in a small, heavy frying-pan. Add the mushroom caps, sprinkle with lemon juice (to preserve their whiteness), salt and pepper, and toss over a low heat for 8–10 minutes until lightly coloured. Add to the casserole.
9 Set the casserole over a low heat and slowly bring to simmering point. Cover tightly and transfer to the oven.
10 Bake the casserole until the pheasant is meltingly tender. If it is a young bird, it will be done in 50–60 minutes. An older one will take considerably longer. Turn the pheasant and baste occasionally with the wine sauce as it cooks to keep it moist, adding a little chicken stock to the casserole if the sauce evaporates too quickly.
11 To serve, transfer the pheasant to a heated serving dish and remove the trussing threads and skewer. Discard the liver and the shallots. Surround with glazed onions and sautéed mushroom caps. Taste the sauce and correct the seasoning, skim off the fat if necessary and spoon the sauce over the pheasant. Serve immediately.

Chartreuse of partridge

GAME PIES

Game pies make a traditionally English meal, either steaming hot under a crisp pastry lid – warming and hearty on a winter's day, or cold and meaty – ideal for a picnic or a buffet centrepiece.

The rich, strong flavour of game makes it an ideal ingredient in a pie, combined with mouth-watering golden pastry – either a chilled pie where the pastry encloses the filling of meat set in jelly, or a lighter single-crust hot pie.

Game in pies is frequently used in combination with another less expensive meat. However, game has such a strong flavour that it will predominate.

Added texture is given to the pie by combining complete portions of meat, such as the breast of a game bird, with strips of meat or cubed or minced meat, as well as extra ingredients such as mushrooms or hard-boiled eggs.

Puff or shortcrust pastry will not withstand heat for very long so, when making either a single- or double-crust pie, the meat must be cooked first. Cool it before putting together the pie, as a hot filling will make the pastry soggy.

Chilled game pies

By using a cake or bread tin or a special pie mould and decorating the lid with pastry trimmings you can create a centrepiece fit for any table.

The cooked pie is allowed to cool, then extra stock is poured through a funnel inserted in slits in the pastry lid to bind the filling together, closing any gaps that will have appeared if the meat has shrunk during cooking. These pies are served well chilled, and are best with a light accompaniment such as a crisp green salad.

Hot game pies

Moist, meaty pie fillings under a single pastry crust make a simple, hearty main-course filler. When game, such as quail, is included in the filling it adds an extra touch of sophistication. Using a proper pie dish makes it easier to knock up the edge of the pie, which will in turn secure the lid. If you are not using a pie funnel (and one is not really necessary if you have a fairly firm filling), pile the meat up in a dome in the centre of the dish. This will help to support the pastry in the initial stages of cooking, so it will not collapse if the meat shrinks away from the lid while cooking.

Quail and beefsteak pie

Quail and beefsteak pie

In this hot pie, inexpensive shin of beef supplements the quails and gives added texture to the succulent filling.

3 hours, plus cooling

Serves 4
4 quails
700 g /1½ lb shin of beef, cut into 15 mm /½ in cubes
425 ml /15 fl oz beef stock, home-made or from a cube
salt
freshly ground black pepper
15 g /½ oz butter
15 ml /1 tbls olive oil.
beurre manié, made by mashing together 25 g /1 oz butter and 30 ml /2 tbls flour
100 g /4 oz flat mushrooms, quartered
350 g /12 oz made-weight puff pastry, defrosted if frozen
flour for dusting
1 egg yolk, beaten

1 In a large saucepan bring the stock to the boil. Add the beef and season with salt and pepper to taste. Bring back to the boil, then cover and simmer slowly for 2 hours. Drain, reserving the stock in a clean saucepan.
2 Heat the butter and olive oil in a large frying-pan. Season the quails with salt and freshly ground black pepper. Place in the frying-pan and brown slowly all over for about 15 minutes, turning them with a spatula.
3 Remove the quails from the pan. Split in half and remove all the meat from the bones. Add the quail meat to the cooked beef.
4 Bring the beef stock to the boil. Whisk in the *beurre manié*, a piece at a time, and boil for 2 minutes, or until thickened. Turn into a bowl, correct the seasoning and leave to cool.
5 Pile the cold meats, liquid and mushrooms into a dome shape in a 1.7 L /3 pt pie dish. Heat the oven to 230C /450F / gas 8.
6 Roll out the puff pastry evenly on a lightly floured board to a thickness of 5 mm /¼ in and cut a lid for the pie a little larger than the dish. Moisten the rim of the dish and place the pastry lid on top. Knock up and flute the edge to decorate. Cut a vent in the centre to allow steam to escape. Cut decorations from the pastry trimmings and stick to the pie with a little beaten egg yolk. Brush the pastry with egg yolk and bake for 10 minutes.
7 Lower the temperature to 190C /375F / gas 5. Bake for a further 15 minutes, or until the pastry crust is golden brown. Serve hot.

● Tiny quails are extremely fiddly to bone out. It is easy to remove the backbone with scissors, but if you give up on the rest of the birds and resort to the cleaver, warn your guests to watch out for tiny bones!

Wild rabbit pie

This delicious pie is equally good for a picnic or as a supper dish. It can be made with tame rabbit but will not taste as gamey.

3 hours 40 minutes, plus cooling and overnight chilling

Serves 4–6

1 wild rabbit, jointed
1 L /2 pt beef stock, home-made or from a cube
15 ml /1 tbls powdered gelatine (if using stock cubes rather than home-made stock)
225 g /8 oz button mushrooms, thinly sliced
50 g /2 oz butter
5 ml /1 tsp freshly grated nutmeg
2.5 ml /½ tsp dried sage
5 ml /1 tsp dried marjoram
salt and freshly ground black pepper
225 g /8 oz smoked ham, in julienne strips
3 medium-sized eggs, hard-boiled and sliced
30 ml /2 tbls port or brandy
flat-leaved parsley, to garnish
raw onion rings, to garnish

For the pastry

225 g /8 oz flour
a pinch of salt
150 g /5 oz butter
50–75 ml /2–3 fl oz iced water
flour for dusting
milk
1 medium-sized egg yolk, beaten

1 Put the rabbit and the stock in a large saucepan and bring to boiling point over high heat. Turn the heat to low and simmer gently for about 1 hour, or until the rabbit is tender.

2 Meanwhile, make the pastry. Sift together the flour and salt and rub in 125 g / 4 oz butter with your fingertips until the mixture resembles fine breadcrumbs. Gradually add iced water until the dough is soft but not wet. Chill 30 minutes.

3 Flour a board and roll out the pastry fairly thinly. Cut off a third and reserve for the lid and trimmings. Roll out the remainder large enough to line a 1.7 L /3 pt rectangular dish or small roasting tin. Cut off a third of the reserved pastry for decorations and roll out the remainder into an oblong for the lid. Roll out the remaining pastry thinly and cut out 6 leaves, rolling what is left into a long, thin piece between the palms of your hands. Cut in half and twist the 2 pieces together, pinching at the ends to join them.

4 Grease the loaf tin with the remaining 25 g /1 oz butter and line with the large piece of pastry.

5 Remove the rabbit from the stock with a slotted spoon and leave to cool. Meanwhile boil the stock hard until it has reduced to about 300 ml /10 fl oz, and keep warm. If using stock made from cubes rather than home-made, dissolve the gelatine in 30 ml /2 tbls water and add to the stock.

6 Sauté the sliced mushrooms in the butter until they begin to give off their juices, then drain and reserve.

Wild rabbit pie

7 When the rabbit is cool, remove all the flesh from the bones and divide into 2 portions. Finely chop half and put the other half through the mincer.

8 Heat the oven to 200C /400F /gas 6. In a bowl, mix the minced rabbit with the nutmeg, sage and marjoram. Put half the chopped rabbit in the bottom of the lined loaf tin and season with salt and pepper. Cover with half the mushrooms, then add a layer of half the minced rabbit and season.

9 Add the ham in one layer, then slices of hard-boiled egg. Cover with the remaining minced rabbit, then the rest of the mushrooms, finishing with a layer of chopped rabbit. Add the port or brandy to the stock and pour enough over the rabbit to just cover the top layer of meat. Reserve the remainder, keeping it in a warm place so it does not set.

10 Brush the outer edges of the pastry lining the tin with milk and put on the lid, pressing firmly. Make 3 slits in the lid. Place the pastry twist around the edge of the lid, and the leaves around the slits, brushing the pastry with milk to fasten. Brush with beaten egg yolk and bake for 20 minutes.

11 Lower the heat to 150C /300F /gas 2 and bake for a further 30 minutes, covering the pie with foil if it is browning too much. Remove from the oven and cool.

12 When it is cold, pour in more stock through the slits in the lid until the pie is full. Refrigerate overnight and serve well chilled, garnished with parsley and onion.

STAR MENU & RECIPE FILE

Here is a menu for a rather special occasion, perhaps a small dinner party to celebrate a winter birthday. Start your meal with deep-fried chicken liver turnovers. These tasty half-moons of deep-fried puff pastry are filled with a piping hot, herby mixture of chicken liver and onion, moist but still firm. They're so easy for a dinner party – you do all the preparations ahead of time and chill the prepared turnovers until you are ready to fry them, just before the meal. Then quickly pop them in the hot oil, arrange them on individual plates, garnish and serve. Piping hot and golden, they look and taste deliciously intriguing.

Wild duck Normandy comes from a countryside of orchards and dairy cattle. This beautiful dish of mallard braised with apples and calvados has the rich, fruity flavour characteristic of the area and is finished in style with cream sharpened with lemon juice. Use frozen mallards if fresh birds are unavailable.

Crumbed carrots, accompanying the birds, are tender inside and crisp outside, to contrast with the creamy sauce served with the duck. Garnish them as I suggest with miniature 'carrot tops' to add a little extra colour. There is nothing complicated about this pretty garnish; just use tiny bouquets of parsley for the tops.

Do justice to the wild duck and drink with it a truly first-class wine. I suggest a young Figeac. This wonderful claret from St. Emilion is full-bodied and matures rather more quickly than most Bordeaux wines.

After the rich duck, serve a palate-cleansing green salad as a separate course. Serving the salad after you've finished off the wine means that both will be at their best – your carefully chosen wine would not be fully appreciated if drunk with the sharp salad dressing. For the salad, a simple combination of crisp lettuce leaves and peppery watercress sprigs, would be appropriate.

Cherry praline bombe is a delicious dessert. For preference, make your own vanilla ice cream, but even if you buy this basic ingredient, the bombe should be a wow! Stir the crunchy caramelized praline into the softened ice cream to give it an irresistibly nutty flavour. Line the bombe mould with this and fill the centre with a light mousse studded with maraschino cherries. Made and frozen the day before, it will be a simple thing to unmould and decorate the bombe between courses. Don't forget to remove it from the freezer between the first and the main course and leave it to soften a bit in the main part of the refrigerator while you eat the duck.

Deep-fried chicken liver turnovers

Wild duck Normandy

Crumbed carrots

Cherry praline bombe

Wine: Figeac

Plan-ahead timetable

Two days before the meal
Cherry praline bombe: make ice cream and freeze.

On the day before the meal
Cherry praline bombe: make the praline, leave to cool and harden, then crush and add to the softened ice cream. Line the mould, cover and freeze. Make the mousse, pour into the centre of the bombe, cover and freeze.
Deep-fried chicken liver turnovers: make and chill the puff pastry, if wished. Cook the chicken livers with the bacon and onion, cool and mince. Season the filling and chill.

Three hours before the meal
Deep-fried chicken liver turnovers: defrost the pastry, if frozen.
Wild duck Normandy: season the ducks with freshly ground black pepper and bring to room temperature.

Two hours before the meal
Deep-fried chicken liver turnovers: roll out the pastry, cut out circles, fill, place on a tray and chill.
Crumbed carrots: prepare, cook, drain and dry carrot strips.

One hour before the meal
Wild duck Normandy: season the ducks with salt and brown them. Sauté the apples. Assemble the casserole and place in oven.

Twenty minutes before the meal
Wild duck Normandy: add the cream and lemon juice.
Cherry praline bombe: whip the cream and refrigerate.

Ten minutes before the meal
Crumbed carrots: Coat the carrot strips with beaten egg, then with breadcumbs. Transfer to a buttered baking dish, season and dot with butter, then bake.
Deep-fried chicken liver turnovers: heat the oil, deep fry the turnovers, drain on absorbent paper and keep hot.

Just before the meal
Deep-fried chicken liver turnovers: transfer to heated plates, garnish and serve.

Between the first and the main course
Wild duck Normandy: transfer ducks to a wooden board and cut in half. Arrange on a heated serving platter with the apple rings. Correct seasoning of sauce, spoon over the ducks and serve.
Crumbed carrots: transfer to a heated serving dish, garnish with parsley and serve.
Cherry praline bombe: unmould onto a serving dish and place in the main part of the refrigerator to soften.

Between the main course and the dessert
Cherry praline bombe: decorate with whipped cream and maraschino cherries and serve.

Deep-fried chicken liver turnovers

Makes 24

250 g /8 oz made-weight puff
   pastry, defrosted if frozen
flour for dusting
1 egg yolk, beaten
oil for deep frying
For the filling
65 g /2½ oz streaky bacon
100 g /4 oz chicken livers

1.5 ml /¼ tsp dried thyme
½ bay leaf, crumbled
½ small onion, finely chopped
salt and ground black pepper
5 ml /1 tsp brandy
For the garnish
1 bunch watercress, trimmed
4 double lemon twists

1   Prepare the filling. Remove the rind from the bacon and cut into small dice. Sauté in a large frying-pan over a low heat until the fat runs.
2   Meanwhile, remove any fat, membranes or greenish patches from the chicken livers. Add to the bacon with the dried thyme, crumbled bay leaf, and finely chopped onion. Raise the heat to moderate. Sauté for 3 minutes, tossing with a spatula, until the livers are browned but still slightly pink in the centre. Transfer to a bowl and leave to cool.
3   Put the cooled liver mixture through the finest blade of a mincer into a bowl or work in a food processor until smooth. Season to taste with salt and freshly ground black pepper and stir in the brandy. Chill.
4   On a lightly floured board, roll out the pastry very thinly. Using a plain 6.5 cm /2½ in pastry cutter, cut out 24 circles. Brush the edges with a little beaten egg yolk and place 5 ml /1 tsp of the chicken liver mixture in the centre of each circle. Fold each circle in half and seal the turnovers with your fingers, pressing down gently. Place the turnovers on a tray and chill for at least 30 minutes.
5   Heat the oil in a deep-fat frier to 190C /375F. Deep fry the turnovers in batches for 3 minutes, or until cooked through and golden brown, turning them once with a slotted spoon during cooking. Drain well on absorbent paper and keep hot while you fry the remaining turnovers.
6   Arrange 6 turnovers on each of 4 individual heated plates. Garnish each plate with watercress and a double lemon twist and serve at once.

 1½ hours including chilling

Wild duck Normandy

Serves 4
2 × 700 g /1½ lb wild ducks, dressed weight
freshly ground black pepper
salt
50 g /2 oz butter
30 ml /2 tbls olive oil
2 large tart dessert apples
90 ml /6 tbls calvados
300 ml /10 fl oz thick cream
30 ml /2 tbls lemon juice

1   Rub the duck cavities with freshly ground black pepper and bring the birds to room temperature.
2   Heat the oven to 190C /375F /gas 5.
3   Season the birds with salt. In a frying-pan large enough to take the 2 ducks comfortably side by side, heat 25 g /1 oz butter and the olive oil. When the foaming subsides, brown the birds on all sides, then remove from the pan and keep warm.
4   While the ducks are browning, peel and core the apples and slice them into thick rings.
5   In an ovenproof casserole large enough to take the 2 ducks comfortably side by side, melt the remaining butter and sauté the apple rings for 2-3 minutes on each side, or until lightly browned, turning with a spatula.
6   Arrange the ducks on top of the apple slices. Add the calvados and cook in the oven for 30 minutes, basting frequently.
7   Add the thick cream and the lemon juice and cook for a further 20-30 minutes, or until the ducks are tender and the sauce is creamy and thick.
8   Transfer the ducks to a wooden board and cut each in 2. Arrange on a heated serving platter and surround with the apple rings. Correct the seasoning of the sauce and spoon the sauce over the duck halves. Serve immediately.

 bringing to room temperature, then 1½ hours   Figeac

Crumbed carrots

Serves 4
10 even-sized, well-shaped carrots
salt
1 egg, lightly beaten
50 g /2 oz dry white breadcrumbs
25 g /1 oz butter
freshly ground black pepper
tiny sprigs of parsley, to garnish

1   Heat the oven to 190C /375F / gas 5. Peel the carrots and cut them into quarters lengthways, trimming off the ends to make even-sized strips.
2   Bring a large saucepan of salted water to the boil, add the carrot strips and simmer for 10 minutes or until tender. Drain, rinse under cold running water and drain again. Dry on absorbent paper.
3   Place the lightly beaten egg in a shallow dish and the breadcrumbs in a separate shallow dish. Grease an ovenproof serving dish generously with some of the butter.
4   Toss the prepared carrots in the beaten egg, shaking off the excess, then in the dried breadcrumbs to coat, patting them on firmly with the palms of your hands.
5   Transfer the coated carrots to the buttered dish, arranging them in 2 neat rows or in rings. Season generously with freshly ground black pepper and dot with the remaining butter. Cook in the top of the oven for 20 minutes, or until crisp and golden brown.
6   To serve, arrange tiny sprigs of parsley at 1 end of each crumbed carrot strip. Serve as soon as possible.

|| 1 hour

Cherry praline bombe

Serves 4
425 ml /15 fl oz vanilla ice cream,
* home-made or bought*
50 g /2 oz sugar
2 egg yolks
30 ml /2 tbls thick cream,
* lightly whipped*
30 ml /2 tbls quartered maraschino
* cherries and 10 ml /2 tsp syrup*
1 egg white

For the almond praline
50 g /2 oz sugar
2.5 ml /½ tsp lemon juice
50 g /2 oz almonds, blanched
* and toasted*
flavourless oil for greasing
To decorate
whipped cream
maraschino cherries

1   If using the freezing compartment of the refrigerator, turn it to its coldest setting about 1 hour before you start. At the same time, put a 600 ml /1 pt bombe mould to chill and transfer the ice cream to the main part of the refrigerator to soften slightly.
2   Make the praline. In a heavy saucepan, combine the sugar and 30 ml /2 tbls water with the lemon juice, stirring over a gentle heat until the sugar has dissolved. Raise the heat and boil to a rich golden caramel. When the caramel is ready, stir in the almonds. Lightly oil a baking tray and pour in the praline mixture. Leave to cool and harden, then ease off with a spatula. Crush finely in a food processor or with a rolling pin.
3   Add the praline to the softened ice cream and work in until evenly mixed, without stirring too much. Line the mould with the ice cream, making an even layer about 20 mm /¾ in thick. Cover and freeze to set.
4   Meanwhile, put the sugar in a small heavy-based saucepan with 50 ml /2 fl oz water and stir over a gentle heat until the sugar is dissolved, then boil to 102C /217F. Leave to cool slightly.
5   In the top pan of a double boiler, beat the egg yolks until light and creamy. Pour in the hot but not boiling syrup gradually, beating constantly with a wire whisk. Cook over simmering water, beating constantly, until thick and doubled in bulk, about 10–15 minutes. Remove from the heat and plunge the pan into a bowl of iced water. Whisk until the mousse is thick and cold.
6   Turn the mousse into a bowl, add the cream, cherries and the syrup, folding them together lightly. In another bowl, whisk the egg white until stiff but not dry. Fold it into the mousse and pour into the centre of the bombe. Cover and freeze overnight.
7   About 15 minutes before serving, unmould the bombe onto a flat serving dish and place in the main part of the refrigerator to soften.
8   To serve, spoon the cream into a star-nozzled piping bag and decorate the bombe with piped cream and whole cherries.

 making ice cream if wished, 1½ hours,
then overnight freezing

Hunter's rabbit

Serves 4
1 rabbit, jointed
freshly ground black pepper
salt
15 ml /1 tbls olive oil
40 g /1½ oz butter
½ Spanish onion, finely chopped
10 ml /2 tsp tomato purée
60 ml /4 tbls dry white wine
300 ml /10 fl oz chicken stock, home-made or from a cube
100 g /4 oz mushrooms, thinly sliced
10 ml /2 tsp lemon juice

1   Season the rabbit portions with freshly ground black pepper and leave to come to room temperature. Just before cooking, season the portions to taste with salt.
2   In a flameproof casserole large enough to take the rabbit portions comfortably in a single layer, heat the olive oil and 25 g /1 oz butter. When the foaming subsides, lay the rabbit portions side by side in the hot fat and sauté over a moderate heat for 4 minutes each side, or until browned. Remove with a slotted spoon and keep warm while making the sauce.
3   To the fats remaining in the casserole, add the finely chopped onion and sauté for 7–10 minutes, or until soft, stirring with a wooden spoon.
4   Stir in the tomato purée and pour in the white wine and chicken stock. Bring the sauce to the boil, stirring frequently, then return the rabbit portions to the casserole. Season to taste with salt and freshly ground black pepper. Cover and simmer gently for 1–2 hours, until the rabbit is tender, turning the pieces occasionally.
5   When the rabbit is almost cooked, heat the remaining butter in a small frying-pan. Add the thinly sliced mushrooms and sauté for 1 minute, or until the mushrooms are coated in butter. Add the lemon juice and season to taste with salt and freshly ground black pepper. Sauté for a further 4 minutes, or until tender, stirring occasionally with a wooden spoon. Keep warm.
6   Remove the rabbit portions with a slotted spoon and arrange on a heated serving dish. Correct the seasoning of the sauce and spoon over the rabbit portions. Sprinkle the sautéed mushrooms over each portion and serve immediately. The 2 front legs are served together as 1 portion.

● The cooking time depends on the age and origin of the rabbit.

bringing to room temperature,
then 1½–2½ hours

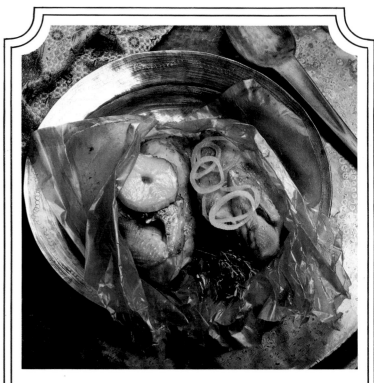

Pheasant en papillote

Serves 2
1 young pheasant, halved
olive oil
15 g /½ oz butter
salt and freshly ground black pepper
a pinch of dried thyme
1 thin slice of Spanish onion
1 ring of cooking apple, cored
sprig of thyme, to garnish

1   Heat the oven to 220C /425F /gas 7. Take a strong white or glazed brown paper bag large enough to hold the pheasant halves comfortably. Grease your hand with olive oil and run it over the bag, both inside and out.
2   In a frying-pan large enough to take the 2 pheasant halves comfortably side by side, heat the butter and 15 ml /1 tbls olive oil. When foaming subsides, sauté the pheasant halves until well browned on both sides, turning them over with a spatula. Remove to a plate with a slotted spoon. Sprinkle with salt, freshly ground black pepper and a generous pinch of thyme. Reserve.
3   Separate the thin slice of Spanish onion rings. In the fat remaining in the pan, sauté the apple ring and the onion rings for 1–2 minutes each side, or until golden, turning them with a spatula. Remove the sautéed apple and onion rings from the pan with the slotted spoon and arrange on top of the pheasant.
4   Carefully slide the pheasant halves into the oiled paper bag, taking care not to tear or pierce the bag. Seal the bag tightly with a piece of string or wire and place on a wire rack in a roasting tin.
5   Roast in the oven for 30 minutes, then remove the wire rack. Crumple some aluminium foil and use it to line the tin so that it fits tightly round the bag. Slit the bag open and fold the paper back.
6   Return to the oven for a further 15 minutes, or until the top is browned and the bird is cooked through but still juicy. The juices should run clear when you pierce through the thickest part of the inside leg with a skewer.
7   Place the pheasant in its bag on a heated serving dish and serve immediately, garnished with a sprig of thyme.

1¼ hours

Salmis of woodcock

Serves 4

4 × 175 g /6 oz woodcock, dressed
  weight
salt and ground black pepper
8 thin strips pounded pork fat, or
  unsmoked streaky bacon
275 ml /10 fl oz dry white wine
275 ml /10 fl oz beef stock, home-
  made or from a cube
juice and finely grated zest of 1
  lemon

15–30 ml /1–2 tbls Dijon
  mustard
freshly grated nutmeg
beurre manié, made by
  mashing 15 g /½ oz butter
  and 15 ml /1 tbls flour
  together
50 g /2 oz mushrooms, thinly
  sliced
30 ml /2 tbls finely chopped fresh
  parsley

1   Heat the oven to 220C /425F /gas 7. Pluck any stray feathers
from the woodcock. Season the birds generously both inside and out
with freshly ground black pepper and leave to come to room
temperature. Just before cooking, season with salt. Cover the birds
completely with thin strips of pounded pork fat or unsmoked bacon
and secure with string.
2   Place them on a rack in a roasting tin and roast for 15 minutes,
basting frequently.
3   Divide each woodcock in half along the backbone and breastbone. With scissors, trim off the backbone, leaving the meaty breast
on the bone. Reserve the backbone. Remove the skin. Put the
woodcock pieces into a flameproof casserole, sauté pan or chafing
dish and cover. Set aside.
4   Chop the backbones up with a cleaver or heavy knife. Put the
chopped bones into a saucepan and pour in the dry white wine, beef
stock and lemon juice. Stir in the finely grated lemon zest and Dijon
mustard and season with salt, freshly ground black pepper and
freshly grated nutmeg to taste. Simmer for 20 minutes.
5   Strain the stock into a clean saucepan and bring to the boil.
There should be about 425 ml /15 fl oz; if necessary make up the
quantity with extra stock. Add the *beurre manié* in tiny pieces,
stirring until the butter has completely melted. Simmer for 2–3
minutes, until the sauce has thickened.
6   Pour the sauce over the woodcock pieces. Add the mushrooms.
Simmer over a low heat for 5–10 minutes, or until tender. Sprinkle
with finely chopped parsley and serve immediately.

● Partridges, which are often easier to buy, can be substituted for
the woodcock. Choose young partridges as old partridges tend to be
tough, and require prolonged cooking.

⦙⦙ bringing to room temperature,
   then 1½ hours

Sautéed quail with grapes

Serves 6

6 quail
75 g /3 oz flour
6 × 15 mm /½ in slices white bread, crusts removed
100 g /4 oz butter, half of it melted
salt and freshly ground black pepper
For the garnish
duchesse potatoes
sprigs of watercress
For the grape sauce
250 g /8 oz seedless white grapes
100 g /4 oz butter
125 ml /4 fl oz port
a pinch of ground cloves
100 g /4 oz button mushrooms, thinly sliced

1   Heat the oven to 170C /325F /gas 3. Split each quail along the
backbone and open the birds. Turn them skin side up and press
down on the backbone of each to flatten completely. Coat the quail
with flour on all sides.
2   To make the canapés, trim each slice of bread to make a
rectangle a little larger than the quail. Trim the corners of each
rectangle to make a 'cameo' shape, and brush each slice on both
sides with melted butter. Place on a baking tray and bake in the
oven for 20 minutes or until golden brown, turning once.
3   Heat the remaining butter in 2 large pans: a large, flameproof
casserole and a frying-pan are suitable. Sauté the quail over a
moderate heat for 15 minutes, or until golden brown. Season the
birds with salt and freshly ground pepper, arrange them on the
canapés on a heated serving dish, garnish and keep warm.
4   To make the grape sauce, bring the grapes and 225 ml /8 fl oz
water to the boil. Drain the grapes and place them in a pan with the
butter, port and ground cloves. Cover the pan and simmer for 6
minutes. Stir in the sliced mushrooms and simmer for 5 minutes
more. Place in a warmed sauce-boat and serve with the quail.

● For the duchesse potato garnish, beat 25 g /1 oz butter, 1 egg, a
little milk and salt, pepper and nutmeg to taste into 500 g /1 lb
mashed potatoes. Pipe into rosettes on a lightly greased baking sheet
and bake in an oven heated to 200C /400F /gas 6 for 20–25 minutes.

⦙⦙ cooking potatoes,
   then 1 hour

Chicken & turkey: basic information

You can buy chicken in a variety of sizes and forms to suit your requirements: from a tiny poussin which will feed only one to a large capon which will make a meal for eight. You can buy them fresh, chilled or frozen; whole, in quarters or in smaller cut portions; cooked or even smoked. The giblets and livers are also sold separately by weight. Packs of frozen chicken livers are available from large supermarkets.

Most chickens nowadays are reared under controlled conditions designed to put on maximum flesh in minimum time. This results in uniformly young and tender birds, and choosing one in preference to another is largely a matter of the weight and number of servings required.

Buying chicken

Fresh chicken: whole birds can be bought fresh from farms, poulterers and butchers, sold by weight and usually oven-ready (i.e. plucked, drawn and trussed). Look for a plump breast, smooth, unbroken skin and pliable breastbone tip. If the chicken is wrapped, check that the film covering looks fresh and is unbroken. Never buy bruised or discoloured birds. The giblets (neck, gizzard, heart and liver) are often, but not always, tucked inside the bird in a polythene bag. If you particularly want giblets, remember to ask for them.

New York dressed birds, i.e. those with the head and feet left on, plucked, but not drawn, should be ordered in advance from your butcher. You pay for the pre-dressed weight. The marks of a young bird are pale yellow legs with small scales, and a pliable beak. For the amount to buy see the buying guide chart.

Chilled chicken: whole birds and portions are sold from refrigerated (as distinct from frozen food) cabinets in large supermarkets. Before it is packed in film bags and refrigerated, the chicken is air chilled, which keeps the flesh dry, unlike the iced-water chilling method often used for frozen birds. Check for freshness against the 'sell by' date on the bag.

Frozen chicken: whole birds and portions are sold from frozen food cabinets (operating at −18C /0F or below) in supermarkets and freezer centres. The birds are sealed in moisture/vapour-proof bags and frozen immediately. As frozen chicken stays frozen without deteriorating during transport, distribution costs are lower and frozen birds are usually slightly cheaper than fresh or chilled. Check that the wrapper is undamaged and that there are no obvious signs of excess frozen liquid inside the bag when buying frozen chicken.

Chicken portions are convenient for single servings or for a recipe requiring a particular cut, and are available fresh or chilled as well as frozen. They are sold singly, by the kg /lb or in multiple packs of quarters or legs, thighs, breasts or wings, usually presented in a single layer so you can easily see the number and size of all the portions in the pack.

Storing chicken

Both raw and cooked chicken is very perishable and, unless it is handled with care, can be a health hazard, especially under warm and humid conditions. But this can be avoided by taking the following simple precautions when storing raw or cooked chicken.

Fresh and chilled chicken: immediately after buying, discard the wrapping and remove the giblets, if any, from inside the bird. Refrigerate the chicken right away, loosely covered with cling film or aluminium foil so that air can circulate freely. Use within 2 days, or 24 hours if kept in a cool larder.

Chicken giblets: raw or cooked, these are very perishable, so if you cannot use them immediately, freeze them in polythene bags for up to 2–3 months.

Cooked chicken: cool as rapidly as possible in a cold, airy place, or by standing casseroles in ice-cold water. When cold, keep in the refrigerator; cold roast chicken can be kept for 3–4 days, casseroles for 1–2 days. When reheating, bring to simmering point and maintain for several minutes at this temperature before serving.

Chicken for the freezer

When buying whole frozen birds or portions transfer them, while still solidly frozen, to your freezer. Use whole birds within 9–12 months and portions within 6 months. If the giblets are inside the bird it must be used within 2–3 months as giblets can only be kept for that length of time. Cooked chicken portions can be cooled quickly, wrapped in foil and frozen for 1–2 months.

Thawing: it is essential to thaw frozen chicken completely, otherwise it cannot cook through evenly, and undercooked poultry can cause food poisoning. Remove the chicken from its wrapping, stand on a plate and cover loosely with foil. Slow thawing in the refrigerator is ideal, because it maintains the texture of the chicken better, but it takes longer than thawing at room temperature. If the bird contains a bag of giblets, remove this as soon as it is sufficiently thawed. For thawing times see the chart.

Buying turkey

Turkeys are available either fresh, chilled or frozen. Whichever you buy, the breast should be plump and white, the drumsticks firm and rounded.

Thawing times for frozen chickens

Weight	in a refrigerator	at room temperature
up to 1.8 kg /4 lb	approx. 24 hours	approx. 12 hours
1.8–2.7 kg /4–6 lb	24–36 hours	12–24 hours
2.7–3.6 kg /6–8 lb	36–48 hours	30 hours
portions	4 hours	1½–2 hours

Buying guide for chicken

Type (alternative names in brackets)	General description	Weight range	Average servings	Best ways to cook
Poussin (double poussin)	bird up to 6 weeks old	small: about 500 g /1 lb large: about 1 kg /2 lb	1 2	fry, spit-roast, casserole whole or halve and grill
Small oven-ready chicken (roaster; spring chicken; U.S.– broiler/fryer)	young, tender bird, ideally sized for quartering	1–1.4 kg /2–3 lb	3–4	joint into portions and grill, fry, casserole or bake
Large oven-ready chicken (roaster)	young, tender bird for cooking whole	1.6–2.3 kg /3½–5 lb	4–8	oven- or spit-roast, pot-roast or casserole, poach
Capon (poularde = hen reared like capon)	cock bird castrasted and reared to produce more white meat	2–3.6 kg /4½–8 lb	6–12	oven-roast, pot-roast or poach
Boiling fowl	retired breeding bird aged over 1 year	1.8–3.6 kg /4–8 lb	6–10	poach
Boiling hen	retired egg-producing bird	1.6–2.3 kg /3½–5 lb	4–8	poach

New York dressed turkeys, plucked but not drawn and with their head and feet still attached, are the ones favoured by traditionalists, but they do work out more expensive as you pay for the weight of the head, innards and feet as well as the edible part of the bird.

Chilled and frozen turkeys are both sold oven-ready, ranging in weight from 2.3–11.3 kg /5–25 lb. Frozen turkeys are the cheapest, though the weight includes extra water. Lengthy, slow thawing is necessary before cooking to make the bird tender and safe to eat (see chart).

Turkey joints and breasts, as well as escalopes cut from the breast, are available, either frozen or chilled, from many shops. These are ideal when you want to eat turkey at one meal only, or when a particular cut is required for a recipe.

Turkey rolls, cooked or uncooked, consist of boned and rolled turkey meat. They may be made of white or dark meat only, or a combination. Sometimes they are sold barded with pork back fat. Uncooked turkey rolls may be roasted, or braised in a sauce.

Smoked turkey is much loved in central Europe and is becoming more popular elsewhere. Usually sold precooked, it has a delicate, smoky flavour.

Quantities to buy

If you are buying turkey joints, one drumstick or wing will usually be sufficient for one person, while for breast meat you should allow 175 g /6 oz, since there is no bone or fat to consider. For a cold buffet a turkey roll is ideal, as it is quick to carve and there is no wastage. Allow 125–175 g /4–6 oz per person.

See Roasting chicken and turkey, *page 8*, for servings from a whole bird.

Storing turkey

A fresh turkey or turkey roll, loosely covered on a plate, will keep for up to 2 days in the coldest part of the refrigerator. Giblets should be kept separately and cooked on the day of purchase: you can use them to make stock. Follow the manufacturer's instructions for storing chilled turkeys and turkey rolls.

Turkey for the freezer

Fresh or frozen whole (unstuffed) turkeys or turkey joints can be frozen wrapped first in aluminium foil, then in freezer bags, for up to 1 year. Cooked turkey can be frozen for up to 3 months. Freeze giblets raw (with the liver packed separately) or cooked, wrapped in freezer bags, for up to 3 months.

Thawing frozen turkey should be done with the bird on a rack over a tray at the

bottom of the refrigerator (see chart for thawing times). Remove the wrapping and extract the bag of giblets from inside as soon as possible. Never try to speed up the thawing process – a partially defrosted bird may never reach a sufficiently high oven temperature to kill any bacteria present, and so is dangerous to eat.

Joints and breasts obviously need less time than a whole bird, but should still be thawed for at least 12 hours in the refrigerator or approximately 6 hours at room temperature.

Roasting times for turkey

Weight	Hours
4–4.5 kg /9–10 lb	3½–4
4.5–5.4 kg /10–12 lb	4–4½
5.4–6.8 kg /12–15 lb	4½–5
6.8–7.7 kg /15–17 lb	5–5½
7.7–9 kg /17–20 lb	5½–6
9–11.3 kg /20–25 lb	6–7

Roasting times for chicken

Type	Time	Temperature
Spring and roasting chicken	20 minutes per 500 g /1 lb	190C /375F /mark 5
Poussin		
500 g /1 lb	45 minutes	180C /350F /gas 4
500–900 g /1–2 lb	approx. 60 minutes	

Thawing times for frozen turkey, duck and goose

Weight	in a refrigerator	at room temperature
2.3–2.7 kg /5–6 lb	30–36 hours	24 hours
2.7–3.6 kg /6–8 lb	36–48 hours	30 hours
3.6–4.5 kg /8–10 lb	48–56 hours	not advisable
4.5–5.4 kg /10–12 lb	56–60 hours	not advisable
5.4–6.8 kg /12–15 lb	60–70 hours	not advisable
6.8–7.7 kg /15–17 lb	3 days	not advisable
7.7–9 kg /17–20 lb	4 days	not advisable
9–11.3 kg /20–25 lb	4–5 days	not advisable

Duck, goose & guinea fowl: basic information

Ducks bred domestically are larger than wild ducks. The terms duck and duckling are used fairly loosely, although strictly speaking a duckling should be between 6 and 12 weeks old. Ducks have a high fat content and do not have all that much meat in proportion to their frame, but their dark-coloured flesh is deliciously rich and succulent, with a distinctive flavour. They are available all the year, being at their best in early to late spring.

Duck

New York dressed birds are plucked but not drawn and have the head and feet still attached. You pay less per kg /lb for birds dressed this way, but you pay for the head, feet and innards, which can amount to one third or even more of the total weight. If you do buy birds prepared this way, look for flexible bills (or soft beaks) and feet: the webbing of the feet should be soft enough to be easily torn. Ducks should be plump but not over-fattened, or there will be a layer of fat beneath the skin which makes it difficult to get the skin crisp when it is roasted.

Oven-ready birds are cleaned, plucked and trussed, ready for the oven. Many poulterers sell the birds this way, and giblets may or may not be sold with the birds. Pre-packaged oven-ready birds are also available from chilled cabinets in supermarkets.

When buying duck allow at least 500 g /1 lb per serving. Duck can be stored in the refrigerator for up to 2 days before cooking. Put it on a plate, separate from the giblets, if there are any, and cover with foil or greaseproof paper. Giblets should be cooked within 24 hours. If you cannot use them immediately, freeze them in polythene bags.

Frozen ducks are available all year round from supermarkets and freezer centres. Transfer frozen birds while still solidly frozen to your freezer. Store for up to 6 months. Frozen birds must be totally thawed before cooking (see chart on page 105), but great care is needed when defrosting: spoilage is likely to be more rapid than it would be with chicken or turkey because of the fatty flesh.

Goose

Goose is traditionally roasted, then served with a variety of stuffings and sauces. Potato and onion or chestnut and apple stuffing absorbs the fat effectively, and the sharpness of apple or cranberry sauce also sets off the richness of the meat. Roast goose is one of the traditional Christmas dishes in Britain and is especially popular in Poland and Germany. The Germans baste the skin with beer about 15 minutes before the end of cooking time to make the skin crisp, then serve it with red cabbage or sauerkraut.

Smoked goose breast, served raw and thinly sliced, is considered a great delicacy in Germany and Poland. Goose can also be dry-cured and pickled. Potted goose is made by mincing the breast of the bird and pounding it to a smooth paste with butter.

Goose giblets: these are the neck, gizzard, heart, liver, wing tips and feet. For a delicious gravy to serve with roast goose, make a stock from the giblets, then blend 50 ml /2 fl oz soured cream with 10 ml /2 tsp flour and 20 ml /4 tsp water. Add this to 400 ml /14 fl oz stock, bring to the boil, stirring constantly, and simmer until thick.

The goose liver is much prized, and may be specially fattened by forcible feeding (sometimes up to 1.8 kg /4 lb) to make the rich and luxurious *pâté de foie gras*. Goose liver can also be cooked as a main dish.

Buying goose: geese are larger than ducks, but the proportion of bone to meat is even higher. Allow 700 g /1½ lb goose per serving. Geese are not seasonal, but are at their best from winter to late spring. In fact it can be difficult to obtain a fresh goose during the summer months. Frozen geese are available all year round in supermarkets and freezer centres. A frozen bird will be only about half the price of a fresh one, though the quality may not be as high. Frozen birds must be completely thawed before cooking. Take great care when defrosting since spoilage is likely to be more rapid because of the fatty flesh (see chart on *page 105*).

Guinea fowl

Guinea fowl are bred domestically so they are not seasonal, but they are at their best from spring to early summer. They are about the same size as pheasants or small chickens. Judge the appearance as you would for chicken: look for a plump breast, white flesh and smooth-skinned feet. The flesh is much drier than that of chicken so extra fat needs to be added during cooking.

Frozen guinea fowl are also available all year round. Like duck and goose, they must be completely thawed before cooking (thaw as for chicken, see chart on *page 105*).

A good-sized guinea fowl will usually serve four people; smaller birds serve two.

Roasting times for duck, goose and guinea fowl		
Type	**Time**	**Temperature**
Duck	approx. 25–30 minutes per 500 g /1 lb	180C /350F /gas 4
Goose	15 minutes per 500 g / 1 lb plus 15 minutes	200C /400F /gas 6
	25–30 minutes per 500 g /1 lb	180C /350F /gas 4
Guinea fowl	approx. 45 minutes or longer according to size	220C /425F /gas 7

Game: basic information

To conserve game bird stocks there are closed seasons while the birds are breeding and shooting is not permitted. However, frozen game birds may be available out of season from some butchers and larger supermarkets.

Buying and storing game birds

If you buy game it will already be hung and dressed ready for cooking. If you are given it, you should hang it until you can get a poulterer or butcher to prepare it. He will usually clean and pluck the bird for you for a small charge.

Hang birds by the neck or beak in a cool, dry, airy place. The length of time for hanging depends partly on the weather, partly on your taste. In mild weather the flesh matures more quickly than in cold weather.

If hanging birds yourself, hang them securely by the beak, unplucked and undrawn in a cool, airy place. Take care that they do not touch each other and make sure they are safe from pets. As a general rule game birds are ready for cooking when the tail feathers can be plucked out easily, but check at regular intervals because a warm, humid atmosphere hastens the maturing process. Test occasionally by plucking some feathers round the vent at the back end of the bird and sniffing to see if you get a gamey whiff.

The longer older birds are hung the more tender they will be when cooked, particularly if the recipe requires a short cooking time and if you want the flesh to have a slight pinkness. Hanging may take up to 10 or even 14 days if the birds are to be 'high', though a very strong flavour is less popular now than it used to be.

Once plucked, game birds can be kept, loosely wrapped in the refrigerator, for up to 2 days before cooking.

Cooking game birds

Young birds are delicious served plainly roasted with the traditional accompaniments of game chips (wafer-thin deep-fried potatoes) or fried breadcrumbs and gravy or bread sauce.

Very small birds like quail and snipe can be grilled, and for this they are usually spatchcocked. To do this cut the bird along the backbone and then turn it over and open it out. Press hard on the middle of the backbone to make the bird completely flat (*see page 16*).

Older birds are best braised or casseroled and are delicious if well marinated before casseroling. Partridge is traditionally cooked in a casserole with cabbage to make a chartreuse. Rich sauces containing port or redcurrant jelly are a popular accompaniment to serve with game birds.

Pigeon pie is a classic English recipe, while a raised game pie is delicious eaten cold, and is perfect for a picnic as it cuts so easily. Any leftover meat from a roasted game bird can be used for a tasty pâté or terrine.

Freezing game birds

Game birds should be fully hung, then plucked and drawn as near freezing time as possible. If the bird already smells high, overwrap in foil (first overwrapping the legs in foil if they protrude), then seal the bird in a freezer bag and label. Freeze for up to 6 months at a constant temperature of −18C / 0 F or below.

A good way to freeze birds for braising or casseroling is in a marinade; this adds flavour and saves time. Combine 300 ml /10 fl oz red wine, 30 ml /2 tbls olive oil, 6 crushed peppercorns, a crumbled bay leaf and a pinch of dried thyme in a large freezer bag. Add the birds, expel all air, seal, label and freeze. Defrost them in the bag for 24–36 hours in your refrigerator, turning the bag regularly.

Buying frozen game birds is a convenience – and often your only option if supplies are uncertain (with the exception of quail which is not available frozen). Remember that frozen birds are more likely to be tough (there is no way to check quality). Unless you have great confidence in your supplier, you would do better to braise or casserole them rather than roast or grill.

Defrost game birds slowly in the refrigerator for 24 hours. Cook them within 24 hours or they are likely to become higher. Dishes of cooked game can be frozen for 1 month, though in general it is not good practice to defrost game, cook the dish and then freeze it.

Buying and storing venison

The seasons for shooting male and female venison, as well as the different species, vary, but some venison, either fresh or frozen, is available all year round. Some butchers stock stewing venison which is already chopped.

Venison should be dark and firm, the fat a clear, creamy white. Even when very high it should have only a gamey, meaty smell with no trace of ammonia. Venison is by nature dry and tough, but these problems are easily overcome – the first by barding or larding the meat, the second by hanging and marinating it.

Venison should be well hung. The exact length of time depends on how high you like it, but 12–21 days is average. As it is a very rich meat, a portion of 175 g/6 oz boneless venison (225 g /8 oz on the bone) should be adequate.

Store venison in the refrigerator in a marinade. It can be kept for up to 3 days, provided it is completely submerged in the liquid all the time.

Venison for the freezer

If you order venison for freezing you may have to take a whole haunch or shoulder. It should be fully hung before freezing. If the meat is already frozen, ask the butcher to cut the part you want for immediate use and keep the remainder frozen. You can then store this in your own freezer for up to 6 months (depending on its initial date of freezing). Fresh venison should be cut into small joints, steaks or chops, wrapped individually in cling film, then put into polythene bags and frozen. Stewing venison can be chopped and frozen in a marinade – just put the meat and marinade in a large freezer bag, expel all air and seal. Defrost in the bag for 36 hours in your refrigerator, turning regularly.

Buying and storing rabbit

Rabbit is widely available as tame or 'hutch' rabbit. More delicate in taste than wild rabbit, it is easily distinguished by its uniformly pale flesh. The flesh of the wild rabbit is much darker than the flesh of tame rabbit, especially at the joints.

A wild rabbit should always be eaten when young, but a tame rabbit will be tender even when old. If a wild rabbit's kidneys are buried in fat, the animal is sure to be tender; if the fat is a golden yellow, it will be particularly tasty.

Rabbits are not normally hung but drawn immediately on killing and should be eaten within 3 to 4 days. Rabbit – both wild and tame – is available all year round, either fresh or frozen.

Tame rabbit should be cooked within 24 hours of purchase. Wild rabbit can be kept in a marinade for up to 3 days, in either a cool place or the refrigerator, as long as the meat is completely covered by the marinade all the time.

Buying and storing hare

Unless your local butcher or poulterer specializes in game, you will probably have to order hare. Specify whether you want a young or older animal and whether you want it hung. The dressed weight of a leveret is 450–700 g /1–1½ lb, that of a young hare 1.1–1.4 kg /2½–3 lb, and that of an older hare up to 2 kg /4½ lb. An older hare will feed six people, a young hare four, but a leveret only two. Hare is in season from late summer to early spring, but is at its best in early winter.

Hare should hang by its hind legs, un-skinned and in a cool place, for 4 or 5 days. A bowl is placed under the head to collect the blood. Your butcher will skin and paunch the hare (remove the entrails) for you after hanging.

If you want the blood of the hare, ask for it to be hung and the blood collected and kept for you, together with the heart, liver and kidneys.

After hanging, the meat may be kept in a marinade for up to 3 days in a cool place or the refrigerator, provided it is completely submerged. The liver, kidneys and heart must be submerged as well. Add 5 ml /1 tsp vinegar to the blood and refrigerate.

Freezing rabbit and hare

Rabbits should be skinned and paunched immediately for freezing. Joint if wished and wrap. Rabbit portions will keep for 6–8 months, but should be casseroled, not roasted, when they are thawed.

If you are buying a hare for freezing, ask for it to be fully hung and discard blood and entrails. If you are hanging it yourself, collect the blood after the first day, add 5 ml /1 tsp vinegar and freeze immediately. After fully hanging, do not freeze the remaining blood or offal.

After skinning and cleaning the hare should be thoroughly dried and then cut into joints ready for cooking. Wrap well and freeze for up to 6–8 months. Frozen hare should be casseroled rather than roasted when it is thawed.

The weight of both wild and tame rabbit, dressed, is 700 g–1.1 kg /1½–2½ lb when young, up to 1.6 kg /3½ lb if older. One rabbit will feed four; one front leg and half a saddle make up one portion.

You will probably have to order wild rabbit. You can tell if it is young by the ears, which tear easily. The butcher will skin and paunch it for you. Age is not important when buying a tame rabbit, unless you want to sauté it. In that case, look for small, plump legs and a small saddle as that will give the most tender meat.

Most butchers now sell frozen tame rabbit, much of which comes from China. Many supermarkets also sell blocks of frozen, boneless rabbit; this is best used for casseroles or pies.

Storage and thawing times for frozen game

Type	Storage time	in a refrigerator	at room temperature
Game birds	6 months 12 months for strong flavour	up to 7–8 hours	up to 3–4 hours
Venison	12 months	10–12 hours per kg/ 5–6 hours per lb	not advisable
Rabbit	6–8 months	10–12 hours per kg/ 5–6 hours per lb	not advisable
Hare	6–8 months	10–12 hours per kg/ 5–6 hours per lb	2–4 hours per kg/ 1–2 hours per lb

Buying and roasting game birds

Birds and servings	Approximate hanging time	Temperature and roasting time
Grouse 2	2–4 days	190C /375F /gas 5 35 minutes
Partridge 1–2	3–5 days young birds 10 days older birds	220C /425F /gas 7 30 minutes
Pheasant hen 3; cock 4	3 days young birds 10 days older birds	220C /425F /gas 7 50–60 minutes
Pigeon 1	not hung (empty crop quickly)	220C /425F /gas 7 20 minutes
Snipe 2 birds each	3–4 days	220C /425F /gas 7, 6– 15 minutes undrawn
Wild duck (mallard) 2–3	2–3 days (drawn)	220C /425F / gas 7 40–50 minutes
Teal 1	2–3 days (drawn)	220C /425F /gas 7 10–15 minutes
Widgeon 1	2–3 days (drawn)	220C /425F /gas 7 15–25 minutes
Woodcock 1	3 days	220C /425F /gas 7, 10– 15 minutes undrawn
Quail 1	Not hung (empty crop quickly)	220C /425F /gas 7 25 minutes

Buying and roasting furred game

Game and servings	Approximate hanging time	Temperature and roasting time
Venison 175 g /6 oz (225 g /8 oz on the bone) per portion	12–21 days	180C /350F /gas 4 20 minutes per 500 g /1 lb
Rabbit (tame and wild) 4	not hung	190C /375F /gas 5 1½–1¾ hours
Hare leveret 2 young hare 4 older hare 6	4–5 days	190C /375F /gas 5 1½–1¾ hours

Index